# Learning and Leading for Transdisciplinary Literacy through Multi-Tiered Systems of Support

This comprehensive guide gives an overview of Multi-Tiered Systems of Support (MTSS) for K-12 teacher leaders and other school professionals with practices toward achieving transdisciplinary success for lifelong literacy in schools. MTSS is a holistic teacher leadership approach that focuses on transdisciplinary networks of instruction and intervention. For MTSS to be effective, teacher-colleagues and teacher leaders need to be prepared to understand the complexities of the systems and the multiple tiers of support needed within each system, as well as their roles in the process.

This book details an illustrative list of tiers for seven systems within an MTSS framework, including multi-tiered systems for:

- Assessment and Evaluation
- Professional Learning (e.g., literacy coaches, literacy leadership teams, online/offline professional learning)
- Family Engagement (e.g., newsletters, parent nights, parent workshops, Parent–Teacher Associations)
- Transdisciplinary Curriculum Content (e.g., media centers, leveled book rooms, schools, districts, and state resource teachers)
- Community Engagement (e.g., social services, school outreach, counseling services, health services)
- Distributive Teacher Leadership (e.g., School Advisory Committee, college/university courses, professional pathways)
- Response to Intervention/Instruction

With examples of instructional practices, connections to researched resources, and implementational plans, this book will be useful for teacher leaders, literacy coaches, and curriculum leaders, as well as school board officials and school administrators, to leverage their knowledge and skills for transdisciplinary literacy learning in their schools.

**Mary E. Little** is a Professor in the Exceptional Student Education program at the University of Central Florida, USA.

**Enrique A. Puig** is Director of the Morgridge International Reading Center at the University of Central Florida, USA.

**Also Available from Routledge Eye On Education**
(www.routledge.com/eyeoneducation)

**Teaching Reading and Literature with Classroom Talk: Dialogical Approaches and Practical Strategies in the Secondary ELA Classroom**
Dawan Coombs

**Building Proficiency for World Language Learners: 100+ High-Interest Activities**
Janina Klimas

**Student-Centered Literacy Assessment in the 6-12 Classroom
An Asset-Based Approach**
Sean Ruday

**Teach This Poem, Volume I: The Natural World**
Madeleine Fuchs Holzer and The Academy of American Poets

**Close Reading in Elementary School: Bringing Readers and Texts Together, 2nd edition**
Diana Sisson and Betsy Sisson

**The Antiracist English Language Arts Classroom**
Keisha Rembert

**The Literacy Coaching Handbook: Working With Teachers to Increase Student Achievement, 2nd edition**
Diana Sisson and Betsy Sisson

# Learning and Leading for Transdisciplinary Literacy through Multi-Tiered Systems of Support

Mary E. Little and Enrique A. Puig

Routledge
Taylor & Francis Group
NEW YORK AND LONDON

Designed cover image: © Getty Images

First published 2025
by Routledge
605 Third Avenue, New York, NY 10158

and by Routledge
4 Park Square, Milton Park, Abingdon, Oxon, OX14 4RN

*Routledge is an imprint of the Taylor & Francis Group, an informa business*

© 2025 Mary E. Little and Enrique A. Puig

The right of Mary E. Little and Enrique A. Puig to be identified as authors of this work has been asserted in accordance with sections 77 and 78 of the Copyright, Designs and Patents Act 1988.

All rights reserved. No part of this book may be reprinted or reproduced or utilised in any form or by any electronic, mechanical, or other means, now known or hereafter invented, including photocopying and recording, or in any information storage or retrieval system, without permission in writing from the publishers.

*Trademark notice*: Product or corporate names may be trademarks or registered trademarks, and are used only for identification and explanation without intent to infringe.

ISBN: 978-1-032-70796-9 (hbk)
ISBN: 978-1-032-69936-3 (pbk)
ISBN: 978-1-032-70797-6 (ebk)

DOI: 10.4324/9781032707976

Typeset in Optima
by SPi Technologies India Pvt Ltd (Straive)

With esteem, appreciation, and warmth we dedicate this book to Dr. Sandra L. Robinson. She understands what it takes to produce this kind of text at a time when an abundance of education is needed to ensure equitable quality education and promote lifelong learning opportunities for everyone. She introduced us to each other over 20 years ago and the collaboration has never stopped.

# Contents

| | |
|---|---|
| About the Authors | x |
| Acknowledgments | xi |
| Glossary | xiii |
| Prologue | xvii |

| | | |
|---|---|---|
| 1 | Multi-Tiered Systems of Support | 1 |
| 2 | Design Thinking in Multi-Tiered Systems of Support | 28 |
| 3 | Multi-Tiered System for Assessment and Evaluation | 47 |
| 4 | Multi-Tiered System for Ongoing Professional Learning | 71 |
| 5 | Multi-Tiered System for Family Engagement | 92 |
| 6 | Multi-Tiered System for Transdisciplinary Curriculum Content | 109 |
| 7 | Multi-Tiered System for Community Engagement | 127 |
| 8 | Multi-Tiered System for Developing Distributive Teacher Leadership | 149 |
| 9 | Multi-Tiered System for Response to Intervention/Instruction | 175 |
| | Epilogue | 199 |

# About the Authors

**Mary E. Little**, Ph. D. is a Professor in the Exceptional Student Education program at the University of Central Florida and the Coordinator of Graduate Programs. She has led the writing, development, and evaluation of almost $30 million in external grants from state, federal, and foundation sources focused on research, personnel development, and innovative programs. She has served as a special education teacher, program coordinator, college professor, program evaluator, and consultant. Dr. Little has been leading, learning, and engaged with university–school partnerships to positively impact learning through school- and university-based professional learning, clinical practice, mathematics interventions, and action research throughout her career. Her current research interests include teacher efficacy, teacher inquiry, interventions in mathematics and reading, school reform, and student learning related to teacher learning within a collaborative partnership approach.

**Enrique A. Puig**, Ed.D. is an award-winning educator and internationally recognized presenter. He has experience as a classroom teacher, literacy interventionist, literacy coach, and university instructor and has presented various aspects of transdisciplinary literacy learning and leading, at state, regional, national and international conferences. Enrique is the director of the Morgridge International Reading Center – College of Community Innovation and Education – at the University of Central Florida. He teaches graduate and undergraduate courses on K-12 diagnostic reading, reading in the content areas, and reading practicum courses. He is an author and co-author of several articles, chapters, and books. His research interest is in transdisciplinary literacy learning and instruction with low-progress learners. Enrique continues to work with teacher-colleagues and students in classrooms to further his knowledge of learning and leading.

# Acknowledgments

Quoting Sir Isaac Newton, "If I have seen further than others, it is by standing upon the shoulders of giants." We were able to see further standing on the shoulders of many giants. First and foremost, we have to acknowledge Routledge/Taylor & Francis Group and our editor Megha Patel for her kindness, guidance, and patience, and her belief in the project. We would also like to acknowledge the following teacher-colleagues and teacher leaders for expanding and continuing to expand our knowledge of Multi-Tiered Systems of Support and transdisciplinary literacy over a period of many years which assisted us in writing this text: Darliny Katz, colleague and friend who was instrumental in starting us on this journey; Elsie L. Olan at University of Central Florida for generously sharing her time and knowledge with us to enhance this text; Jennifer Manak, our thought-partner and critical friend at Rollins College; Jayme Hartman and Kelli D'Amato at SJCS; Carla Kay at Duquesne University; Rachelle Savitz at Eastern Carolina University; Amy Broemmel at the University of Rhode Island; Denise N. Morgan at Western Carolina University; George G. Hruby at the University of Kentucky; Karen L. Ladinsky, friend and therapist who continues to inspire us; Evan Lefsky, a perpetual source of inspiration for teacher leadership; Craig Cosden, who continues to update our vocabulary; Gay Su Pinnell, emerita at the Ohio State University, for being a muse, friend and colleague in addition to a constant source of inspiration and knowledge; Mary Ann Poparad at National Louis University for her powerful coaching language; Mary Ann Colbert in Palm Beach County Schools for helping us reimagine multisensory instruction; OCPS Superintendent Maria F. Vasquez and colleagues Bridget Williams, Bonnie Toffoli, and Kim Wood; Principals Betsy

# Acknowledgments

Theis, Seth Daub, Sean McGuire, and Patty Harrelson, and practitioner scholars Ellice Richards, Virginia Milam, Loisann Murphy, Michael Hart, in Orange County Public Schools, Florida. Teacher Quality Partnership colleagues Melissa Carli, Cheryl Van de Mark, Dena Slanda, Elizabeth Bagley, Taylar Wenzel, Susan Kelly, and Norine Blanche. John and Carrie Morgridge and the Morgridge Family Foundation, for their generosity in supporting UCF in creating the Morgridge International Reading Center; to our colleagues at UCF – Naim, Kapucu, Andrea C. Borowczak, Mark Hartman, Daniel Eadens, Karen Biraimah, Su Gao, Enrique Ortiz, Deshawn Chapman, Earlisha Whitfield, Viki Kelchner, Vassiliki Zygouris-Coe, Sherron Roberts, and Michelle Kelley for ongoing boundary-spanning conversations. We additionally want to express a special acknowledgement to ALL the school-based practitioner scholars from across the United States and other countries who over time have invited us into their classrooms and schools and have made us better learners. A very special thank you to Dean Grant Hayes at the University of Central Florida for his warm, caring, and ongoing words of encouragement.

We continue to acknowledge with the utmost respect and admiration the influential and seminal work of Urie Bronfenbrenner, Grace Fernald, Louise Rosenblatt, Maxine Greene, Maria Montessori, Brian Cambourne, Lev Vygotsky, and Marie M. Clay for their extraordinary research, passion, and endeavors. At a time when much seminal work is ignored, their work perseveres and converges disciplines. Through their work, and formidable words, they have transformed the face of education so that we continue to learn as transdisciplinary literate citizens to ensure equitable quality education and promote lifelong learning opportunities for everyone.

# Glossary

**Andragogy**  the art, science, and craft of learning and leading adults.

**Artifact-mediated**  learning through the manipulation of various items or data that represent the learner's attempts (i.e., writing samples, oral reading records, etc.)

**Artifacts**  residual items from an event.

**Broad-spectrum Model**  model for learning and leading that can support a variety of learners and orientations.

**Differentiated Instruction**  providing instruction tailored to individual needs based on their strengths that accounts for content (age appropriateness), context (learning environment) and process (instructional practices).

**Confluency**  in-the-head working systems flowing, running, blending together to construct meaning and make sense.

**Comprehension**  the ability to use multisensory input to construct, deconstruct, and reconstruct defensible interpretations.

**Ethnographic Approach**  a scientific method of gathering data to understand, that does not start with a question to be resolved, but rather questions are formed from triangulating participant observations, non-participant observations, and artifact collecting.

**Feedforward**  cognitive mechanisms used to promote predicting and anticipating.

**Fluency**  integrating all language working systems to construct meaning efficiently and effectively.

# Glossary

**Generative response**  a positive interaction that promotes questioning and independent learning behaviors.

**Graphophonic Working System**  in-the-head knowledge of the association between the letters and the sounds in language for encoding and decoding.

**Hebegogy**  the art, craft, and science of learning and leading adolescent students (ages 10-24).

**Lexical Working Systems**  in-the-head knowledge of the productive and receptive vocabulary that includes affixes, in addition to Greek and Latin origins of words.

**Literacy**  Reading, writing, speaking, listening, viewing, and thinking across disciplines at a level appropriate for the society in which one lives.

**Metacognition**  ability to know "in our heads" what strategic activities we are using or need to use to comprehend and communicate.

**Macro Tier**  universal broad-spectrum level of support to improve transdisciplinary instruction in a Multi-Tiered Systems of Support Model.

**Meso Tier**  Specific and targeted level of support to improve transdisciplinary instruction in a Multi-Tiered Systems of Support Model.

**Micro Tier**  Precise and intensive level of support to improve transdisciplinary instruction in a Multi-Tiered Systems of Support Model.

**Multi-Tiered Systems of Support**  a synergistic and holistic solution-seeking leveled approach to improving learning and leading for all stakeholders within a given environment.

**Non-participant observers**  someone who observes with no participation or interaction in an event.

**Participant Observer**  someone who observes while participating or interacting in an event.

**Pedagogy**  the art, craft, and science of learning and leading children.

**Phonemic Awareness**  in-the-head levels of sensitivity to the individual sounds of spoken language.

**Phonics**  An understanding of using a rule governed association of sounds and letters.

**Phonological Awareness**  knowing how spoken words can be used, and that words may be segmented, they consist of syllables, onsets, and rimes.

# Glossary

**Pragmatic Working Systems**  in-the-head ability for knowing the context and how it can be made comprehensible to the reader or writer.

**Program**  a series of actions with one goal in mind.

**Rationales**  theoretical understandings

**Reading as a Process**  a working system of predicting and anticipating, monitoring, searching further at difficulty, and self-correcting that incorporates sources of information using a variety of strategic activities to construct, deconstruct, and reconstruct meaning.

**Response to Intervention/Instruction**  a three tiered approach that increases in instructional intensity to support transdisciplinary student learning.

**Scaffolding**  A temporary support system provided by a more knowledgeable person to assist growth grounded on a learner's strength.

**Schematic Working Systems**  in-the-head ability to access appropriate background knowledge to make sense.

**Self-reflective Practice**  the ability to stand back and make a critical analysis of how you are doing.

**Semantic Working Systems**  in-the-head ability for making meaning of comprehensible text that allows us to "recode" information for personalization.

**Syntactic Working Systems**  in-the-head knowledge of the grammatical or structural organization of a language.

**Tier 1 Instruction**  Universal core whole group instruction in a Response to Intervention/Instruction model.

**Tier 2 Instruction**  Targeted small group instruction in a Response to Intervention/Instruction model.

**Tier 3 Instruction**  Intensive individual instruction in a Response to Intervention/Instruction model.

**Transdisciplinary**  using knowledge from a variety of disciplines for creating new knowledge to solve real world issues at a variety of levels (personal, interpersonal, and global).

**Transformational Model**  an approach to learning and leading that focuses and creates change; a synergistic model of learning and leading where all involved change.

# Glossary

**Transmission Model**  an approach to learning and leading where knowledge is transmitted or transferred to a learner. Teacher is in control of the content and to some degree the context.

**Transaction Model**  an approach to learning and leading that is contingent on the interaction between the teacher and the learner.

**Vocabulary**  the lexicon of a language; the in-the-head inventory of productive and receptive words.

**Working Systems**  in-the-head functional schemes that a reader or writer uses to construct meaning and communicate across disciplines.

**Writing as a Process**  a working system of predicting and anticipating, monitoring, searching, and self-correcting that incorporates sources of information using a variety of strategic activities to compose and construct meaningful text to communicate, inform, entertain, persuade, or reflect.

**Zone of Distal Development**  a conceptual third space that is beyond what a learner can learn independently or with the support of a more knowledgeable other. Curiosity and questioning develop in the ZDD.

**Zone of Mesial Development**  a conceptual third space where independent learning occurs. Self-efficacy along with self-monitoring and self-regulating behavior develop in the ZMD.

**Zone of Proximal Development**  a conceptual third space where learning occurs with the support of a more knowledgeable other. Optimal learning opportunities occur in the ZPD.

# Prologue

A prologue in any text provides background information or context about the content. It sets the tone for the work and introduces central themes. This prologue for *Learning and Leading for Transdisciplinary Literacy through Multi-Tiered Systems of Support* is intended to specifically illustrate the genesis of the aspirational model for Multi-Tiered Systems of Support introduced in this text. It may contradict your current thinking and other models of Multi-Tiered Systems of Support, but we are confident that the Multi-Tiered Systems of Support model presented here is well grounded in sound theory and research-validated instruction practices, and supported by hours of ethnographic research in real schools and classrooms with real students, teacher-colleagues, and teacher leaders. Additionally, you will notice that we tend to spell out and repeat key terms and phrases. This is an intentional move on our part, to ensure that novel language is internalized to support and sustain emerging understandings.

In 2015, the United Nations adopted *Transforming our World: the 2030 Agenda for Sustainable Development* that includes 17 sustainable goals. In particular, goal number 4 specifically addresses education to "ensure inclusive and equitable quality education and promote lifelong learning opportunities for all." Then, in November 2022, the United States government published *Convergence Education: A Guide to Transdisciplinary STEM Learning and Teaching* which addresses the subject of engaging students where disciplines converge. Notice the United States government is now talking about "learning and teaching," not the more traditional "teaching and learning." We will circle back to that critical shift in wording later. Nonetheless, both of these documents started to prime our thinking about

Prologue

the potential role of Multi-Tiered Systems of Support to accomplish the United Nations' Sustainable Goal in Education to ensure inclusivity and equitable, quality transdisciplinary education to promote lifelong critical learning and thinking within a pre-kindergarten through graduate school transdisciplinary framework for instruction. Consequently, based on the information from these organizations, we began to wonder, "What would a practical model look like at the district, province, school, and classroom level?" Of course, at the top of our list was that it had to be grounded on sound theory and supported by research-validated instructional practices. Hence, we started our collaboration on this aspirational text by listening to and learning from many teacher-colleagues and teacher leaders through structured interviews, focus groups, ethnographic fieldnotes, and observations. In addition, we conducted multiple online searches.

Our work is informed by the following principles: 1. Language is a tool for critical thinking, 2. Knowledge is socially constructed within diverse learning environments, and 3. Developing a common language is critical for forward shifts to occur. Shifts in thinking take time and are more likely to occur when we continuously update our language. Updating our language aids in changing our thinking to envision and articulate new transdisciplinary vistas and possibilities. We cannot critically communicate in a discipline without acquiring the language of the discipline at some level. Layer on to that the social aspect of learning, especially across content areas. All learning environments are social hubs. From a pre-kindergarten classroom to a doctoral seminar, various levels of knowledge are accessed through social activity – online and offline. For forward shifts to occur to improve transdisciplinary instruction within a district, province, and school, the development of a growing common language is paramount.

After decades of experiences in the field, we realize that these three tenets are paramount for sustaining the United Nations' goal 4 for an inclusive and equitable quality education. Our initial work started with teacher leaders at various levels to define what we mean by Multi-Tiered Systems of Support.

A simple online search revealed over 63,000 documents whose definitions vacillated between Multi-Tiered "System" of Supports and Multi-Tiered "Systems" of Support, adding to the confusion at the ground level. Some sites even defined it as "formerly" Response to Intervention/Instruction. It makes sense, then, that through our firsthand work with teacher leaders and teacher-colleagues that most thought of Multi-Tiered Systems of Support as synonymous with Response to Intervention/Instruction. We started to realize quickly that developing a common language was our starting point. So, we recognized that it was time to reframe our questions with these experienced and knowledgeable teacher leaders who were so graciously sharing their time with us. Consequently, rather than asking these teacher leaders to define the term, we reframed the question to, "What multi-tiered systems do you have in place, for example, for curriculum content? Professional learning? Community engagement? Family engagement? Assessment and evaluation? Distributive teacher leadership? Response to Intervention/Instruction?" The moment we reframed the questions, the biggest shock of awareness was "that makes perfect sense, but we've just never thought of it that way." Their emerging understanding was critical, and it was a pivotal moment in the conversation and our collaborative solution seeking.

From our collaborative conversations, seven systems emerged that would have sustainable and positive outcomes to improve instruction. We then had to revisit the idea of tiers in order for colleagues to refresh their understanding. Within this model of Multi-Tiered Systems of Support, we needed to get away from the current use of Tiers 1, 2, or 3, so strongly associated with Response to Intervention/Instruction, to shift our thinking so that Multi-Tiered Systems of Support were NOT synonymous with Response to Intervention/Instruction. At this crossroad, the work of Urie Bronfenbrenner's ecological systems theory (1994) offered a lexical solution to the Tier 1,2, 3 issue.

Bronfenbrenner's systems theory addresses a broad-spectrum "macro tier", a connective "meso tier", and a human-centered "micro tier" which elegantly overlapped with our Multi-Tiered Systems of Support model and its focus on universal, targeted, and intensive instructional interactions among all stakeholders, to sustain and improve transdisciplinary instruction over time with the goal of promoting lifelong learning. The "macro tier" is intended to create broad-spectrum support exposing learners to novel concepts and practices focused on updating language as a tool for thinking, while, by design, the meso tier provides more intentional tailored support grounded on learners' strengths and needs. Implementation of the micro tier brings to the forefront a more intensive concentrated effort focused on specific strengths and needs. Relationships among the tiers are bi-directional, where learning is a responsive, symbiotic activity capable of changing the beliefs and actions of the participants involved. Each tier is distinguished by the interactions among students, teacher-colleagues, and teacher leaders, where the individuals do not function independently but are interrelated and assert influence on each other. The tiers account for cultural and political influences that may impact the learning experience or curating a learning environment.

With the understanding that school is a place of learning for everyone, each overlapping system and tier in the model is intended to inform and improve professional learning and instruction over time. In other words, the Multi-Tiered Systems of Support model introduced in this text is intentionally designed to strengthen a school's transdisciplinary ecosystem (context) for literacy learning and leading to support a world class education that fosters a global-minded student population capable of finding solutions for current and future issues.

At the beginning of each chapter, we have included a purposeful quote to pique your curiosity and set the tone for the chapter. Additionally, each quote is also intended to prompt professional conversations about the topic at hand. Each chapter in *Learning and Leading for Transdisciplinary Literacy through Multi-Tiered Systems of Support* has an application section that briefly reviews the macro, meso, and micro tier within each system of support. Moreover, the "medical" model for research is held as the platinum standard for any research in education (Zhao, 2018). With that in mind, we have also added a section in each chapter about potential side effects, or unintended consequences, to better prepare for sustainability. Think of any drug commercial you see on television or in a magazine. The benefits are always highlighted, but so are the side effects; so, the consumer can make an informed decision in consultation with a professional.

*Learning and Leading for Transdisciplinary Literacy through Multi-Tiered Systems of Support* begins with Chapter 1, which critically defines our aspirational model of Multi-Tiered Systems of Support to help schools, districts, provinces, and states in developing a common language to enable forward shifts in emerging understandings. In Chapter 2, we proceed with a discussion on the importance of Design Thinking as a vital component to sustain Multi-Tiered Systems of Support. We then move on into Chapter 3, where we review the indispensable role of assessment and evaluation in data-informed (not data-driven) decision-making from an asset-based perspective. Many experts in the field claim that the number one factor in impacting the quality of learning in the learning environment is the classroom teacher. With that in mind, Chapter 4 fleshes out a Multi-Tiered Systems of Support for ongoing professional learning. It is universally accepted that a student's first teacher is the family. Consequently, Chapter 5 addresses developing a Multi-Tiered Systems of Support for family engagement. Similarly essential to any learning experience is the idea of curriculum content. Chapter 6 takes a broad-spectrum and inclusive view of curriculum that goes beyond content and resources. The community of any learning environment (school, classroom, district, province) is also an important source of support to ensure learning occurs on a grand scale. Chapter 7 looks at community engagement as a Multi-Tiered System of Support to engage and sustain lifelong learning. In Chapter 8, we review the importance of developing distributive teacher leadership within Multi-Tiered Systems of Support to ensure that schools, districts, and provinces have a constant source of sustenance and stimulant to sustain learning and a teaching population of passionate and dedicated professionals. Finally, Chapter 9 revisits the idea of Response to Intervention/Instruction within a broader Multi-Tiered Systems of Support model.

We end *Learning and Leading for Transdisciplinary Literacy through Multi-Tiered Systems of Support* with an Epilogue that concludes with lessons learned and emerging understandings. Written for teacher-colleagues and teacher leaders, our ultimate goal for this text is that it will serve schools, districts, states, and provinces as a springboard to fulfill the United Nations' 2030 Agenda for Sustainable Development and further. To be sustainable, the model presented in this text is intended to be a dynamic model where all stakeholders (students, teachers, teacher leaders, and communities) play a role in its design and implementation.

# Multi-Tiered Systems of Support

*All things appear and disappear because of the concurrence of causes and conditions. Nothing ever exists entirely alone; everything is in relation to everything else.*

–The Buddha

The word "system" implies multidirectional connections and reciprocal relationships (Chen-Levi, Schechter, & Buskila, 2021). Multi-Tiered Systems of Support is a holistic teacher leadership approach that focuses attention on networks of instruction/intervention. It is a model for visualizing wholes. For Multi-Tiered Systems of Support to be effective, teacher-colleagues and teacher leaders need to be prepared to understand the complexities of the systems and the multiple tiers of support needed within each system, as well as their roles in the process. The tiers of support within each system cannot be reduced to a simplistic cause-and-effect relationships or decision trees. It is a way of supporting teacher-colleagues and teacher leadership in dealing effectively with adaptive challenges that schools encounter while improving learning and instruction. Multi-Tiered Systems of Support stresses the ability to identify critical elements of systems and the interconnectivity among a variety of factors that contribute to improving learning and leading.

Conceptually, Multi-Tiered Systems of Support is an organic framework constructed, deconstructed, and reconstructed over time by a genuine professional learning community of practice with a growth mindset (Dweck, 2016) that accounts for teamwork, goals-setting, information gathering, collaborative decision-making, and solution-seeking endeavors for forward shifts in learning for all stakeholders – students, families, teachers, and teacher leaders. Schools are complex organizations designed with an extensive variety of intermingling purposes, people, and goals. The essence of Multi-Tiered Systems of Support is to understand an array of influencing factors, such as relationships, processes, connections, interconnections, disciplinary content, and contexts to improve learning and leading for all.

Informed by teacher colleagues and teacher leaders, our aspirational concept to reality framework for Multi-Tiered Systems of Support is founded on Conditions of Learning (Crouch & Cambourne, 2020) as it applies to all stakeholders, and scaffolded by Universal Design for Learning, Systems Thinking in unison with Design Thinking from a transdisciplinary literacy learning perspective that crosses curricular disciplinary boundaries with a focus on a global citizenry to solve real-world issues. Our thinking and conversations throughout the text are meant to be transformational and ongoing. Although, we have written this text with an end in mind; in reality, there should not be an end in sight. Like pi, growth is infinite.

## Systems Thinking

Multi-Tiered Systems of Support stresses the ability to identify critical elements of systems and the interconnectivity among a variety of factors that contribute to improving learning and leading. The heart of Multi-Tiered Systems of Support is to understand an array of compelling factors, such as relationships, processes, connections, and contexts to improve learning and instruction within complex organizations called schools (Connolly, Keenan, & Urbanska, 2018). The complexity of schools addresses varying demands, perceptions, identities, cultures, and beliefs of all within the system which impact decisions, practices, and occurrences within a continuous school improvement process.

Sustained school improvement requires "systems thinkers"; that is, people who can address the entire system at all levels: school and community, district or local education authority, and state/province or national policy (Fullan, 2005). Systems thinking involves attempts to understand and improve complex systems, examines systems holistically, and focuses on the way in which a system's parts interrelate and work together to accomplish a common goal. Systems thinking assists in dealing with complexity because it is an approach that places the study of wholes before that of the parts.

Systems thinking is an effective means of managing organizations since it facilitates group learning, shared decision-making, and improved organizational resilience. Specifically, systems thinking offers a harmonic comprehensive way of conceptualizing learning and practicing teacher leadership within an entire school setting, which leads directly to enhancing the quality of collaborations. Continuous collaborations create a sense of commitment among school faculty members and enable them to achieve more together that they would as individuals (Shaked & Schechter, 2017).

The essence of Multi-Tiered Systems of Support introduced in this text is an asset-based conceptual framework that fosters high-quality, research-validated instructional practices based on students' strengths and needs (Freeman, Miller, & Newcomer, 2015). Using dynamic and static assessments, strengths and needs are identified by continuously observing, monitoring, and responding to student learning over time. Contingent teaching is the watchword. Teacher decision-making and changes to instruction and interventions are based upon students' response to instruction. Within classrooms in our schools, Multi-Tiered Systems of Support promotes a coherent and intentional system of instruction by connecting multiple factors to enhance student learning. Ideally, Multi-Tiered Systems of Support provides and matches high-quality instructional practices and curricular resources to students' strengths and needs academically, socially, and behaviorally (Freemen, Miller, & Newcomer, 2015).

The Multi-Tiered Systems of Support framework introduced in this text is an integrated system of behavioral, social, emotional, and academic support that includes educators, families, and communities, considers all students and systems, and attends to equitable access, opportunity, and positive outcomes with each school's ecosystem of supports for transdisciplinary learning and leading. To accomplish this asset-based vision for Multi-Tiered Systems of Support within classrooms and schools, educators implement equitable, multi-level systems of support to provide equitable services, practices, and curricular resources to every learner based upon responsiveness to effective high-quality instruction and intervention. The triadic Multi-Tiered Systems of Support framework presented here draws upon 1. systems thinking, 2. design thinking, and 3. Universal Design for Learning within tiers of instruction and interventions as the foundation for high-quality instruction, enhanced curriculum designs, strategic use of data, and collaboration within a continuum of support to facilitate student success through continuous professional learning. Each of these systems interplay and intersect each other with the Conditions of Learning (see Figure 1.1). Schools are complex organizations designed with an extensive variety of intermingling purposes, people, and goals. The essence of the triadic Multi-Tiered Systems of Support framework is to understand and implement fully functional systems of support given an array of compelling factors, such as relationships, processes, connections, and contexts to improve learning and leading.

The conceptualization of the various systems within the triadic Multi-Tiered Systems of Support model (Figure 1.1) depicts multiple factors needed for the harmonic, comprehensive, and collaborative systems approach to Multi-Tiered Systems of Support implementation within classrooms, schools, and districts. In addition, the strengths and needs of all students are addressed by considering the intersectionality of the conditions of learning (Crouch & Cambourne, 2020) and curriculum design features of Universal Design for Learning. Collaboration and teamwork among families, educators, and communities are also key features of systemic implementation of Multi-Tiered Systems of Support. Continuous learning and improvement to meet the educational needs of all students within our asset-based multisensory classrooms and schools are the foundation of successful implementation.

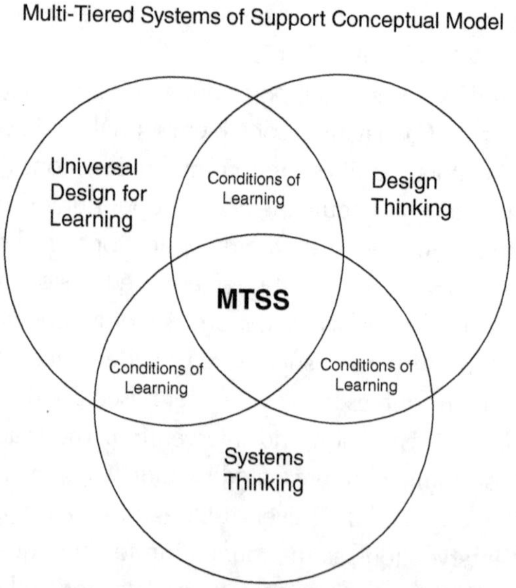

Multi-Tiered Systems of Support Conceptual Model

*Figure 1.1* Triadic Multi-Tiered Systems of Support Model

Multi-Tiered Systems of Support

In the next few paragraphs, we will review and discuss Cambourne's Conditions of Learning and how each condition contributes to an effective and efficient implementation of Multi-Tiered Systems of Support. Understanding the intersectionality of Cambourne's Conditions of Learning is critical for intentional and coherent implementation of Multi-Tiered Systems of Support.

# Conditions of Learning

The expertise of many giants in education has influenced our awareness, design, and construction of our triadic Multi-Tiered Systems of Support model. As the triadic model in Figure 1.1 illustrates, the metaphorical glue that holds it all together is the Conditions of Learning. Brian Cambourne (1988) conducted a study on the dawn of literacy learning by examining the development of oral language over time. In his study, he found that certain conditions were in place, at a universal level, to enable the development of oral language learning. When these Conditions of Learning are present, he theorized that students will be more likely to be enmeshed in the process of learning. Cambourne found that there are eight universal conditions of learning that are in place during oral language learning. As stated earlier, although his work is originally on the conditions "of" learning, we refer to them as conditions "for" learning from a teacher's and teacher leader's perspective and use them as a guide to create supportive coherent K-12 transdisciplinary literacy learning environments.

The eight Conditions of Learning that Cambourne unfolded are: immersion, demonstration, approximation, response, responsibility, engagement, use, and expectation. When learning is taking place, these eight conditions occur in tandem. Here we will address each one separately, while acknowledging that learning occurs when they are all in place in what Cambourne refers to as a "synergistic network."

By studying the conditions for learning, you can then start to examine the learning environment. These conditions can shape the groundwork for creating a supportive multisensory transdisciplinary learning environment. In the next few paragraphs, we will describe in detail each condition. As we highlight each condition, remember that there is no specific order for the conditions. When real learning is occurring, the conditions transpire simultaneously. Also keep in mind that the conditions for learning are not to be turned into a matrix of classroom activities to check off, but a "synergistic network" to scaffold our thinking when organizing a multisensory transdisciplinary learning environment. The intersectionality of Cambourne's Conditions for Learning should help us assemble an intentional and coherent K-12 transdisciplinary literacy framework for multisensory instruction and a powerful model for implementing Multi-Tiered Systems of Support.

## Demonstration

Although each condition is dependent and builds on each other, the condition of demonstration is one that every single one of us refers to as one manner of learning something. Ask any group how they learned something, and everyone will mention that they observed someone involved in what they attempted to learn. For example, think about how you learned to do any routine activity. In every situation, we observed someone engaged in the activity that made it look simple, so simple in fact, that we felt we could learn to do it too.

Through multiple exposures to an activity, we acquired not only a sense that we could achieve the activity, but we also began to recognize the value of engaging in the activity. The benefit of engaging in the activity could be for any number of reasons: for entertainment, to further another activity, to support a sense of independence, or to assist us in helping others, just to mention a few. Let us take driving a car as an example. After many demonstrations in the society we live in, driving a car provides us with the independence to go to the theatre, grocery shopping, and visit relatives and friends. All of these activities are what Cambourne (1988) refers to as contextually relevant.

We are reminded by Cambourne that demonstrations have to be continuously repeated and that there is no defined length of time that each demonstration should last. This understanding is key when curating a multisensory learning environment. These two caveats should have a tremendous impact on transdisciplinary literacy learning and leading. By taking a look at ourselves first, we will realize that the demonstrations that we observed were always demonstrations of an entire or whole activity. Shifting gears, turning on the windshield wipers, or braking by itself were never demonstrated as isolated activities but rather functions of the entire or whole concept of driving a car. This concept should have an incredible impact on the function of a teacher in supporting students in making accelerated progress and teacher leaders on planning for professional learning opportunities.

## Responsibility

Teacher-colleagues and teacher leaders should be viewed as "lead-learners" by showing students that they accept full responsibility for their learning. Teacher-colleagues, teacher leaders, and students need to show that they are self-monitoring, self-regulating, and self-directed. The condition of responsibility in learning emphasizes the significance of the learner being in control of their learning. No one can learn for someone else, but everyone can learn from a more knowledgeable other. The condition of responsibility in learning manifests itself when learners are willing to make decisions about their learning and more knowledgeable others trust that learners will be involved in the demonstrations provided.

There are certain behaviors that foster responsibility in learning. Responsibility is encouraged in classrooms and schools when learners are invited to try something before requesting help. When help is required, it is presented in a collaborative solution-seeking spirit. Schools and classrooms that offer choice in a transdisciplinary information-intensive learning environment are urging learners to seize responsibility for their learning and upgrading self-efficacy (Bandura, 1998).

It is a fundamental responsibility of a teacher and teacher leader to continuously checking themselves so that decisions are produced by collaborative solution seeking instead of didactic decision-making. Didactic decision-making confiscates the element of responsibility from the learner and places it on the more knowledgeable other. We have heard the question – if the teacher is doing all the work, who is doing all the learning?

## Approximation

Most adults that interact with children are familiar with approximation as a condition in learning. The baby that begins to coo and make sounds is approximating the oral language they are exposed to through multiple demonstrations provided by other siblings, children, and adults. The kindergartener that draws squiggles on paper approximates writing based on many demonstrations they have faced. Many of us have observed young children approximate reading a story by clasping a book and pretending (or approximating) to read. As adult learners, we are constantly approximating, predicting, and anticipating an outcome based on our present-day level of knowledge or lived experiences.

Cambourne (1988) tells us that when we think of learning as a model for hypothesis testing, approximations are critical for processing information. Approximations are essential for learners to build a feed-forward mechanism that operates to make learning efficient. A feed-forward mechanism is our "in-the-head" ability to predict and anticipate. Approximations are predictions and anticipation that starts transdisciplinary information processing. Without approximations, transdisciplinary information processing is immobilized, and refined processing and learning becomes an impossibility (Greene, 1988). Subsequently, learning environments ought to be set up for learners to feel free to approximate to begin transdisciplinary information processing.

Part of a teacher's responsibility is to safeguard that a multisensory learning environment is engineered for all learners (children and adults) to approximate, learn, and grow. Constructing an environment where learners are free to take risks is vital. Without approximations being accepted, the probability of forward shifts in learning will not occur. This applies to adults as well. We have to acknowledge that making errors is part of learning. Students will make mistakes in their learning. Teacher-colleagues and teacher leaders will make mistakes in implementing research-validated instructional practices.

## Response

Learning does not occur in a vacuum. All learning is complemented or driven by generative responses from more knowledgeable others during the process of learning. We borrow from Cambourne (1988) the term "response" instead of "feedback". Cambourne has described "feedback" as a mechanistic behaviorist term. Feedback indicates a one-sided point of view irrespective of the learner and does not reflect the responsive nature of the interaction. Traditionally, education has focused on providing corrective feedback. In providing "corrective" feedback, we are weakening the significance of approximations and removing the responsibility of learning from the learner. By giving a generative response, we are respecting and broadening the learner's approximations to foster forward shifts and the construction of a self-extending system (Clay, 2015).

We compare feedback to a transmission model of learning that centers on memorization of content and response to a transformational model of learning that stimulates critical thinking. It will be up to the teacher to evaluate the advantages of feedback and response in relation to the recognized crucial theme or concern. Responses in learning are grounded on the interaction between the learner and the more knowledgeable other. Affording a response is contingent on the learner's experiences and the experiences of the more knowledgeable other to support independent learning behaviors. A generative response is made considerately and thoughtfully to a learner's approximations.

The matter of response is vital for teacher-colleagues and teacher leaders to boost critical thinking. Ordinarily, responses at school concentrate on recognizing, commending, or collaboratively seeking solutions centered on a demonstration provided by either students or teacher-colleagues. Responses fall into three distinct groups. They focus on knowledge or skill level, unfolding the learner's understanding, or leading toward a particular resource.

## Immersion

When we were learning to speak, we were surrounded by oral language, regardless of the heritage language spoken at home. From the day we were born, we were immersed in oral language with people talking to us, about us, and around us. Consequently, because we were immersed in this oral language, learning to speak was facilitated.

Taking our cue from oral language learning, we need to immerse our students in a transdisciplinary information-intensive multisensory learning environment where thinking, reading, writing, speaking, listening, and viewing is coherent and intentional. By immersing everyone in a transdisciplinary information-intensive multisensory environment, we are utilizing disciplinary knowledge and appreciating the available technology that our students are growing and comfortable with in their everyday lives.

In addressing immersion as a condition for learning, we prefer to use the term information-intensive learning environment rather than the popularly used print-rich or literacy-rich environment. It seems to us that in order to prepare students for career, college, and global citizenship, print alone will not suffice.

The task of the teacher and teacher leader is to consider and plan how to create a multisensory transdisciplinary information-intensive environment where all involved will benefit. Creating a transdisciplinary information-intensive learning environment means providing online and offline materials for students. In elementary classrooms (K–5), this might include workboards, interactive whiteboards, electronic tablets, word walls/theme charts, computers, books/ebooks (narrative and non-narrative), and dictionaries/thesauruses. In secondary classrooms (6–12), a transdisciplinary information-intensive environment may include class agendas, content area textbooks/ebooks, affix charts, interactive whiteboards, electronic tablets, computers, books/ebooks (narrative and non-narrative), primary sources, and reference materials. In separating the grades to highlight the impact of creating an information-intensive environment, we are bringing to the forefront the need for adjusting the multisensory learning environment between a pedagogical perspective and a hebegogical perspective (Elliott-Johns, Booth, Rowsell, Puig, & Paterson, 2012).

At the school level, consideration needs to be given as to how the school is addressing the creation of a multisensory information-intensive learning environment for everyone involved. Immersion at the school level investigates strengths and needs to include updating technologies, community involvement, providing professional magazines and books/ebooks across core content areas, looking at professional learning opportunities, and creating an environment where everyone feels free to take risks. Too many times we have seen middle and high school students immersed inappropriately in a learning environment where elementary instructional practices are, although well intended, ineffectively used with adolescents.

## Expectation

For effective implementation of Multi-Tiered Systems of Support, expectation needs to be considered from the perspective of all stakeholders – students, families, community, teacher-colleagues, and teacher leaders. If the expectation among all involved in a school is not congruent, forward shifts will be impeded. Rosenthal and Jacobson (1968) addressed the importance of expectation in their study and revealed the importance of expectation in learning. Additionally, expectation is interrelated to self-esteem in learners (Cambourne, 1988) and self-efficacy (Bandura, 1998). The idea of truly knowing students and colleagues supports our notion of what we expect. Consequently, our expectations have a powerful influence on learners' emotions, learning, and memory when processing information (Rushton, Eitelgeorge, & Zickafoose, 2003) provided we assess and reflect on the learners' strengths and needs.

When our expectations are too low, a "this too shall pass" attitude and apathy is likely to manifest in learners. Mindful teacher-colleagues and teacher leaders know that these emotions are counterproductive to learning. When our expectations are too high, learners may develop a defeatist attitude prompted by assignments, texts, and projects that are too demanding to accomplish. Once again, these emotions are counterproductive to learning. Therefore, striking a perfect balance on our expectations becomes a critical point for consideration for teacher-colleagues and teacher leaders when we consider that emotions are accepted as a gateway to long-term memory (Caine & Caine, 1994; Lyons, 2003).

Our expectations should be grounded on our developing understanding of students' Zones of Mesial Development (Puig, 2019), Zones of Proximal Development (Vygotsky, 1978), and Zones of Distal Development (Moll, 2014; Spear-Ellinwood, 2011). The plural "zones" is used to imply that learners have multiple zones of development across core disciplines over time. Through mindful and intentional assessments and evaluations, teacher-colleagues and teacher leaders can develop a theory or rationale of students' strengths, what they can learn and/or do independently and needs, and what they cannot absolutely do or learn yet or what they can do or learn with the support of a more knowledgeable other.

# Engagement

A critical condition for learning is what Frank Smith (1981) calls "engagement." Cambourne (1988) found that there are four principles for true engagement to take place. The first principle is that the learner believes that if they delve into a learning situation, they will be successful. Think of it this way: why would you attempt to do something that you knew you would fail if you attempted to do it? This principle highlights the point that one factor that needs to be in place for learners to be engaged is the idea that if they attempt to do something, they expect to be successful. There has to be a sense of self-efficacy in place to be engaged (Bandura, 1998). No one wants to attempt something they know they will fail.

Cambourne (2007) positions the condition of engagement at the heart of learning. It has been our experience that engagement progresses within the learner's Zones of Proximal Development (Vygotsky, 1978) or instructional zones where learners can take on a task with the support of a more knowledgeable other. Deducing from the work of Tharp and Gallimore (1991), we realize that within the condition of engagement there are four levels that learners go through from subject-centered experiences to solution-seeking learning with complex sublevels occurring within each. As a framework for thinking when learning is taking place, the first level of engagement appears to exist at a social stage with interaction among learners and more knowledgeable others. At the second level of engagement, learners are consciously self-regulating. As the learner progresses through the levels of engagement that we have identified, the learning behavior becomes "fossilized" (Vygotsky, 1978) or habitual. The fourth level of engagement occurs when the learner recognizes what they have learned and what they still do not know. The fourth level is where learning is recursive, and the learner returns to the first level with new learning occurring.

Teachers and teacher leaders should always keep this expectation in mind when executing a plan that will directly impact students. Teacher-colleagues also need to feel that if they implement a new instructional practice, they will be successful in promoting learning in their classrooms. Understanding the purpose and the benefit in an activity or learning situation is a second principle identified by Cambourne.

It is understanding "what's in it for me." Without this sense of purpose or clear understanding of benefits, learners are not likely to be engaged. Interestingly, most professional learning opportunities focus on understanding the features of an instructional practice. Seldom is the grounding theory and benefit – the "whys" told. Consequently, it is up to the teacher to ensure that students understand the importance of acquiring prominent levels of multiple literacies (ways of communicating) where features and benefits are highlighted. Artificial Intelligence and social media are changing the ways we communicate. These multiple literacies have to be considered if we want to engage students.

Cambourne's third principle of engagement is the idea that if I attempt to learn something, there will not be any negative impact during the process of learning. To ensure engagement by a learner, the learner needs to feel safe to take risks. When a teacher plans for a lesson, consideration should be given to ensure that all involved understand that everyone is safe to take risks in attempting new learning. Here we have found that maintaining a good sense of humor and celebrating half-rights or productive failures are vital.

The fourth principle of engagement, according to Cambourne, is the concept that the learner respects and admires the person providing the demonstrations. Think of your own learning and teaching experiences. The students that are usually engaged during your demonstrations are the ones that respect and admire you as a teacher and as a person. Most of us are engaged in learning when the demonstrations provided are by someone we respect or admire. Even if we do not agree with the person providing the demonstrations, we are respectfully engaged because of our respect and admiration for that person or their work.

Cambourne's four principles of engagement are key points to consider as a teacher or teacher leader to ensure that all participants are engaged in all demonstrations. These principles should prompt you to think that learners need to be convinced that they are liked, and respected; special attention should be given to the kinds of demonstrations provided; and a certain level of awareness of the principles of engagement should be in place.

## Use/Employment

Research in neuroscience tells us that practice assists us in taking information into long-term memory (Jensen, 1998; Lyons, 2003; Wolfe, 2001). Although not empirically proven, Gladwell (2008) claims that the key to success in any field is a matter of practicing a specific task for a total of about 10,000 hours. The concept of use is not new in society or education. We have all grown up in school with use or practice incorporated into all aspects of our schooling. Although not necessarily the most effective instructional practice, many of us remember rote practice, committing information into long-term memory for further use in the future in other learning enterprises (or not). Effective instructional practices bands practice with social interaction in order for new learning to take place. Cambourne has stated that new learning is a by-product of social interaction and personal reflection. Vygotsky (1978) and Caine and Caine (1997) further validate this concept when they claim that learning is amplified through socialization with others.

We have reviewed Cambourne's Conditions for Learning as they apply to our work with students, teacher-colleagues, and teacher leaders. This information alone is still insufficient for us to make truly informed decisions regarding instruction based on assessment and the professional learning opportunities that need to be in place to improve instruction within a Multi-Tiered Systems of Support framework. To increase the likelihood of improving transdisciplinary literacy learning and leading we have to understand the confluence of the conditions for learning and the concept of instructional coherence. In the next section we will share some of our insights from research, theory, and experience regarding the intersectionality of the Conditions of Learning and the design features of Universal Design for Learning (UDL) to conceptualize our triadic model of multi-tiered systems of support.

## Universal Design for Learning

When considering Cambourne's Conditions for Learning and the advances in neurosciences and research over the last forty years, it is clear that there are multiple pathways for accessing, engaging, and demonstrating learning. Universal Design for Learning is a framework for instruction organized into three principles based on learning sciences and research. These principles guide curriculum design for instruction to address the learning strengths and needs of all students (Rose & Gravel, 2010). The framework is organized around three networks within the brain: recognition, strategic, and affective (Rose, 2002). To support recognition of learning, there are multiple means of representation – that is, how we explain and demonstrate *what* we learn. To support strategic acquisition of learning, we provide multiple means of action and expression – that is, *how* we express what we know. Finally, to support affective learning, we provide multiple means of engagement supporting the motivation and rationale of *why* we learn.

The principles of Universal Design for Learning are designed to reduce barriers for all students to access learning by providing multiple pathways when planning, teaching, and assessing learning by students. Through the effective use of these principles within curriculum design, Cambourne's Conditions for Learning are actualized to meet the diverse learning strengths and needs of students to access and demonstrate learning. The Universal Design for Learning principles are included in our model to address curriculum design thinking to reduce barriers of access to learning by all students.

# Design Thinking-Networked System of Tiers within MTSS

The triadic Multi-Tiered Systems of Support framework introduced in this text is designed to be a harmonic, comprehensive, school-wide continuum of services provided within an asset-based framework to support all stakeholders through high-quality, research-validated practices based on students' strengths and needs through curriculum design (Freeman et al., 2015; Lemons, Vaughn, Wexler, Kearns, & Sinclair, 2018). Within the Multi-Tiered Systems of Support framework presented in this text is Response to Intervention/Instruction (RtI/I), which addresses academics, behaviors, and social needs (Mundschenk, Fuchs, & Simonson, 2017). The framework builds upon a public health model for prevention and is tailored to address the strengths and needs of each student to ensure academic and social success. Using data from diagnostic, formative, and summative assessments, teacher-colleagues, and teacher leaders determine students' strengths and needs to provide preventative, targeted, and intensive support. Data collected are then used to promote forward shifts through a continuous solution-seeking model.

Multi-Tiered Systems of Support is a tightly networked and coordinated system of tiers of increasing intensity that not only addresses academics, but also addresses behavioral, social, and emotional supports. This networked and coordinated system of macro, meso, and micro tiers are a nested and aligned arrangement of dynamic interactions and collaborations to address individual strengths and needs of students by teams of transdisciplinary educators collaborating with caregivers and the community to consider all students to improve learning over time (Freeman et al., 2015). Additionally, the Multi-Tiered Systems of Support framework introduced in this text centers instruction within the school but draws on the home and community for support and resources to collaboratively develop and implement solutions.

Specifically, the Multi-Tiered Systems of Support framework should be fluid and flexible, allowing all stakeholders to move within the macro, meso, and micro tiers to address students' academic and/or behavioral strengths and needs. The labeled tiers in the framework are not to be confused with the enumerated tiers in a Response to Intervention/Instruction model. At the macro tier, teacher-colleagues and teacher leaders investigate improving instruction from a broad-spectrum perspective that will impact all stakeholders. The meso tier is meant to be an intermediate tier that is considered a midpoint towards tackling adaptive challenges. Finally, the micro tier addresses refinement to a plan of action. The tiers in the Multi-Tiered Systems of Support framework are not to be confused or synonymous with the core, targeted, and intensive tiers of Response to Intervention/Instruction.

The framework presented in this text addresses schools and districts foci on improving instruction as an ecosystem from an andragogical, pedagogical, and hebegogical vantage point. Whereas Response to Intervention/Instruction specifically addresses transdisciplinary literacy learning and its impact on students. To accomplish such a task, teachers and teacher leaders use multiple sources of both static and dynamic assessments to address students' learning, collecting frequent data to inform instructional decision-making. Teacher-colleagues and teacher leaders are responsible for learning to implement methods, and to coach each other to continuously improve and enhance their use of research-validated instructional practices. Collaboration is important to help identify, use, and interpret multiple sources of data to ensure students are successful in the classroom.

To summarize, high-quality instruction, additional resources, collaborative expertise, interventions, differentiation, and scaffolded support must be considered and implemented within classrooms within the multiple, networked systems of supports (Bender & Shores, 2007; Little, 2009). Classroom instruction may be differentiated and intensified based upon the instructional needs of the students, within the large group and as individuals within the classroom. Static and dynamic assessments are the primary sources of information about the student's learning which serves as the basis for instructional decisions.

This nested arrangement of structures and tiers are interdependent in addressing transdisciplinary literacy learning for students. The harmonic and comprehensive systems approach also encourages diverse ways of work to meet the learning goals of all stakeholders. Each of the educational professionals must also be supported within a nested arrangement of multiple structures to develop and implement this vision for learning by all, which will be explored and described within this book.

Since the goal is to increase learning and leading for all stakeholders, teacher-colleagues and teacher leaders must be the primary participants in the Multi-Tiered Systems of Support process. This harmonic, comprehensive, and continuous process, however, may include other educators on the school-based team to help identify and participate in solution seeking to improve learning and leading. This may require us to learn new methods and use new curricular resources to teach and differentiate instruction within dynamic and complex systems of support.

This transdisciplinary, harmonic, comprehensive, and continuous system of assessment and instruction provides all stakeholders with networked systems of support to address educational goals to engage productively in society. Research-validated practices, services, and curricular resources are based upon continuously determined student educational strengths and needs, which may include more intensive interventions through initiative-taking processes of instructional decision-making. According to the National Center on Intensive Interventions (NCII, n.d.), the following are essential features of Multi-Tiered Systems of Support: (a) instruction and intervention delivered using research-validated practices; (b) data-informed decision-making; (c) universal screening procedures and instruments for early identification; (d) formal and informal assessment and progress monitoring; (e) responsive instruction and intervention; (f) multi-tier instruction; and (g) a taxonomy of intervention that addresses frequency and duration in response to student strengths and needs (Barrio, Lindo, Combes, & Hovey, 2015; Fuchs & Fuchs, 2007; Murawski & Hughes, 2009; Vaughn & Fuchs, 2003).

# Data-Informed Decision-Making at the Nexus of MTSS Systems

Data use and instructional solution seeking are central to effective classroom instructional decision-making by teacher-colleagues and teacher leaders within the Multi-Tiered Systems of Support framework. Although the process of instructional decision-making has become part of educational nomenclature and practice, questions remain regarding how to effectively interpret and use data within this process for instruction and intervention (Katz &

Dack, 2014). This data collection and evaluation cycle is at the nexus of classroom decision-making to reconceptualize and interpret the use of data into pedagogical/hebegogical content knowledge to address unique student strengths and needs through innovative interplay of curriculum content and teaching variables within transdisciplinary systems (Mandinach, Honey, Light, & Brunner, 2008).

Data use is influenced by teachers' and teacher leaders' knowledge of how to interpret and respond to data (Horn, Kane, & Wilson, 2015). Background information and initial assessment data define the instructional issue to address as contextualized by the teacher-colleagues and teacher leaders. This initiative-taking process of instructional decision-making through data use has been also described to improve student outcomes while advancing and refining the art, science, and craft of teaching (Datnow, Park, & Kennedy-Lewis, 2012). However, although teachers collect classroom data through formal and informal assessment procedures, instructional decision-making requires "sensemaking" of the data (Mandinach, 2012) to determine necessary research validated instructional methods and resources (Little, 2012).

Enhancing data-informed decision-making means carefully analyzing and reflecting throughout this recursive process, either alone or with colleagues (Cain, 2011). This collaborative process of 'sensemaking" by teacher-colleagues and teacher leaders facilitates professional learning through discussions, interpretations, and conclusions (McNiff, Lomax, & Whitehead, 2004) so colleagues can apply across disciplines (Bradley-Levine, Smith, & Carr, 2009). In this way, the effects of data-informed decision-making can extend beyond the walls of one classroom and have a much greater influence. Data-informed decision-making processes enhance depth of understanding and interpretations of data as a result of discussions with other educators within a professional learning communities of practice, especially if the focus is on the impact of teaching on student learning (Marsh, Bertrand, & Huguet, 2015).

## Meeting the Instructional Strengths and Needs of All Learners

Classroom instruction and interventions within networked systems of support drive the renewed emphasis on improving learning for all students. It is important to build on this knowledge and magnify, enhance, and increase learning to address these adaptive challenges to make positive differences. Transdisciplinary collaboration within systems of support is critical to determine and enact solutions to address the educational changes and reforms. Instruction *must* address the strengths and needs of the learner by addressing the Conditions for Learning through the use of differentiated, instructional practices for each individual student. Teaching, therefore, calls for the knowledge and use of various research-validated instructional practices, as well as multiple strategic moves and techniques to scaffold instruction to assure students reach and exceed increasing levels of competencies and understandings (Little, 2009).

Effective teaching within our Multi-Tiered Systems of Support framework is contingent teaching. It is changing and adapting lessons and designing curriculum content and context that meets the specific strengths and needs of our students. No two lessons or units will be the same as teachers use their knowledge and skills to adapt and enhance lessons based upon *their* students' strengths and needs. We use instructional planning and decision-making process (a.k.a., instructional solution seeking) to make these important instructional decisions to meet the strengths and needs of students. This instructional planning and decision-making process is used by teachers and teacher leaders within schools on a daily basis. The instructional decisions and the results of student learning collected by progress monitoring assessments and documented classroom observations are essential in the Multi-Tiered Systems of Support process.

As we implement instructional decision-making processes within complex educational systems, considerations and variables to the Multi-Tiered Systems of Support need to be identified and addressed. Pedagogical/hebegogical content knowledge and deep understandings are needed to enhance and diversify instructional approaches, explanations, and supports to meet students' strengths and needs. Knowledge of students' strengths and needs must be identified to make decisions about the multiple curriculum content and instructional variables of learning and leading. During the instructional process of assessing, evaluating, planning, teaching, and re-assessing student learning, strategic use of research-validated instructional practices are important to meet the strengths and needs of students.

## Multi-Tiered Systems of Support

Traditionally, Multi-Tiered Systems of Support focus on improving instruction for students. We make the claim that for Multi-Tiered Systems of Support to make an impact on instruction, we need to simultaneously focus on the professional learning community of practice, as well. The vision, then, for equitable multi-level, harmonic, comprehensive systems of support include continuous professional learning and implementation of research-validated practices by teacher-colleagues supported by teacher leaders at varying levels. However, there are multiple factors that are also key to the successful implementation of a harmonic comprehensive Multi-Tiered Systems of Support framework (Curran, Bauer, Mittman, Pyne, & Stetler, 2012). Through teacher leader focus groups, structured interviews, literature reviews, and micro-ethnographies, we have identified seven specific "systems" that successful schools and school districts have in place to ensure professional learning and student success. These systems are a networked arrangement of complex structures of data-informed instruction, implementation decision-making, transdisciplinary cooperation, teacher leadership, and continuous professional learning. Figure 1.2 is a graphic representation of the unique interpretative and transformational framework espoused in this book introducing macro, meso, and micro tiers, distinguishing it from being synonymous with Response to Intervention/Instruction.

Throughout this book, we will be describing and expanding the key components of Multi-Tiered Systems of Support that include:

1 Multi-Tiered System for Assessment and Evaluation (e.g., formative/dynamic and summative/static).
2 Multi-Tiered System for Ongoing Professional Learning for everyone that interacts with students (e.g., literacy coach, literacy leadership team, online/offline professional learning).
3 Multi-Tiered System for Family Engagement (e.g., newsletter, parent night, parent workshops, Parent–Teacher Association/Organization).
4 Multi-Tiered System for Transdisciplinary Curriculum Content (e.g., media center, leveled book room, school, district, and state/province standards).
5 Multi-Tiered System for Community Engagement (e.g., social services, school outreach, counseling services, health services).

## Multi-Tiered Systems of Support framework

**Multi-Tiered System for Assessment and Evaluation**
Macro Tier – Static universal assessment and evaluation
Meso Tier – Static diagnostic assessment focused on item knowledge
Micro Tier – Dynamic diagnostic assessment focused on processing

**Multi-Tiered System for ongoing Professional Learning**
Macro Tier – Assemble a transdisciplinary literacy leadership team
Meso Tier – Employ a transdisciplinary literacy coach
Micro Tier – Foster transdisciplinary peer coaching

**Multi-Tiered System for Family Engagement**
Macro Tier – Ongoing communication for family support
Meso Tier – Mixed mode communication for family support or involvement
Micro Tier – Face to face engagement for family involvement

**Multi-Tiered System for Transdisciplinary Curriculum Content**
Macro Tier – Focus is on state/province K-12 standards
Meso Tier – Comprehensive K-12 transdisciplinary literacy framework
Micro Tier – Instructional resources (print, non-print, technology)

**Multi-Tiered System for Community Engagement**
Macro Tier – Community member leadership team
Meso Tier – Utilizing community services off campus
Micro Tier – Employing community services on campus

**Multi-Tiered System for Developing Distributive Teacher Leadership**
Macro Tier – State and district pathways
Meso Tier – School level pathways
Micro Tier – University degree/ certificate pathways

**Multi-Tiered System for Response to Intervention/Instruction**
Tier one – Broad-spectrum core instruction
Tier two – Targeted small group instruction in addition to Tier 1 instruction
Tier three – Intensive 1-1 instruction in addition to Tier 1 instruction

*Figure 1.2* Multi-Tiered Systems of Support Framework

6 Multi-Tiered System for Developing Distributive Teacher Leadership (e.g., School Advisory Committee, college/university courses, professional pathways).
7 Multi-Tiered System for Response to Intervention/Instruction (e.g., Tier 1 universal core instruction for all students, Tier 2 targeted instruction/intervention for approximately 20% of students, Tier 3 intensive instruction/intervention for approximately 5% of students).

## Unintended Consequences

In education, with the best of intentions, innovations are implemented that impact learning for all stakeholders and seldom is consideration given to any potential negative side effects or unintended consequences before implementation. Taking the lead from the medical field, we have to acknowledge the potential of unintended consequences in preparation to pivot and change directions when forward shifts are not occurring. Acknowledging potential unintended consequences from the start empowers schools and districts. In the medical field, patients are always given practical solutions and potential negative side effects. By doing so, medical professionals are empowering patients with an informed choice. Likewise, when implementing Multi-Tiered Systems of Support, all stakeholders need to be aware of the benefits as well as potential unintended consequences so that all stakeholders can make an informed decision. This simply means that if implementation does not go as planned, stakeholders have considered a plan B.

Throughout the following chapters on the seven systems introduced in this text, each system presented includes a section on unintended consequences to assist schools and districts in making informed decisions. The sections of unintended consequences within each chapter defining the seven systems listed in the framework are an illustrative list. This is not an exhaustive list as we recognize the uniqueness of each school and community. As a Multi-Tiered Systems of Support framework is implemented, the goal is for each school and district is to stop and reflect collaboratively to develop a plan B. For example, we recognize that each system will have some unintended consequences and, when combined, it may create different unintended consequences. A system for assessment and evaluation may be wrought with misinterpretations and false positives. A system for professional learning may lead to ineffective instructional practices with a particular class or school. The point in considering what works and what does not is to increase the likelihood of forward shifts and continuous improvement that is sustainable over time.

## Emerging Understandings

In this chapter, we have introduced our asset-based triadic model of Multi-Tiered Systems of Support grounded in (1) Systems thinking, (2) Design thinking, and (3) Tiers of instruction/intervention, intersected by the Conditions of Learning and the principles of Universal Design for Learning to improve professional learning and student learning. Using micro-ethnographic methodologies, teacher led focus groups, and contemporary literature, we have also established seven specific systems that need to be in place for Multi-Tiered Systems of Support to be a productive construct that teacher-colleagues, teacher leaders, schools, and school systems can utilize for forward shifts to occur and sustain. The rest of the text will revisit each of the seven multi-tiered systems in detail to assist schools, districts, and provinces in decision-making and implementing Multi-Tiered Systems of Support effectively and efficiently to support lifelong transdisciplinary literacy learning.

## Professional Reflection Question

Professional collaborative and reflective conversations generate forward shifts when the goal is improving instruction. Developing a common language is the first step toward seeking solutions to adaptive challenges. The following reflection questions are presented to prompt the vital professional conversations that need to take place and promote the development of a common professional language:

- How do systems of multiple assessments provide needed data and information for data-informed decision-making by educational teams?
- What multiple systems for continuous professional learning and support for everyone that interacts with students need consideration as part of a school's ecosystem (e.g., literacy coach, literacy leadership team, online/offline professional learning)?

- What are critical practices for engaging families and community members within the Multi-Tiered Systems of Support in schools, districts, states, and provinces?
- What are the enhanced roles for teacher leaders and teacher-colleagues within a distributive leadership system?
- How will multiple systems be developed and implemented at the macro-tier, meso-tier, and micro-tier within each of the critical components to improve instruction: design thinking; assessment and evaluation; professional learning; family engagement; transdisciplinary curriculum content; community engagement; distributive teacher leadership; and Response to Intervention/Instruction (RtI/I)?

# References

Bandura, A. (1998). *Self-efficacy: The exercise of control*. New York: Freeman.

Barrio, B. L., Lindo, E. J., Combes, B. H., & Hovey, K. A. (2015). Ten years of response to intervention: Implications for general education teacher preparation programs. *Action in Teacher Education, 37*, 190–204.

Bender, W. N., & Shores, C. (Eds.). (2007). *Response to intervention: A practical guide for every teacher*. Thousand Oaks, CA: Corwin Press.

Bradley-Levine, J., Smith, J., & Carr, K. (2009). The role of action research in empowering teachers to change their practice. *Journal of Ethnographic & Qualitative Research, 3*(3), 191–197.

Cain, T. (2011). Teachers' classroom-based action research. *International Journal of Research & Method in Education, 34*(1), 3–16.

Caine, R. N., & Caine, G. (1994). *Making connections: Teaching and the human brain*. New York: Addison-Wesley.

Caine, R. N., & Caine, G. (1997). *Unleashing the power of perceptual change*. Alexandria, VA: Association of Supervision and Curriculum Development.

Cambourne, B. (1988). *The whole story: Natural learning and the acquisition of literacy*. Auckland: Ashton Scholastic.

Cambourne, B. (2007). Biomimicry and education innovation. *Bioinspired, 5*(1), 7–9.

Chen-Levi, T., Schechter, C., & Buskila, Y. (2021). Exploring systems thinking in schools: Mental models of school management teams. *International Journal of Educational Reform, 30*(2), 116–137.

Clay, M. M. (2015). *Change over time in children's literacy development*. Portsmouth, NH: Heinemann.

Connolly, P., Keenan, C., & Urbanska, K. (2018). The trials of evidence-based practice in education: A systematic review of randomised controlled trials in education research 1980–2016. *Educational Research, 60*(3), 276–291.

Crouch, D., & Cambourne, B. (2020). *Made for learning: How the conditions of learning guide teaching decisions.* Richard C. Owen Publishers

Curran, G. M., Bauer, M., Mittman, B., Pyne, J. M., & Stetler, C. (2012). Effectiveness-implementation hybrid designs: Combining elements of clinical effectiveness and implementation research to enhance public health impact. *Medical Care, 50*(3), 217–226.

Datnow, A., Park, V., & Kennedy-Lewis, B. (2012). High school teachers' use of data to inform instruction. *Journal of Education for Students Placed at Risk (JESPAR), 17*(4), 247–265.

Dweck, C. S. (2016). *Mindset: The new psychology of success.* New York: Ballantine Books.

Elliott-Johns, S. E., Booth, D., Rowsell, J., Puig, E., & Paterson, J. (2012). Using student voices to guide instruction. *Voices from the Middle, 19*(3), 25–31.

Freeman, R., Miller, D., & Newcomer, L. (2015). Integration of academic and behavioral MTSS at the district level using implementation science. *Learning Disabilities: A Contemporary Journal, 13*(1), 59–72.

Fuchs, L. S., & Fuchs, D. (2007). A model for implementing responsiveness to intervention. *Teaching Exceptional Children, 39*(5), 14–20.

Fullan, M. (2005). The meaning of educational change: A quarter of a century of learning. In *The roots of educational change: International handbook of educational change* (pp. 202–216). Dordrecht: Springer Netherlands.

Gladwell, M. (2008). *Outlier: The story of success.* New York: Little Brown.

Greene, M. (1988). *The dialectic of freedom.* New York: Teachers College Press.

Horn, I. S., Kane, B. D., & Wilson, J. (2015). Making sense of student performance data: Data use in teachers' learning opportunities. *American Educational Research Journal, 52*(2), 208–242.

Jensen, E. (1998). *Teaching with the brain in mind.* Alexandria, VA: Association of Supervision and Curriculum Development.

Katz, S., & Dack, L. A. (2014). Towards a culture of inquiry for data use in schools: Breaking down professional learning barriers through intentional interruption. *Studies in Educational Evaluation, 42*, 35–40.

Lemons, C. J., Vaughn, S., Wexler, J., Kearns, D. M., & Sinclair, A. C. (2018). Envisioning an improved continuum of special education services for students with learning disabilities: Considering intervention intensity. *Learning Disabilities Research & Practice, 33*(3), 131–143.

Little, M. (2012). Action research and response to intervention: Bridging the discourse divide. *The Educational Forum, 76*, 69–80. doi: 10.1080/00131725.2012.629

Little, M. E. (2009). *Response to intervention (RtI) for teachers: Classroom instructional problem solving.* Denver, CO: Love Publishing Company.

Lyons, C. A. (2003). *Teaching struggling readers: How to use brain-based research to maximize learning*. Portsmouth, NH: Heinemann.

Mandinach, E. B. (2012). A perfect time for data use: Using data-driven decision making to inform practice. *Educational Psychologist, 42*(2), 71–85.

Mandinach, E. B., Honey, M., Light, D., & Brunner, C. (2008). A conceptual framework for data-driven decision making. In E. B. Mandinach & M. Honey (Eds.), *Data-driven school improvement: Linking data and learning* (pp. 13–31). New York: Teachers College Press.

Marsh, J. A., Bertrand, M., & Huguet, A. (2015). Using data to alter instructional practice: The mediating role of coaches and professional learning communities. *Teachers College Record, 117*(4), 1–40.

McNiff, J., Lomax, P., & Whitehead, J. (2004). *You and your action research project* (2nd ed.). London & New York: Routledge Falmer.

Moll, L. C. (2014). *L.S. Vygotsky and education*. New York: Routledge/Taylor & Francis Group.

Mundschenk, N., Fuchs, W., & Simonson, S. (2017). Statewide change in teacher preparation: An inside job. *The New Educator, 13*(4), 392–407.

Murawski, W. W., & Hughes, C. E. (2009). Response to intervention, collaboration, and co-teaching: A logical combination for successful systemic change. *Preventing School Failure: Alternative Education for Children and Youth, 53*(4), 267–277.

National Center for Intensive Interventions (n.d.). https://intensiveintervention.org/

Puig, E.A. (2019). Rethinking the intersectionality of the Zone of Proximal Development: The challenges of disruptive and transformative change to improve instruction. In A. E. Lopez & E. L. Olan (Eds.), *Transformative pedagogies for teacher education: Critical action, agency, dialogue in teaching and learning contexts* (pp. 69–86). Charlotte, NC: Information Age Publishing.

Rose, D. (2002). *Teaching every student in the digital age: Universal design for learning*. Association for Supervision and Curriculum Development (ASCD).

Rose, D. H., & Gravel, J. W., (2010). Universal design for learning. In P. Peterson, E. Baker, B. McGraw (Eds.), *International encyclopedia of education* (3rd ed.). Elsevier, pp. 119–124.

Rosenthal, R., & Jacobson, L. (1968). Pygmalion in the classroom. *The Urban Review, 3*(1), 16–20.

Rushton, S. P., Eitelgeorge, J., & Zickafoose, R. (2003). Connecting Brian Cambourne's conditions of learning theory to brain/mind principles: Implications for early childhood educators. *Early Childhood Education Journal, 31*, 11–21.

Shaked, H., & Schechter, C. (2017). Systems thinking among school middle leaders. *Educational Management Administration & Leadership, 45*(4), 699–718.

Smith, F. (1981). Demonstrations, engagement, and sensitivity: A revised approach to language learning. *Language Arts 58*(6), 634–642.

Spear-Ellinwood, K. (2011). *Re-conceptualizing the organizing circumstance of learning*. Unpublished doctoral dissertation. College of Education, University of Arizona, USA.

Tharp, R. G., & Gallimore, R. (1991). *Rousing minds to life: Teaching, learning, and schooling in social context*. Cambridge University Press.

Vaughn, S., & Fuchs, L. S. (2003). Redefining learning disabilities as inadequate response to instruction: The promise and potential problems. *Learning Disabilities Research & Practice, 18*(3), 137–146.

Vygotsky L. S. (1978). *Mind in society: The development of higher psychological processes*. M. Cole, V. John Steiner, S. Scribner, & E. Souberman (Eds.) Cambridge: Harvard University Press.

Wolfe, P. (2001). *Brain matters: Translating research into classroom practice*. Alexandria, VA: Association of Supervision and Curriculum Development.

# 2 Design Thinking in Multi-Tiered Systems of Support

*Study the science of art. Study the art of science. Develop your senses – especially learn how to see. Realize that everything connects to everything else.*

–Leonardo Da Vinci

From a Multi-Tiered Systems of Support (MTSS) perspective in a K-12 transdisciplinary literacy model, Design Thinking is a flexible and responsive process in which teacher-colleagues and teacher leaders strive to recognize all stakeholders' strengths and needs, face conventions, and reinterpret issues to name research validated practices and results that might not be immediately evident at our current level of comprehension. Simultaneously, Design Thinking provides a mindful, respectful, and humane solution-seeking approach to unravelling tangled complex issues and concerns (Razzouk & Shute, 2012). It is a collaborative professional learning community of practice for thinking and doing. To conceive, construct, and implement MTSS we have found that adopting a Design Thinking course of action is most productive. Although many schools implementing MTSS successfully, do not acknowledge the concept of Design Thinking, many followed the concepts and phases without naming it. Like collaborative action research processes (Little, Slanda, & Cramer, 2024), a Design Thinking course of action is a respectful and mindful human-centered approach to solution seeking that involves a recursive non-linear 5-step process toward seeking solutions to given adaptive challenges (Becker & Mentzer, 2015; Carroll et al., 2010; Donar, 2011; Mentzer, Becker, & Sutton, 2015).

Implementing MTSS at the school and district levels can be complex and overwhelming. Here is where Design Thinking practices are helpful in moving stakeholders from idea to impact. Design Thinking practices provide the models and support necessary to take a complex issue and simplify it. As teacher-colleagues and teacher leaders determine how to leverage MTSS in ways that serve all stakeholders, the ability to solve unstructured issues and to engage in complex communication will be at the outset for forward shifts to occur. Design Thinking within MTSS is a transdisciplinary approach towards solution-seeking. With MTSS in mind, we want to revisit the idea that the Design Thinking model is all about innovative solution seeking that is not necessarily sequential or lockstep. It is not a linear sequence of tidy steps, but a humane, creatively reflexive, and practical approach to generating novel concepts and solutions (Brown, 2008). Furthermore, phases of Design Thinking can be seen as a transdisciplinary concept which fosters innovative work while explicitly complementing disciplinary thinking (Manak & Puig, 2021; Puig & Froelich, 2021). Figure 2.1 is a graphic model of Design Thinking for MTSS in education.

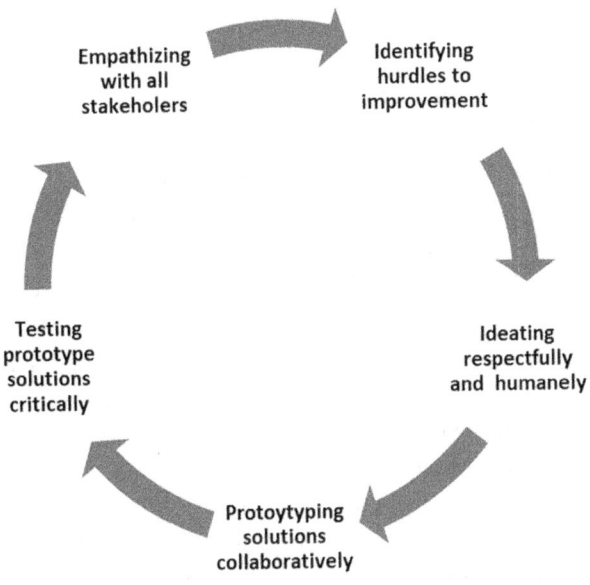

Figure 2.1 Design Thinking Model for MTSS in Education

Design Thinking, a human-centered construct, is one approach that can provide teacher-colleagues and teacher leaders with the abilities and mindset to navigate away from the traditional school model established during the Industrial Revolution to a stakeholder-centered goal where colleagues collaboratively design learning experiences at the intersection of curriculum content, stakeholders' strengths, and research validated practices (Luka, 2014). Design Thinking within MTSS is a method with an emphasis on developing instructional mindsets with empathy, imaginative confidence, and an acceptance of productive failure. In addition, it strengthens self-efficacy and helps teacher-colleagues and teacher leaders embrace necessary changes to tackle adaptive challenges to improve instruction with community engagement in mind. Think Maslow before Bloom. In other words, we need to consider, initially, hierarchical human needs over learning objectives by levels of complexity.

## Design Thinking as a Process to Develop MTSS

Often, as with many activities in education, Design Thinking is seen as a checklist of activities to accomplish and move on. Like learning itself, Design Thinking is a cumulative, non-linear, and recursive model that fosters teacher-colleagues' and teacher leaders' mindset toward steering change in a positive, lifelong learning trajectory. Subsequently, it is a series of fluid actions between the periods of inspiration, ideation, and implementation, to perpetually improve upon a potential solution (Shively, Stith, & Rubenstein, 2018).

The periods of inspiration, thinking, and implementation have been expanded to transactional phases of empathizing, defining, ideating, prototyping, and testing. Design Thinking as a process can be used to identify issues, seek solutions, and explore opportunities for forward shifts to occur. Please note that simply going through these phases is where most teacher-colleagues and teacher leaders misunderstand Design Thinking and do not see the results they hoped for. These phases exist to support the development of an action-oriented growth mindset where productive failures are accepted and dissected in the name of lifelong learning. Time is always a commodity in schools and districts. The enterprise moves quickly from identifying an issue to designing and then evaluating a solution to getting generative responses. Each of the five phases – empathizing, identifying, ideating, prototyping, and testing – has various practices to facilitate critical and unique experiences based on your school, district, and community.

# Phase 1: Empathizing

The first phase, acting with empathy, is what makes Design Thinking distinctive. Empathizing in Design Thinking as a process is considering what advantages are in it for all stakeholders. With MTSS in mind, how is the MTSS framework going to benefit students, teacher-colleagues, teacher leaders, and the community? At this point, the work is concerned with stakeholders and the impact MTSS will have on them and students. During the empathy phase, you observe a variety of demonstrations at the classroom, school, and district levels, engage as a participant and non-participant observer, and immerse yourself in the experience of those you are designing for. This can involve continuously asking "Why?" to understand why things are the way they are. Keep in mind that asking "Why?" questions may make some colleagues and community members uncomfortable. As with anything we say, the tone in which questions are asked is important. The goal during this phase is to recognize stakeholders' strengths and needs and what is meaningful to them. This phase is where we see the most challenges, yet it is also the most critical.

One adaptive challenge during this phase is to not speak directly to the stakeholders, as this may cause teacher-colleagues to speculate about students' strengths and needs, and, similarly, families or teacher leaders to give their opinions about teachers' strengths and needs. While initially you may begin empathizing with teacher-colleagues and teacher leaders, eventually you must speak directly to all stakeholders. As you engage in Design Thinking, the goal is to seek solutions on a variety of levels – physical, emotional, and contextual – to clearly understand who the stakeholders are and what is important to them. Mindfully watching what stakeholders do and how they interact with the learning environment will serve as a window into how they think and feel (Besharat, Komninos, Papadimitriou, Lagiou, & Garofalakis, 2016). Intentionally watching physical interactions will enable inferences to unfold perceptions. Perceptions will give you inspiration for creative solutions to adaptive challenges. When seeking solutions, the most memorable solutions are derived from perceptions grounded in human behavior. Notice body positions and facial expressions, since not everything has to be said. Becoming a keen observer brings its own challenges, of course. Our minds are cluttered with preconceived notions and speculations that have the potential to veil, distort, and cloud our observations. Here, new learning involves seeing with a fresh pair of eyes and empathizing with a lens for that to occur.

Interacting directly with stakeholders uncovers a huge amount of information about how they reason and what they value. At times, stakeholders' reasoning and what they value are not clearly noticeable. A good dialogic conversation can surprise both designers and stakeholders by bringing to light unimagined insights. Personal texts and narratives are usually strong indicators of profound beliefs and worldviews. High-quality designs are constructed on a foundation of crystalizing those beliefs and worldviews. At this phase, designers are seeking stories to understand "why".

Empathizing involves four processes: witnessing, participating, seeing, and hearing. Witnessing involves paying attention to stakeholders' behaviors in the context of their world. In addition to interviewing stakeholders, either formally or informally, we must notice how they navigate their world. Observing how they navigate their work will sometimes bring contradictions with what they say about navigating their world. The contradiction between what someone says and what they do may be an opportunity for deeper conversations to bring root causes to the surface and to make the invisible visible.

Dialogic conversations play a vital role during the empathizing phase. These conversations should be warm, caring, inviting, and nonjudgmental and should also encourage transformational participation. If the conversation begins to sound like a one-sided interview with twenty questions, stop. Ideally all those involved should be engaged in asking respectful, thought-provoking, and clarifying questions. Credibility and trustworthiness are major watchwords at this stage. During these conversations, you are looking for personal and intimate stories that will prompt you to deepen the conversation. Asking genuine "Why?" questions will assist in uncovering deeper meanings. "Why?" questions need to have a tone of clarification rather than interrogation. The questions must be grounded in seeking understanding and not come across as doubting beliefs and worldviews.

Witnessing and participating should be carried out in tandem. Personal texts and narratives are embodied in artifacts. Noticing clothing, style, jewelry, photos, friends, tattoos, piercings, preferred artists, and pets say a lot about individuals and what is important to them. The living and learning environment should provide a wealth of data to establish a caring relationship. Placing all these tangible artifacts onto an Empathy Map will scaffold teacher-colleagues and teacher leaders in developing a common vision and language that will support subsequent phases in design mapping as a process. An Empathy Map is a graphic organizer which is divided into four quadrants. Each of these quadrants should be given a label as follows: Says – Thinks – Does – Feels. As Design Thinkers, understanding stakeholders and their motivation is an essential feature for designing and implementing an innovation at the classroom, district, or school level. Think of an Empathy Map as a picture of how stakeholders (teachers, teacher leaders, students, and community) interact and are impacted by the school. When producing an Empathy Map, use relevant quantitative (i.e., standardized assessment scores, end of unit exams, attendance records) and qualitative (i.e., documented observations, student work samples, interest inventories, motivation profiles) data for tackling any adaptive challenge to improve instruction. In addition to student artifacts, photographs of classrooms, school, and community can serve to develop empathy for all stakeholders. The Empathy Map is a comprehensive illustration of stakeholders' actions, vexations, ideals, ambitions, and more within a single text to promote professional dialogic solution-seeking and decision-making conversations. Equipped with this information, teachers and teacher leaders will be in a better position to seek solutions for adaptive challenges to improve instruction within an MTSS framework. Figure 2.2 illustrates a sample Empathy Map.

Unfolding all the collected personal data starts the transition into the Defining phase of Design Thinking. Unfolding means that you are starting to uncover and untangle to create a big picture of what will impact all stakeholders; it is an opportunity to reflect on the information gathered with the goal of making the invisible visible. Here you start posting pictures, notes, and other tangible artifacts that portray feelings and evidence about the stakeholders. Combined, all the tangible artifacts serve as an aid to understanding stakeholders' strengths and needs. This visible documentation is the start of the synthesis process that will take you into the Defining stage.

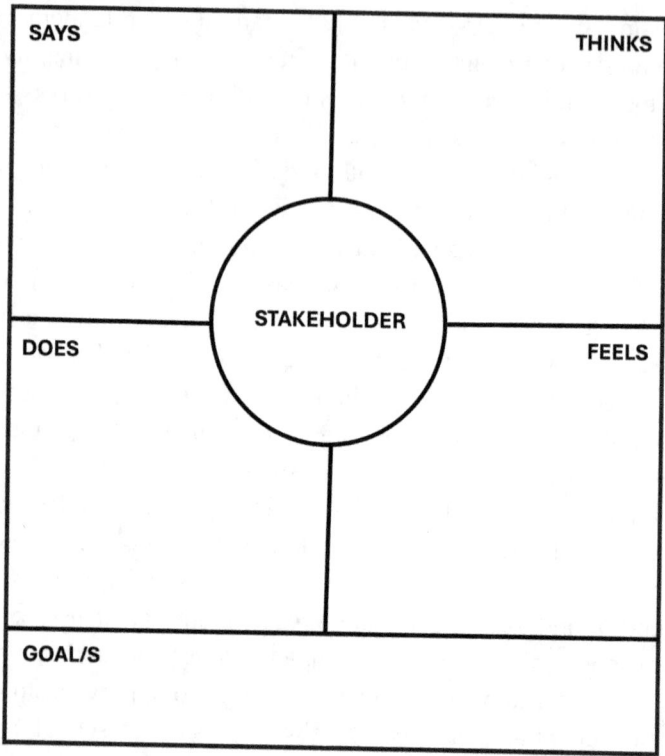

*Figure 2.2* Empathy Map

## Phase 2: Identifying

During the Identifying phase, you unfold the empathy findings and create an actionable issue statement often starting with, "How might we...." "How might we" emphasizes a positive perspective reflecting the potential for forward shifts, but it also invites stakeholders to think critically about how this can be a collaborative solution-seeking approach. We choose to use the word "unfold" instead of the popular "unpacking" throughout the entire process. When definitions or concepts are unfolded, they are opened up for all involved to get a more holistic view or understanding. Unpacking, on the other hand, usually leads to putting away over time. When you unpack something, it implies that you have packed something away. In many cases, the concepts being "unpacked" are novel and have never actually been packed by you in the first place.

The Identifying phase in Design Thinking as a process is concerned with bringing clarity and intentionality. In this phase, you consider: Who are the stakeholders? What are their strengths, needs, issues, and level of tolerance to change? What issues do we need to work toward and seek solutions? This phase is foundational since this is the phase during which decisions will impact the solution-seeking enterprise. It is an opportunity to define the adaptive challenges ahead grounded in what was learned about all stakeholders. After developing expertise in all stakeholders and the context in which they all exist, you start to draw meaningful conclusions on the broad-spectrum data you have collected. One side note to ponder at this point: *No one is ever a complete expert on a subject, but as lifelong learners we always want to be developing expertise.* Developing expertise keeps us fresh. Consequently, the goal of the Identifying phase is to draft a mindful and realistic solution statement. In the Defining phase this is referenced as a point of view. The ultimate question here within MTSS is: From what point of view is a classroom, school, or district functioning? The solution or the tentative answer should be derived from a focus on the strengths and needs of the stakeholders. Mindful and realistic solutions emerge by synthesizing the data collected to unfold personal stories, connections, and patterns of behavior over time. The Identifying phase is all about making meaning, especially within MTSS, to improve instruction and make school a place of learning for all stakeholders.

An affinity, by definition, is a comparison of attributes suggesting a connection or a likeness in characteristics. At this stage, many Design Thinking professionals find the use of Affinity Mapping, as a graphic organizer, to be beneficial in structuring and examining qualitative data to identify overall themes and patterns to seek sustainable solutions. To start Affinity Mapping, collaboratively summarize or condense the collected data from observations (this may also include photographs), instructional resources available, and interviews on to Post-it notes and organize them into groups on a board or table visible to everyone. Then, collaboratively distinguish developing commonalities and tag them with essential terminology or labels. These labels will be the primary headings for the Affinity Map. Finally, generate an Overview Map that synthesizes the comprehensive enterprise by linking all the themes and any additional commonalities noticed to create a holistic portrayal of the vital issues at hand. The key for effective Affinity Mapping is to be open-minded, inquisitive, and cooperative throughout the process, and to let the data inform your investigation and meaning making. Here are some guiding dos and don'ts when employing Affinity Mapping:

Do:

- Start with a crisp focus and series of goals for your evaluation.
- Embrace a diverse assembly of stakeholders to bring several viewpoints to the data.
- Use succinct, comprehensible markers for each data point.
- Foster open-ended dialogue and evaluation of the data.
- Be prepared to reorganize and reshuffle data as new understandings surface.
- Record your final map and understandings for future reference.

Do not:

- Presuppose or foist your own understandings on the data.
- Sidestep clustering data grounded on shallow comparisons or predetermined categories.
- Permit a single stakeholder to rule the conversation or decision-making.
- Avert hastening the process or skipping over data points.
- Get too committed to preliminary categories or classifications.
- Avoid producing too many or too few clusters.
- Disregard recording the process and results.

Affinity Mapping crystalizes issues to support vital decision-making by bringing transparency and emphasis to adaptive challenges, allowing subsequent phases in the Design Thinking as a process to be more efficient. It works because it affords stakeholders to collaboratively categorize qualitative data into affinity spaces specifically related to personal and communal areas of significance. Moreover, it develops a vital common language for sustainable solution-seeking over time that will benefit all stakeholders. Figure 2.3 is a generic sample of an Affinity Map for MTSS to improve instruction with three clusters or themes.

The Identifying phase in Design Thinking as a process is imperative because it results in the development of an intentional point of view toward solution-seeking by identifying potential hurdles to address. The point of view

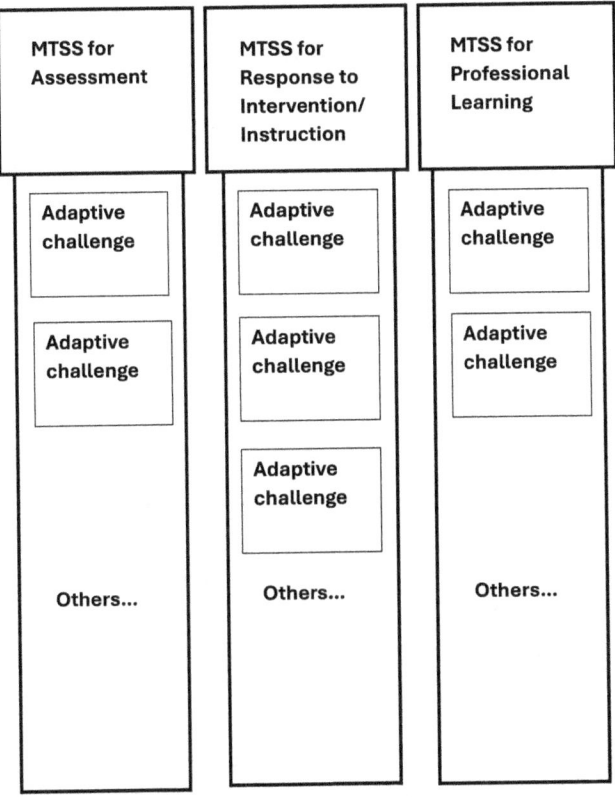

*Figure 2.3* Affinity Map Sample

specifically addresses a precise adaptive challenge based on new learning about the stakeholders and the learning environment. Drafting a specific solution statement tends to create more and better-quality outcomes when brainstorming ideas. The Identifying phase is also an opportunity to reorganize and synthesize disconnected ideas into robust understandings. Along with the collective data from the Empathizing phase, you will have critical insights to leverage solutions seeking behaviors towards tackling adaptive challenges.

To begin, think about what stood out to you during your time as a participant observer and a non-participant observer. Look for patterns in behavior across your documented observations. Be constantly hypothesizing the reasons something occurs and how you are going to be interacting with what occurs. By asking "Why?" questions, you will consistently be making connections with stakeholders and the context of school, district, and community and the need for MTSS to improve instruction. At this point, from an asset-based perspective, you will be synthesizing and highlighting the strengths and needs of all stakeholders to make informed decisions. You will more than likely look at a single salient point. Work to share your current understandings based on the latest data collected by researching and empathizing. Next, articulate a point of view by drawing on information on stakeholders, strengths, needs, and current understandings as a solution statement that will ground the rest of the design endeavor. Deriving an effective and doable point of view solution statement is vital to kick-start the process.

An effective point of view solution statement:

- Draws attention to, and outlines, issues to address (e.g., professional learning opportunities, funding, curriculum content, educational resources, student learning outcomes, and family engagement).
- Motivates the MTSS team.
- Describes conditions for appraising conflicting notions.
- Galvanizes the MTSS team to make decisions independently and analogously.
- Tugs on the heartstrings and stirs the souls of stakeholders.
- Avoids spending time on emerging concepts that are all things to all stakeholders (i.e., a solution statement is discrete, not broad-spectrum)

In the Identifying phase, the MTSS team determines a specific significant adaptive challenge; in the following, Ideating phase the focus will be to produce solutions that deal with the adaptive challenge. A well-designed and stated point of view will be a natural pathway into the Ideating phase. An effective transitional step toward Ideating is to create a list of "How should we…?" free-association topics born out of the solution statement. These free-association topics are usually subcategories of the overall issue at hand which focus on various aspects of the adaptive challenge. This exercise supports moving into Ideating and allows for the selection of a variety of subcategories that will motivate the MTSS team to generate many persuasive solutions. Teacher-colleagues and teacher leaders use ideating all the time in the school setting. In Design Thinking, it is organized brainstorming.

# Phase 3: Ideating

During the Ideating phase, you produce a variety of possibilities for each system within a MTSS framework. The focus here is quantity not quality. Professional conversations and evaluation will come later. You want to create as many possibilities imaginable to see how they may commingle together. Within reason, practicality is not important at this step. The main purpose during this phase is to think not about what is possible but about what *can* be possible. At the end, one of the ideas, or the integration of several ideas, is chosen to elaborate upon in the next phase. This is also a phase in which adaptive challenges occur. It is not just a collaborative activity where a chart tablet is pulled out and ideas jotted down. As adults, ideating is challenging, and is also a characteristic that needs to be nurtured and refined over time. It may simply begin with "What if?" questions that triggers the imagination and promote reflection. Ideating requires the imagination to go into overdrive. By harnessing the synergistic power of the group, ideas will be elevated that build on others' ideas. Supplementing limitations, immersing yourself in inspirational resources, and embracing confusions supports you to exceed further than simply contemplating an issue overall.

Some techniques that have been used during the Ideating phase are:

- Building – where you physically create a tangible item.
- Bodystorming – which is a combination of role-playing and simulation to generate ideas and comprehend issues.
- Mindmapping – where a graphic organizer is employed to generate concepts and their connections to a central theme or issue; and
- Sketching – drawing to propose, explore, refine, and communicate ideas.

A simple online search can reveal many more techniques for ideating. All these techniques have common traits that they are intended to suspend judgement and are meant to separate the production of ideas from the evaluation of ideas to give your imagination and creativity an open vista for exploration. It is recommended that as you shift into the prototyping phase, you start to categorize all the ideas collaboratively into two or three categories to guide the group without diminishing the creative constructive interaction generated during the Ideating phase.

## Phase 4: Prototyping

In the Prototyping phase, the goal is to generate artifacts that support responding to solution-seeking outcomes (i.e., curriculum resources, budgets, instructional frameworks, professional learning schedule). Early on in prototyping, the questions that surface may be broad-spectrum in order to ensure quick and economic reactions and promote generative responses from colleagues and stakeholders. Later, prototypes and questions may be polished and refined. A prototype can be anything that colleagues or stakeholders can interact with, such as data walls, interactive whiteboard, or Post-it notes. During prototyping, emotions may run high because now the rubber is starting to hit the road. Prototyping brings the abstract into the concrete and arouses personal sensitivity.

When ideating and seeking solutions, prototyping is necessary for genuine critical thinking to occur. Prototyping should serve as a conduit for communication that has the potential to promote productive interactions with stakeholders. Initially, prototyping should be a frugal project allowing each idea to be produced with little time and funds invested at the start. Staying frugal at the start allows designers to track a variety of ideas without committing to a specific direction from the beginning. To manage the solution-seeking process, naming a variety of factors supports designers in breaking down larger issues into smaller manageable parts.

At first, prototyping may feel awkward. Jump in. Grab resources and get started. Do not invest too much time in a particular prototype, however. Spending too much time on a single prototype will distract you from other opportunities. Prototyping should be viewed as an opportunity to genuinely see what is being evaluated. Examples of a prototype in MTSS may include an intentional and consistent framework for instruction, a school schedule, or a syllabus for professional learning. This text is a prototype for MTSS. Based on our experiences, we have singled out seven multi-tiered systems. Yet do not be blinded to other potential tangential systems that may arise during implementation which are dependent on the unique realities of classrooms, schools, and districts.

Prototyping and testing are two phases that go hand in hand. Rather than a period of transition. Investigating these two phases in tandem unfolds the layers of evaluating a prototype project. Often organizing and implementing an engaging testing situation is a powerful next step after creating a prototype. When "testing" a prototype, you are looking for an organic and genuine response from stakeholders. A response that should be generative in nature. Do not presume that you are evaluating a product by simply putting curricular resources or a framework for instruction in front of stakeholders. Testing, like MTSS, is a non-linear and recursive process.

# Phase 5: Testing

The Testing phase is when you are looking for generative responses from stakeholders to the prototypes or curricular projects that have been created. The responses are another opportunity to gather data and gain greater empathy for stakeholders. Unlike the Empathizing phase, the Testing phase is an opportunity to acquire better insights into stakeholders' strengths and needs with an actual product. Both empathizing and testing are based on interactions with stakeholders, but you should not confuse the work involved in both. The latter is to evaluate a product that should prompt designers to question why something worked – or did not work – for intended stakeholders. A word of advice-create prototypes as if you are right, but evaluate and test as if you are wrong. Testing is an opportunity to enhance solutions and improve them.

Testing involves an improvement mindset to improve future generations of solutions or prototypes. It is another opportunity to empathize with and learn more about stakeholders through documented observations and active participation that provides a different lens for improvement. Additionally, testing allows designers to reflect and adjust their initial point of view.

There are a variety of ways of "testing" a prototype. Regardless of how you are "testing" a prototype, listening is paramount. Evaluating a product or prototype may involve providing a prototype curricular resource, framework for instruction, or schedule to an intended stakeholder with a specific goal in mind to use with no explanation. By not providing an explanation initially, it gives an observer the chance to look at how words, actions, and materials interact. Yet another form of testing is to provide multiple prototypes for intended stakeholders to compare or contrast. Many times, unconsidered strengths and needs will surface during the comparison or contrasting.

Design Thinking as a process presented in this chapter enumerates the phases, but Design Thinking as a process is non-sequential, non-linear, and recursive (Luka, 2014; Razzouk & Shute, 2012). Each phase presented in this chapter will need to be personalized for the unique variation in classrooms, schools, and districts. One thing is for certain – repetition is vital to useful design. Repetition by reprocessing multiple times or revisiting phases of the process may seem tedious and time-consuming, especially when time is a commodity in schools, but repetition will serve you well when designing with sustainability in mind. Usually as you recycle through Design Thinking as a process, your point of view tapers and you shift from broad-spectrum views to refined details. At the metaphorical end of the day, you will internalize and personalize the process so it will work for your specific situation in classroom, school, or district.

## Unintended Consequences

Although Design Thinking as a process is a formidable solution-seeking model for implementing MTSS (Panke, 2019), it does come with some pitfalls and also has some unintended consequences. Historically, education has a low success rate in implementing new processes (Beverage, 2003), often because teacher leaders and teacher-colleagues are resistant to change as evidenced by the continuing Industrial Revolution schedules (Becker, Hornung, & Woessmann, 2011) and "banking" model of curriculum content (Freire, 2018). Not mastering the Design Thinking process is a failure of application. If only some colleagues are on board with the concept, it will not work. Design Thinking as a process thrives in an environment where colleagues are encouraged to question. Understanding the process necessitates genuine buy-in from the start. It is not a quick fix to persistent issues. Teacher leaders and teacher-colleagues who are interested in employing Design Thinking should carefully consider these untended consequences and amend the practices as necessary to meet their specific strengths and needs.

- Predispositions: As in any human interaction, Design Thinking is susceptible to individual and educational predispositions. It is essential to be perceptive of these predispositions and to try to offset them through diverse viewpoints and methods.

Design Thinking in Multi-Tiered Systems of Support

- Opposition to change: Some stakeholders may oppose change, even if a Design Thinking solution would be advantageous. It may be essential to build harmony and incapacitate opposition in order to employ a Design Thinking solution efficiently.
- Restricted attention on implementation: While Design Thinking is effective in recognizing and outlining issues and seeking solutions, it may not always be as effective in terms of enactment and sustainability.
- Shortage of organization: Design Thinking as a process may appear as a carelessly coordinated process, which can lead to irregularities in the execution and enactment of the process.
- Shortage of robust metrics: Design Thinking as a process does not always provide succinct metrics for measuring the success of solutions or projects, making it problematic to gauge the effect of the Design Thinking process.

Despite these limitations, Design Thinking endures as a constructive tactic for solving complex education issues and producing innovative solutions. Knowing the unintended consequences and tackling them up front as adaptive challenges, schools, districts, and state/provinces can augment the benefits of Design Thinking. Preparation is a critical practice for teacher leaders and teacher-colleagues to implement MTSS effectively over time using Design Thinking as a process. Nonetheless, there are adaptive challenges that may hinder successful development. These adaptive challenges include intellectual restrictions, ecological restrictions, supply restrictions, and dialogic restrictions. Intellectual restrictions refer to boundaries in the way colleagues process information and make decisions that may lead to biases and impact effective implementation. Ecological restrictions refer to peripheral influences, such as policies and funding, which can shape outcomes. Supply restrictions refer to confining availability of resources, such as schedules, materials, published programs, teachers, and teacher leaders, which can limit the achievability of developing enterprises. Dialogic restrictions account for adaptive challenges in expressing and producing information, which can block helpful teamwork and harmonization. Developing a common language is crucial.

While preparing for Design Thinking as a process may come with several adaptive challenges, there are solutions and approaches to conquer them. Spotlighting effective mindful practices and coherently evaluating and modifying plans based on fluctuating situations, teacher leaders and teacher-colleagues can collaboratively address adaptive challenges more effectively. The adaptive challenges of Design Thinking mentioned in this section have to be faced with collaborative intentionality and mindfulness.

## Emerging Understandings

The primary goal of employing MTSS is to improve instruction for all stakeholders – students, teachers, teacher leaders, and the community. Schools and districts that are implementing MTSS successfully use Design Thinking as a process to seek solutions and tackle adaptive challenges. Although not identifying or claiming their successful implementation to Design Thinking as a process, all schools take into consideration: involving stakeholders and sharing the benefits of change to them; highlighting issues and brainstorming potential solutions; creating specific models of schedules or adopting specific programs for study, and then monitoring progress over time. Teacher leaders and teacher-colleagues may not call this Design Thinking, but the process they engage in collaboratively is the same. Throughout this chapter and book, we assert the Vygotskian theory that language is a tool for critical thinking. In this chapter, we decided that calling Design Thinking by its name affords us the language to think critically about MTSS by updating our language and consequently upgrading our thinking when the professional conversation is about improving instruction over time.

Education is about social reproduction, and it is in the business of fostering critical thinking by respectful, mindful, and productive humans for a better society. Design Thinking as a process begins with empathizing and considering what is in it for stakeholders at the end of the metaphorical day. Since MTSS is intended to address improving instruction for all – students, teachers, teacher leaders, and the community –, improving instruction has to go beyond just academics. In practice, adopting an ubuntu attitude seems to be a natural fit for education in general. Ubuntu is a non-Western African perspective that highlights the interrelation of people and their communities, and the concept that "I am because we are". It is grounded in the thought that people are social individuals who are characterized by their associations with others, and that the existence of the person is contingent on the community in which they thrive.

Keeping an ubuntu perspective to the fore, the next chapter starts going into developing a Multi-Tiered System of Support for assessment and evaluation. We present the seven systems introduced in this text in a numerical order (Chapters 3 then 4 and so on), but the multi-tiered systems themselves are like the phases in Design Thinking; they are not linear or sequential. The seven systems, like the phases in Design Thinking, are synergistic concepts that can stand alone for analysis, but ultimately have to work together to produce an effective outcome. The following professional questions for reflection are meant for teacher leaders and teacher-colleagues to engage in a dialogic conversation for personalized solution seeking within an asset-based model where strengths are recognized first before attempting to support needs.

## Professional Reflection Questions

What are the benefits and features of Design Thinking as a model in education?

a  How does Design Thinking as a process benefit schools, districts, and state/provinces?
b  What are some potential adaptive challenges that will need to be addressed?
c  How can we ensure that successful failure is seen as growth in the right direction?
d  Are the issues to improve instruction clearly understood by teacher leaders, teacher-colleagues, and community?

## References

Becker, K., & Mentzer, N. (2015). Engineering design thinking: High school students' performance and knowledge. In *2015 International conference on interactive collaborative learning (ICL)* (pp. 5–12). Florence, Italy: IEEE.

Becker, S. O., Hornung, E., & Woessmann, L. (2011). Education and catch-up in the industrial revolution. *American Economic Journal: Macroeconomics, 3*(3), 92–126.

Besharat, J., Komninos, A., Papadimitriou, G., Lagiou, E., & Garofalakis, J. (2016). Augmented paper maps: Design of POI markers and effects on group navigation. *Journal of Ambient Intelligence and Smart Environments, 8*(5), 515–530.

Beverage, M. W. (2003). Slow change in a fast culture. *Educause Review, 38*, 10–11.
Brown, T. (2008). Design thinking. *Harvard Business Review, 86*(6), 84.
Carroll, M., Goldman, S., Britos, L., Koh, J., Royalty, A., & Hornstein, M. (2010). Destination, imagination and the fires within: Design thinking in a middle school classroom. *International Journal of Art and Design Education, 29*(1), 37–53.
Donar, A. (2011). Thinking design and pedagogy: An examination of five Canadian post-secondary courses in design thinking. *Canadian Review of Art Education: Research and Issues, 38*, 84–102.
Freire, P. (2018). The banking concept of education. In *Thinking about schools* (pp. 117–127). New York: Routledge.
Little, M., Slanda, D., & Cramer, E. (2024). *The educator's guide to action research*. Blue Ridge Summit, PA: Rowman and Littlefield.
Luka, I. (2014). Design thinking in pedagogy. *The Journal of Education, Culture, and Society, 5*(2), 63–74.
Manak, J. A., & Puig, E. A. (2021). Methods and strategies: Enhancing the STEM framework. *Science and Children, 58*(6), 82–85.
Mentzer, N., Becker, K., & Sutton, M. (2015). Engineering design thinking: High school students' performance and knowledge. *Journal of Engineering Education, 104*(4), 417–432.
Panke, S. (2019). Design thinking in education: Perspectives, opportunities and challenges. *Open Education Studies, 1*(1), 281–306.
Puig, E. A., & Froelich, K. S. (2021). *Teaching K–12 transdisciplinary literacy: A comprehensive instructional framework for learning and leading*. New York: Routledge.
Razzouk, R., & Shute, V. (2012). What is design thinking and why is it important? *Review of Educational Research, 82*(3), 330–348.
Shively, K., Stith, K. M., & Rubenstein, L. D. (2018). Measuring what matters: Assessing creativity, critical thinking, and the design process. *Gifted Child Today, 41*(3), 149–158.

# Multi-Tiered System for Assessment and Evaluation

*Measure what can be measured and make measurable what cannot be measured.*

–Galileo

When considering a multi-tiered system for assessment and evaluation, multiple types of assessments address several purposes for evaluation, instruction, and professional learning opportunities. Universal, diagnostic, formative, and progress monitoring assessments are used as components of the instructional and professional learning planning processes. This chapter describes the types, uses, and categorical tiers (macro, meso, and micro) of various assessments within a Multi-Tiered System of Support framework.

## Understanding the Purposes and Types of Assessment

Teachers and teacher leaders gather a plethora of data from multiple sources, engage in solution-seeking sessions within their grade-level departments or professional learning communities, and create charts and graphs to share with stakeholders to improve student outcomes. Although the process of data collection has become part of educational nomenclature and practice, questions remain regarding decision-making through effective interpretation and use of data (Katz & Dack, 2014). Data *use*, not just *collection*, is at the nexus of teacher and teacher leadership decision-making (Schildkamp, 2019). This can be challenging, as interpretation and use of data is complex and is influenced by teachers' knowledge of how to interpret and respond to data (Horn et al., 2015; Mandinach, 2012). Often referred to as "data literacy" (Lose, 2007), the ability to accurately document, analyze, and respond to a variety of multiple sources of data is necessary for the purpose of continuously improving learning and leading. To do this well, teachers and teacher leaders must have the ability to make use of multiple data sources, interpret data accurately, and engage in productive collaborative inquiry with their colleagues (Allington, 2011).

Therefore, the effective use of data requires educators to develop knowledge and skills to analyze, interpret, and convert data into action (Datnow & Hubbard, 2016). Further, teachers and teacher leaders need access to resources that assist with the process of selecting research validated practices, intensifying instruction, and intervention; and collecting and analyzing data to meet the varied strengths and needs of diverse learners. Instruction and intervention for all students, especially low-progress readers, should include the following: (a) the targeted involvement of the teacher during design and delivery of research-validated practices; (b) a harmonic, comprehensive, and integrated approach allowing students to experience transdisciplinary literacy as a coherent whole; and (c) the use of static and dynamic assessments allowing for instructional shifts according to student strengths and needs (Fisher & Ivey, 2006).

Current research indicates some educators feel unprepared to work with diverse learners and many feel poorly prepared to provide instruction and intervention in literacy and numeracy for students who may be at risk (Powell et al., 2010). Given the influence an educator has on student outcomes, it is critical that educators acquire the pedagogical content knowledge necessary to provide effective, targeted instruction and intervention to address the identified academic strengths and needs of the students, as aligned with the standards, and grounded in research validated practices.

Formative (dynamic) and summative (static) assessment tasks continuously provide us with information about students' strengths and needs aligned with curriculum content and research-validated instructional practices. Summative static assessments provide an overall summary of learning at the end of a unit, chapter, and/or end of course. Formative dynamic assessments inform teaching and should be viewed as tools to assist teachers and teacher leaders in designing and revising instruction for students and professional learning needs with an end goal of improving instruction. All the information from assessments about students throughout teaching must align with objectives

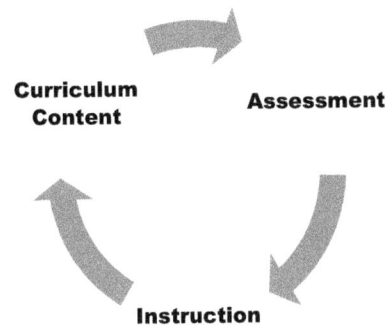

*Figure 3.1* Continuous Cycle

as well as connecting learning with the content standards in a continuous improvement cycle. Figure 3.1 is a visual representation of this cycle.

As we continue the discussion on assessment, we do want to address both formative and summative assessments as the understanding of the two types of assessments can be a source of confusion. First, let us look at summative static assessment. In general, summative static assessment typically documents how much learning has occurred at a point in time to measure students' understanding of content by determining what they know and do not know. Many associate summative static assessments only with standardized tests such as state testing, but they are also used as a part of district and classroom programs. These can include state assessments, district benchmarks assessments, end of chapter or unit tests, and end of term or semester examinations. The purpose of summative static assessment is to measure the level of student understanding, program, or school success. It is important to note that summative static assessment cannot reflect the efficiency of teaching in its process, because assessment is carried out only *after* the instruction every few weeks, months, or once a year.

Formative dynamic assessment, on the other hand, delivers information *during and throughout* the learning/instructional process *before* the summative static assessment. They are usually embedded within the learning/instructional process. Ideally, both the teacher and the student use formative dynamic assessment results to make decisions about what actions to take to promote for forward shifts to occur. It is an ongoing, dynamic process that involves far more than frequent testing, and measurement of student learning is just one of its components.

There are numerous types of static and dynamic assessments that we use to learn as much as we can about our students. Assessments may be used in isolation or in combination with others for the purpose of providing valuable information to use in instructional planning and can range from documented classroom observation to standardized tests. The increased attention on using multiple assessments to assess what students know and how they think encourages us to deepen our knowledge about and use of diverse types of assessments which will impact the implementation of a variety of research validated practices.

The use of static and dynamic assessments within the Multi-Tiered Systems of Support process is to ensure that students receive rich learning experiences and to differentiate instruction to improve learning for all students. Therefore, as we implement Multi-Tiered Systems of Support, we need to use multiple sources of assessment data to determine students' strengths and needs. This information is the foundations for us to continuously analyze, revise, and enhance instruction within the transdisciplinary literacy learning environment. There are four types of assessments that are important in analyzing our instruction: universal screening, progress monitoring, diagnostic, and outcome (summative). We will take a closer look at each of these assessments with definitions and examples.

## Universal

Broad-spectrum results from a group of students (e.g., district, province, school, class) are gleaned from static assessments and are often referred to as "universal assessments." Universal assessments collect student performance data that focus on meeting and exceeding curriculum content standards. They provide important preliminary or baseline information about students' previous and current strengths and needs. One source of universal assessment is often state and/or district grade-level benchmark assessments of curriculum content standards. These standardized static state assessments are provided at the initiation of a school year or the beginning of a unit of study. These screening measures are used by district- or school-based administrators as a broad indicator of students' strengths and needs for the purpose of program planning, instructional services, and potentially professional learning opportunities. For example, student summative static assessment data from state assessments are often the baseline data for the School Improvement Plan. In addition, numerous school districts develop and administer multiple grade-level benchmark assessments several times a school year which are aligned with the state curriculum content standards to provide continuous assessment data related to student learning using a standardized assessment measure. Therefore, these assessments should also become part of the initial, universal screening assessment data of the instructional decision-making and lesson planning processes within the learning environment.

These assessment data become an integral part of the learning and leading process because they provide information about students' learning aligned to state and district curriculum content standards and grade-level benchmarks. A review of previous records provides important assessment information about student strengths and needs, especially if trends or inconsistencies in student learning are noticed. This information will be useful when considering instructional goals, student grouping, necessary resources, and professional learning needs. Consider the following professional reflection questions during a review of records (Table 3.1).

*Table 3.1* Guiding Questions-Review of Records

| Source of Data | Guiding Questions to Consider |
| --- | --- |
| Previous standardized test results | • What are the areas of strength?<br>• What are the areas of need?<br>• Are the areas of strength and need consistent?<br>• Are the areas of need in areas that impact performance?<br>• Are the data consistent or show a trend from previous years? |
| Past summative assessments | • Are the summative assessments from prior units of study consistent?<br>• Are the results of the summative assessments reflective of performance that is consistent with peers? For instance, did most students do very well or very poorly on a specific assessment? |
| Universal screening (such as a grade-level assessment) | • Do the screening data reflect consistencies with the standardized test data?<br>• Are there areas that seem to be consistent?<br>• Are there areas that are not consistent?<br>• What specific content standards are areas of strength and areas for additional instruction? |

Three other informal static assessments provide essential information when planning for instruction during the completion of universal assessments within Multi-Tiered Systems of Support: documented observations, work-sample analyses, and initial curriculum content inventories.

- Documented Observations – In the learning environment, teachers make many decisions and observations on an hourly basis, in some cases, by the minute. Consequently, unless observations are consistently documented, some of this rich and vital data will be lost. Students should be observed while they are working on academic tasks, during whole group instruction, while working independently, and in small groups. Documented observations can and should be completed throughout instruction as they provide continuous information about student learning (Table 3.2).
- Work Sample Analyses – A critical aspect of harmonic and comprehensive broad-spectrum-level assessments for groups of students includes mindful analysis of student artifacts. These artifacts can include performance tasks from in-class assignments, board work, and learning assignments. Considerations and reflection questions during work sample analyses can include some of the following examples (Table 3.3).
- Curriculum Content Inventories – These inventories and assessments are used to evaluate students' performance of specific learning goals. This form of evaluation identifies students' strengths and needs. These assessments can be developed using a scope and sequence from curricular

Table 3.2 Guiding Questions-Observations

| Source of Data | Reflection Questions to Consider |
|---|---|
| Documented Observations | • Does the student appear interested and engaged in the learning?<br>• How often does the student answer questions, or need assistance?<br>• Does the student use classroom resources, etc. often, accurately?<br>• Does the student accurately discuss the topics posed?<br>• What are the areas of strength?<br>• What are the areas of need?<br>• Are the documented observations consistent or show a trend with other sources of assessment data? |

*Table 3.3* Guiding Questions-Work Samples

| Source of Data | Guiding Questions to Consider |
|---|---|
| Work Sample Analyses | • Does the student follow the directions (oral or written) about the task?<br>• Does the student complete all sections of the task? Accurately? Independently?<br>• Does the student use accurate skills when completing the task?<br>• What are the areas of strength?<br>• What are the areas of need?<br>• Are the work sample quality consistent or show a trend with other sources of assessment data? |

*Table 3.4* Guiding Questions-Curriculum Inventories

| Source of Data | Guiding Questions to Consider |
|---|---|
| Curriculum Content Inventories | • Does the inventory align with state and district content standards and grade-level benchmarks?<br>• Do the resources have inventories available?<br>• Were student results consistent with other assessments?<br>• What are the areas of strength?<br>• What are the areas of need?<br>• How will I use this information when planning for instruction? |

resources in the specific subject (as aligned with district and state content standards and grade level benchmarks). Some are also packaged and published commercially (Table 3.4).

# Progress Monitoring

There are a variety of purposes for continuous, formative dynamic assessment as we teach. One is to monitor the instructional engagement, understanding, and progress of students' learning related to the curricular goal. Another purpose is to evaluate and inform you of any necessary changes to instruction. Progress monitoring assessments are usually short and frequent assessments that provide a snapshot of student learning related to the instructional objectives. Through consistent ongoing documented observation and assessment, the teacher and teacher leaders stay informed about the progress of the students (Puig & Froelich, 2007).

The following list includes samples of ongoing progress monitoring. Instructionally relevant assessment data are from broad categories that include:

- Published program assessments (in conjunction with published curriculum content programs).
- Published content assessments/inventories.
- Informal classroom assessments that are teacher-created measures of student strengths as aligned with pre-determined grade-level benchmarks or student's individual prior performance.
- Curriculum-based measurements measuring specific skills in the content areas aligned with curriculum content benchmarks.

Curriculum-Based Measurement is an effective and efficient means of assessing and monitoring students' ongoing progress with disciplinary content. These powerful formative assessments measure students' mastery of content and allows teacher-colleagues to learn how students are progressing in the core academic areas. Curriculum-Based Measurement can specifically address grade-level benchmarks taught and highlight students' increments of growth over time. We can use Curriculum-Based Measurement to assess areas of strengths and needs on a weekly basis for a period of one to five minutes depending on those specific skills being measured. Students are given brief, timed exercises (probes) to complete, using the skills and materials that are drawn directly from students' school curriculum content resources.

This frequent sampling of student knowledge provides current information of progression within the learning environment. In other words, it tells how well students are performing or understanding content. At this level of assessment, teacher-colleagues are excavating how students are processing information and what item knowledge they own. Students are assessed on the accuracy of processing, item knowledge, and disciplinary fluency. Curriculum-Based Measurement provides a clearer view of the rate of learning over time and determines whether there is a need to continue the instruction the same way, or if there is a need to change it. Curriculum-Based Measurement partially informs instruction. Based on students' responses and considering students' strengths, changes can be made to modify

## Multi-Tiered System for Assessment and Evaluation

*Table 3.5* Guiding Questions-CBM

| Source of Data | Guiding Questions to Consider |
|---|---|
| **Curriculum-Based Measurement** | • Does this formative dynamic assessment align with state and district standards and grade-level benchmarks?<br>• Do the curriculum resources have assessments available?<br>• Were student results consistent with other assessments?<br>• What are the areas of strength?<br>• What are the areas of need?<br>• How will I use this information when planning for instruction? |

teaching practices by identifying the amount and type of instruction students' need to make the necessary forward shifts in learning. Consequently, based on diagnostic assessment of strengths and needs, the instructional time can be changed (increased or decreased), or the grouping arrangement can be changed (individual versus small group), or change in material used and teaching techniques, or way of presenting the disciplinary content can take place. Consider the following professional reflection questions when using progress monitoring probes in Curriculum-Based Measurement and the potential for change in instruction (Table 3.5).

# Targeted, Diagnostic Assessment

From assessment results of the multiple measures described in the previous section, there may be indications that a student, or a group of students, may not be mastering the curricular goals. Consequently, additional, more targeted dynamic assessments may need to be administered to smaller groups and/or individual students in order to diagnose strengths and needs. It might be helpful to think of diagnostic assessment as testing that occurs before intervention. Diagnostic assessments are intended to provide additional assessment data to plan-focused, student-centered interventions for students who have not yet achieved grade-level proficiency. They are often conducted with individual students to identify specific strengths and needs in the curricular content or discipline. Assessments are made up of three components: (1) screening measures; (2) observational measures; and (3) diagnostic measures.

Screening measures provide an analysis of students' specific strengths and needs. Simultaneously, these assessments are also employed to identify those who may need more intensive instruction. Documented observational measures are embedded in our daily instruction and provide us with information for monitoring our students' progress and intervention needs. Diagnostic measures provide student profiles that can be used for both dynamic formative and static summative assessment at key checkpoints throughout learning and leading as a gauge to determine student progress because of instruction. Depending on the individual students, these measures do not have to be administered at one time and can be broken up into multiple sessions.

The purpose of targeted, diagnostic assessments is to evaluate the strengths and needs of individual students. The diagnostic assessment data provides specific skills and abilities of specific students to support more intensive intervention, through aligned, but different curriculum content resources and instructional methods. In other words, it allows us to tailor our content and instruction to students' specific academic strengths and needs. Although multifaceted diagnostic assessment often focuses teacher-colleagues' attention to one area or domain of knowledge. Diagnostic assessments can be administered before and/or during instruction and intervention within the classroom. For example, a teacher or literacy coach may administer a diagnostic test specifically targeting a grade-level standard to an identified group of students to determine specific content strengths and needs. In addition, a teacher may administer a diagnostic assessment to check for student understanding of the same knowledge and skills after instruction. The use of diagnostic assessments identifies students who are experiencing problems at an early stage to plan appropriate interventions.

As we teach, we must also consider that diagnostic assessment calls for the continual assessment of students' abilities. The data from targeted, diagnostic assessment provides us with more in-depth and specific information of the strengths and needs of individual students related to the mastery of disciplinary curriculum content. We can carefully examine the actual work samples of individual students to identify strengths and needs. This type of analysis also indicates the students' strengths, and the results can be used by the teacher in lesson planning, providing differentiated instruction, and enhanced learning opportunities. To use diagnostic assessment methods effectively in the classroom, we must provide valid responses to students. This should be done in a timely manner to ensure students recognize areas

*Table 3.6* Guiding Questions-Diagnostics

| Source of Data | Reflection Questions to Consider |
|---|---|
| Diagnostics | • Does the assessment target specific areas of concern?<br>• Do the results answer questions about ability, motivators, triggers for negative behavior, or areas of strength?<br>• Do the results seem consistent with other assessment measures?<br>• Is the data specific enough to create a statement to be used to design a plan of action? |

of strengths and need or to correct error patterns and misconceptions. When developmentally appropriate, students may also be encouraged to explore why their answers are right or wrong through one-on-one, peer chats or small-group discussion. This information from diagnostic teaching and diagnostic assessment assists teacher-colleagues to better individualize instruction and instruction for low-progress students (Table 3.6).

The various assessments described are focused on an individual student to determine specific academic strengths and needs and to develop individualized instructional and intervention plans. Once these plans are developed and implemented with fidelity, progress monitoring probes continue to determine learning by the student. The goal for the multiple assessments for all students, a smaller, targeted group of students, and an individual student is to assure that all students are learning transdisciplinary curriculum content and learning to learn.

# Outcome Assessment

Outcome static assessments provide data related to student's harmonic and comprehensive learning after an established period of instruction and interventions as a final assessment. This can occur at the end of units of study, school year, and/or state and/or district assessments. Usually, the purpose of outcome static assessments and evaluation is related to decisions regarding programs for students to meet their instructional strengths and needs and is also called summative static assessment. These outcome summative static assessments provide a summary of learning by all students in a class, program, or special service. As previously mentioned, numerous state departments of education and school districts use the results of summative state assessments aligned with the state curriculum content standards to make decisions related to promotion and subsequent student programs. Administration and actions from outcome static assessments (summative) are in tandem with implications set in state and school district policy. It is imperative that teachers and teacher leaders are knowledgeable about the implications set in state and school policy for summative static assessments that directly impact future instruction, students, and implications for professional learning opportunities. Student assessment data from these summative static assessments can and should be used by as part of the universal screening assessment data within unit and lesson planning. This cycle of teacher instructional decision-making uses the multiple sources of assessment, aligned with national and state curriculum content standards and grade-level benchmarks, to meet the instructional strengths and needs of students through effective planning within the Multi-Tiered Systems of Support. Figure 3.2 provides a graphic overview of the types of assessments used.

|  | Universal | Progress Monitoring | Targeted, Diagnostic | Outcome |
| --- | --- | --- | --- | --- |
| Definition | Initial determination of broad base of student performance | Skill-based, ongoing sensitive to minor changes in student learning | In-depth, specific information re: knowledge and skills | Final determination of broad base of student performance |
| Uses | Broad benchmark attainment index (initial) | Specific academic or behavioral target | Specific academic domain of knowledge, skills, or abilities | Broad benchmark attainment index (final) |
| Student Focus | School-wide | Class or small group | Individual student | School-wide |
| Frequency | Annually/3-4 times/year | Every 3 weeks/weekly | Annually (or as needed) for in-depth evaluation | Annually |
| Instruction | Class/school curricular/program decisions | Effectiveness of instruction and interventions | Selecting appropriate programs and/or educational placements | Align with curriculum goals and instructional planning process |
| Implication | First step in instruction and intervention planning | Continue and/or revise instruction and/or interventions | Program or curriculum planning | High stakes, based on state and school district policies |

*Figure 3.2* Types of Assessments Used by Teachers

# Using Assessment to Plan Instruction and Interventions

As we think of assessment, we must ask ourselves a few questions: How are all students performing? How are all students responding to instruction/ additional supports (progress monitoring)? What additional information is needed to meet the strengths and needs of the students who do not appear to be making adequate progress (targeted, diagnostic)? To be sure, student learning depends on a variety of key factors. One factor is the knowledge we have about the unique strengths and needs of students; the curricular content we teach; how students are grouped for instruction; and how their learning and mastery of critical content is progressing. Another is the degree to which we effectively integrate research validated instructional practices and interventions within the learning environments. Teacher-colleagues who regularly collect assessment data about student learning gain valuable information to make subsequent instructional decisions. For student data to have a positive influence on learning and leading, we need to locate, analyze, and interpret data to help inform planning, and to provide differentiated instruction and interventions through individualized learning plans, flexible grouping practices, and alternative interventions to address diverse student strengths and needs. The importance here is to remember that it is an ongoing cycle of reviewing transdisciplinary curriculum content, research-validated instructional practices, resources, and assessment informed by multiple, ongoing static and dynamic assessments.

As you look at the item-level analysis for each student, assessment data are used to adjust teaching practices in ways that enhance student learning. Consider the following reflection questions:

- What do the universal assessment results mean when planning for the entire class of students?
- What needs to be known about specific, individual student's strengths and needs?
- Is the current curriculum content and instruction appropriate for all/some students?
- Are the diverse strengths and needs of all students being met?
- Can differentiated instruction be provided based on the data?

- Is targeted instruction and/or interventions through small groups or individual needed in specific disciplines?
- Would pairing students help those who need more practice work?
- Would a review of the concepts by providing supportive resources be beneficial to students?
- What about offering instruction through different learning modalities?
- Would one-on-one interventions or tutoring be helpful?
- How about intensive instruction or enrichment activities?
- Will students benefit from integrating subject or skills to curricular content knowledge?
- Do the data support this?

The data allow us to determine to what degree of emphasis, greater or lesser, than on certain topics or to plan individualized instruction for students. The goal is to decide what the data reveal and to employ new research-validated practices to reach students, make practical educational decisions, meet the strengths and needs of individual students, determine, and re-evaluate our decisions for instructional effectiveness, and to be more effective and productive in the classroom. In other words, it determines our students' strengths, needs, interests, and supports to develop a plan for targeted instruction and/or interventions.

Static, universal assessments are used to understand how well students are responding to the core program and instruction (standards-based curriculum content and high-quality, differentiated core instruction) which may help identify students' strengths and those in need of additional supports and/or interventions. Dynamic assessments are embedded within classroom lessons to provide formative assessment information about students' processing of critical content and skills over time. Our goal with assessment is that we have a harmonic and comprehensive multi-tiered assessment system by using a variety of assessments on a continuum, having a primary purpose for each assessment type, and using multiple resources to create a holistic picture of student progress over time.

The multiple sources of available assessment data provide the vital information about instruction and results to teachers, teacher leaders, and families. Teacher leaders use the results from the assessment data to provide information to the Multi-Tiered Systems of Support team members to inform next steps. In addition, these data can be very motivating for students and can facilitate communication between teachers, teacher leaders, and families. When we learn that students are encountering hurdles to learning, action must be taken to address the adaptive challenges. Sometimes, this instructional planning and decision-making process is carried out by teacher-colleagues; at other times, it is carried out through collaboration with families and other professionals. Student performance will be improved if the process is informed by assessment data that are aligned with the curriculum content benchmarks and the specific strengths and needs of the students.

Formative, dynamic assessments are part of the instructional process and assist in appropriate implementation of instruction. Progress monitoring assessments reflect the rate and growth of a student or students in response to the instruction. In some cases, targeted, diagnostic assessment information may also be available and contribute to the needed information when planning specific instruction and interventions. Each of these types of assessments provides valuable information, as well as opportunities for further investigations. The questions that may be generated differ for each of these sources of information about student learning. For any data source there are also some general reflection questions to ask. These are:

- Do the data reflect a level of motivation that is exceedingly high or low?
- Do the data reflect a level of ability that is exceedingly high or low?
- Do the data reflect the need for more attention, support or services to be provided immediately?
- Are the data inconsistent and needs further investigation or more specific data?

The universal and static assessments, as well as teacher-documented observations during instruction, provide an overview of a student's abilities or performance. There are some students whose initial assessment data raise questions or concerns. When initial results raise questions or concerns, these students are identified for more targeted instruction. A student who is identified through universal screening may never, in fact, have any significant learning gaps. However, there is a reason to ask questions and to monitor the student more closely than others.

In the beginning of the year and at designated times throughout the year, we should have opportunities to ask questions about each student that has been identified. Each student should have assessment results, and these results should be intentionally reevaluated over time. A review may determine that the student had a challenging time with a specific competency or skill but demonstrates competency on all other assessments. These reviews may also indicate significant reasons for concern. For any student with learning gaps, the teacher and teacher leaders should gather more information and collect further data through progress monitoring during and after targeted instruction. The progress monitoring data should be able to indicate if the student is experiencing success in learning or if the student needs additional supports.

In many classrooms and schools, teachers and administrators develop annual goals and pacing calendars based upon state and district curriculum content standards and grade-level benchmarks. The intent is to inform when planning units and lessons to assure forward shifts in learning. In addition, the use of progress monitoring assessments, including curriculum content measures, provides a frequent and important response to teacher-colleagues, as well as teacher leaders and transdisciplinary literacy coaches, about student learning of curriculum content standards and grade-level benchmarks. Expectations for student performance, both learning and timelines, provide intermittent learning goals within the school year. These progress monitoring measures should be sensitive to measure the effects of both instruction and intervention.

No one source of data can fully communicate students' strengths and needs accurately, although each source of assessment data can raise questions or provide vital information. Sources such as previous results from static summative assessments, standardized testing, and records from prior years provide information to examine. In addition, pre-assessments and screening data may also add to the picture for a more accurate view. During instruction, dynamic formative assessments (e.g., curriculum-based assessments, reading records, probes, and work samples) and progress monitoring contribute to the information about student learning. In some cases, targeted, diagnostic assessment data contributes additional information about the strengths and needs of students. Together, all these sources play a significant role when planning for instruction and professional learning needs. The data are used to make decisions and determine if and what kind of additional supports and services are needed for professional learning and instruction. The data also serves to raise questions, confirm, or deny the effectiveness of instruction, or determine approaches to instruction. All these actions are part of the process of differentiated instruction and responsive teaching.

## Professional Learning and Leading

Teachers and teacher leaders continue to strive to enhance their content and pedagogical knowledge to address the diverse strengths and needs of students within elementary and secondary school settings. The complexities of instruction, assessment, and intervention to meet the needs of all students may require additional knowledge of, and experiences with, processes and resources designed to address diverse learning strengths and needs of students within a framework of continuous and responsive sense making during the data-informed decision-making processes. This can be accomplished by ensuring educators have the pedagogical/hebegogical content knowledge and resources as necessary for data-informed decision-making by engaging in the cyclical decision-making process within an asset-based, Multi-Tiered Systems of Support framework. Enhanced academic outcomes for students with diverse learning needs are actualized when educators can analyze, interpret, and convert data into action (Datnow & Hubbard, 2016; Wilson, 2016). Data-informed decision-making further allows educators to intentionally and consistently intensify instruction and intervention across the tiers informed by multiple sources of assessment data. In addition, resources and protocols from state, province, and national centers provide teachers and teacher leaders with the pedagogical/hebegogical content knowledge and resources for data-informed decision-making to meet the strengths and needs of each student. As teachers and teacher leaders continue to strive to meet the instructional strengths and needs of students within the inquiry based, data-informed decision-making process, enhanced professional learning and use of resources provide critical professional experiences.

Instruction and intervention for low-progress readers should include the following: (a) targeted involvement of the teacher during design and delivery of research validated practices; (b) a harmonic, comprehensive, and integrated approach allowing students to experience literacy learning as a coherent whole; and (c) the use of assessments allowing for instructional changes according to student's strengths and needs (Fisher & Ivey, 2006).

Current research indicates some educators feel unprepared to work with diverse learners and many feel poorly prepared to provide transdisciplinary literacy instruction and intervention for students who may be at risk (Powell et al., 2010). Given the influence a teacher has on student learning, especially transdisciplinary literacy development, it is critical that educators acquire the pedagogical/hebegogical content knowledge necessary to provide effective, targeted transdisciplinary literacy instruction and intervention grounded in research-validated practices.

## Improving Outcomes Using Assessments within a Tiered Framework

Responsive instruction through a data-informed decision-making approach is critical to improving transdisciplinary literacy learning outcomes, especially when implemented within a Multi-Tiered Systems of Supports framework. Federal legislation and state initiatives have reiterated the need to strengthen content standards and rigor for *all* students, emphasized the use of research-validated instructional practices to support student learning, and promoted the use of data informed decision-making. In the United States, previously established as a method for identification and eligibility within the Individuals with Disabilities Education Act (IDEA, 2004), Multi-Tiered Systems of Support placed a focus on intensifying support for low-progress students before they experience failure.

Ideally, Multi-Tiered Systems of Support is a harmonic and comprehensive framework that addresses instruction and intervention using research-validated practices within classrooms (Braun et al., 2018). Multi-Tiered Systems of Support are flexible and provide a system in which students can move along the continuum of the tiers as appropriate for their instructional strengths and needs, as well as a venue for professional learning opportunities. Within a tiered framework, teachers and teacher leaders provide support and interventions in literacy with increasing intensity (ESSA, 2015). Multi-Tiered Systems of Support provides a framework within which teachers and teacher leaders engage in data-informed decision-making to rapidly respond to student strengths and needs (ESSA, 2015). Therefore, the Multi-Tiered Systems of Support framework promotes initiative-taking, data-informed instructional decisions to preempt, intercept, and intervene with students experiencing learning difficulties, and serves as the basis for determining a student's eligibility for special services in many states.

As described, Multi-Tiered Systems of Support is an intentional and coherent solution-seeking framework that accounts for research-validated instructional practices for all students (Braun et al., 2018). As teachers and teacher leaders collect multiple sources of formative, targeted, and diagnostic data and adjust instruction, decisions are made about instruction through either frequency (additional sessions) or duration (increased time). Defining characteristics of Multi-Tiered Systems of Support include: (a) research-validated practices; (b) data-informed decision-making; and (c) individualized and targeted intervention (Barrio et al., 2015; Sisk, 2019). Throughout the Multi-Tiered Systems of Support framework, teachers and teacher leaders use data-informed decision-making to identify students who are not responsive to instruction, determine specific instructional goals based upon the data, and provide individualized intervention (Hoover et al., 2008; Lane et al., 2019). Teachers and teacher leaders meet the strengths and needs of students using assessment instruments sensitive to and linked to instruction, allowing them to make decisions about the learning environment, resources, professional learning opportunities, and reinforcements to aide in transdisciplinary literacy learning (Daly III et al., 2007).

## Resources for Data Collection and Analysis

Although educators are skilled at the collection of classroom data through formal and informal assessment procedures, instructional decision-making requires "sense making" of the data (Mandinach, 2012) to determine necessary research-validated practices and resources. Furthermore, educators not only need to know how to interpret data; they also need to be aware of how to intensify instruction using various practices that meet the unique strengths and needs of the student. Data-informed decision-making is a cyclical process through which teachers and teacher leaders engage in continuous decision-making necessary to provide research-validated practices, evaluate the impact of the instruction through static formal and dynamic informal assessments, adjust instruction and intervention in response to student learning, and monitor shifts in learning. If the student is not responsive, the educator adjusts instruction. At the core of the cycle is student learning. There are four specific phases in this data-informed decision-making process.

The data-informed decision-making process includes four key phases that are integral throughout the implementation of a Multi-Tiered Systems of Support framework:

1 Identify the issue.
2 Develop and implement a solution.
3 Collect and analyze data.
4 Reflect and share the results.

Given the current role of educators as diagnosticians and interventionists within the Multi-Tiered Systems of Support framework, additional pedagogical/hebegogical content knowledge and resources related to solution-seeking, research-validated instructional practices, progress monitoring instruments, and data analysis protocols are needed to assist with data-informed decision-making. To assist educators with data-informed decision-making, multiple vetted resources and sites have been developed to provide educators with multiple resources that are readily available for immediate use. These high-quality and fully accessible websites were created by experts to translate research into resources for classroom use. Designed for educators, the sites include guidance on how to incorporate the resources within the classroom to make sense of data and translate data into action. A simple online search will reveal a plethora of available assessment resources.

## Multi-Tiered Systems of Support (Macro, Meso, and Micro)

Within a harmonic and comprehensive Multi-Tiered Systems of Support framework, the use and interpretation of multiple types and sources of assessments assure that all students receive differentiated instruction and unique interventions to improve learning. Therefore, the information included in this chapter is the basis for us to continuously analyze, revise, and enhance our instruction within our classroom through four types of assessments: universal screening, progress monitoring, diagnostic, and outcome (summative). From assessment results of multiple measures described in the previous sections of this chapter, there may be indications that students may or may not be learning the curricular content goals.

Within a harmonic and comprehensive Multi-Tiered Systems of Support framework, initial, overall assessment results from a group of students (e.g., at district, province, school, and class levels) are gleaned from assessments and are often referred to as "universal assessments" at the macro-tier level.

Universal assessments collect student performance data that focus on curriculum content standards. They provide important preliminary or baseline information about students' previous and current strengths and needs. The results from assessments used and interpreted at the macro-tier may indicate that additional information is needed for effective planning and learning and leading. Therefore, additional, more targeted assessments may need to be administered to smaller groups and/or individual students at the meso-tier to diagnose instructional concerns. At the micro-tier of assessment use, the various assessments as described are focused on an individual student to determine specific academic strengths and needs and to develop individualized instructional and intervention plans. Once these plans are developed and implemented with fidelity, progress monitoring probes continue to determine learning by the student. The goal for the multiple assessments for all students, a smaller, targeted group of students, and an individual student is to assure that all students learn the curricular content standards. Additionally, these assessment results have implications of professional learning opportunities.

## Unintended Consequences

With the current emphasis and numerous products focused on the assessment of students, it is critical to focus also on potential unintended consequences and cautions. Primarily, assessment products, use, and results must be understood by the assessor to both administer accurately and interpret the results. Assessment results must address the need for the data for instructional and intervention planning. The disadvantage of assessing learning is that it can sometimes overlook the uniqueness and individual progress of each learner. It may not fully capture the depth of understanding, personal growth, and creativity that individuals bring to their learning journey. In addition, assessments consume both momentous time and resources. If these assessments are not linked to curricular standards or programs, results are difficult to transform into instructional responses.

## Emerging Understandings

The use of various assessments provides valuable information for teachers and teacher leaders to integrate and focus instruction and interventions to specific instructional strengths and needs of students. Teachers use multiple sources of assessment data to plan to improve student learning. This information is the basis for us to continuously analyze, revise, and enhance instruction and determine interventions. The four types of assessments that are important within a Multi-Tiered Systems of Support framework are: universal screening, progress monitoring, diagnostic, and summative. Each type of assessment provides the basis for instructional planning integral to meeting the strengths and needs of all students within classrooms and schools.

Several types of assessments focus instructional concerns of students throughout the school or classroom (macro-tier), groups of students (meso-tier), and individual student (micro-tier). Specifically, there are important guidelines for the successful use and implementation of various forms of assessments. Assessment data are the basis for planning instruction and interventions. Therefore, the alignment of assessments with curricular standards is critical. Although there are multiple assessments available, educators should be knowledgeable about use and interpretation (e.g., standardized assessments, district- and school-mandated assessments, diagnostic and progress monitoring probes). Continuous professional learning about each type of assessment for use by teachers and teacher leaders to assure accurate use and interpretation of results is vital.

Grounded on a variety of student assessment results, in the next chapter we will review Multi-Tiered Systems of Support for ongoing professional learning to improve instruction. We will define and share professional learning opportunities at the macro, meso, and micro tiers.

## Professional Reflection Questions

When considering Multi-Tiered Systems of Support for assessment and evaluation, the following reflection questions need to be discussed as systems and tiers are conceived, constructed, and executed:

a  What universal or standardized assessments will be required by the district, state, or province?
b  At a macro-tier, what summative or static assessments are available for universal administration?

c  At a meso-tier, what formative or dynamic assessments are available to inventory students' developing strengths and needs across disciplines and grade levels?
d  At a micro-tier, will we look at student learning from a processing standpoint or student achievement from a content learning perspective?
e  How will the assessments be used to inform instruction?
f  How will the assessment be used to impact professional learning opportunities?

# References

Allington, R. (2011). *What really matters in response to intervention: Research-based designs*. New York: Pearson.

Barrio, B. L., Lindo, E. J., Combes, B. H., & Hovey, K. A. (2015). Ten years of response to intervention: Implications for general education teacher preparation programs. *Action in Teacher Education, 37*, 190–204.

Braun, G., Kumm, S., Brown, C., Walte, S., Hughes, M. T., & Maggin, D. M. (2018). Living in tier 2: Educators' perceptions of MTSS in urban schools. *International Journal of Inclusive Education, 24*(10), 1114–1128.

Daly, E. J. III, Martens, B. K., Barnett, D., Witt, J. C., & Olson, S. C. (2007). Varying intervention delivery in response to intervention: Confronting and resolving challenges with measurement, instruction, and intensity. *School Psychology Review, 36*(4), 562–581.

Datnow, A., & Hubbard, L. (2016). Teacher capacity for and beliefs about data-driven decision making: A literature review of international research. *Journal of Educational Change, 17*(1), 7–28.

Every Student Succeeds Act, Public Law 114–95, 114th Cong., 1st sess. (2015).

Fisher, D., & Ivey, G. (2006). Evaluating the interventions for struggling adolescent readers. *Journal of Adolescent and Adult Literacy, 50*(3), 180–189.

Hoover, J. J., Baca, L. M., Wexler-Love, E., & Saenz, L. (2008). *National implementation of Response to Intervention (RTI): Research summary*. Washington, DC: National Association of State Directors of Special Education (NASDE).

Horn, I. S., Kane, B. D., & Wilson, J. (2015). Making sense of student performance data: Data use in teachers' learning opportunities. *American Educational Research Journal, 52*(2), 208–242.

*Individuals with Disabilities Education Improvement Act* of 2004, 20 U.S.C. § 1400 et seq. (2004). (reauthorization of the Individuals with Disabilities Education Act 1990).

Katz, S., & Dack, L. A. (2014). Towards a culture of inquiry for data use in schools: Breaking down professional learning barriers through intentional interruption. *Studies in Educational Evaluation, 42*, 35–40.

Lane, K. L., Menzies, H. M., Oakes, W. P., & Kalberg, J. R. (2019). *Developing a schoolwide framework to prevent and manage learning and behavior problems.* New York: Guilford Press.

Lose, M. K. (2007). A child's response to intervention requires a responsive teacher of reading. *The Reading Teacher, 61*(3), 276–279.

Mandinach, E. B. (2012). A perfect time for data use: Using data-driven decision making to inform practice. *Educational Psychologist, 42*(2), 71–85.

Powell, D. R., Steed, E. A., & Diamond, K. E. (2010). Dimensions of literacy coaching with Head Start teachers. *Topics in Early Childhood Special Education, 30*(3), 148–161.

Puig, E. A., & Froelich, K. S. (2007). *The literacy coach: Guiding in the right direction.* Boston, MA: Pearson/Allyn and Bacon.

Schildkamp, K. (2019). Data-based decision-making for school improvement: Research insights and gaps. *Journal of Educational Research, 61*(3), 257–273.

Sisk, D. A. (2019). Differentiation: Using teaching strategies that facilitate learning in the inclusive classroom. In *Cultivating inclusive practices in contemporary K-12 education* (pp. 43–65). Hershey, PA: IGI Global.

Wilson, M. (2016). Becoming data and information rich in education. *BU Journal of Graduate Studies in Education, 8*(1), 5–9.

# Multi-Tiered System for Ongoing Professional Learning

*He who learns but does not think, is lost! He who thinks but does not learn is in great danger.*

–Confucius

Researching and implementing intentional and coherent ongoing professional learning opportunities is another hallmark of an effective and efficient Multi-Tiered Systems of Support framework at the school and district level. When Multi-Tiered Systems of Support is viewed as a continuous improvement model, the role of the literacy coach and a transdisciplinary literacy leadership team is critical as part of a support system to ensure perpetual forward shifts in instruction. Both a quality literacy coach and a resolute transdisciplinary literacy leadership team serve as a catalyst and conduit of information to impact professional learning opportunities with the goal of improving instruction and consequently learning for all in school. The following illustrative reflection questions are designed to help schools and districts engage in critical conversations to determine the type of professional learning opportunities that need to be created and available to bolster teacher-colleagues in making data-informed decisions to support all students:

- How does the professional learning opportunity focus on students' processing of information? (How are students learning?)
- How does the professional learning opportunity focus on what materials or content should be introduced to students? (What are students learning?)

- How does the professional learning opportunity focus teacher-colleagues' attention to interact with students' response to instruction?
- Who is responsible for scheduling and providing relevant professional learning opportunities?
- How are professional learning opportunities humane and respectful of teacher-colleagues' experience, knowledge, and time?
- How are students' strengths and needs being used to inform the type of professional learning opportunities provided?
- How are teacher-colleagues' strengths and needs being used to inform the type of professional learning opportunities provided to foster teacher leadership?

Facilitating a Multi-Tiered Systems of Support team or transdisciplinary literacy leadership team is another form of transdisciplinary literacy coaching to improve K-12 learning and instruction across all grade levels and disciplines. This section is included primarily here for teacher-colleagues and teacher leadership to take note that transdisciplinary literacy coaching on a continuum that involves many structures to support learning for everyone at a school site (Puig & Froelich, 2011). When we view transdisciplinary literacy coaching on a continuum of professional learning experiences, we consider the role of the transdisciplinary literacy coach as less supportive when they are facilitating a study group or literacy leadership team. The transdisciplinary literacy coach in this role is promoting more intra-active reflective behaviors by teacher-colleagues and teacher leadership by encouraging and promoting active solution seeking. At this point on the continuum of coaching, the literacy coach truly embodies a lead learner.

To facilitate a Multi-Tiered Systems of Support team or literacy leadership team with a focus on learning and instruction, a transdisciplinary literacy coach must consider that the group or the team needs to:

- Understand transdisciplinary literacy learning as a process.
- Establish ground rules for the study group or team meetings.
- Understand Cambourne's Conditions of Learning (Crouch & Cambourne, 2020) and how they apply across disciplinary classrooms and grade-level boundaries.
- Develop a common language to minimize misinterpretations.
- Identify and honor team members and their experiences.

- Learn how to control personal pedagogical and hebegogical passions; and
- Address adaptive challenges effectively and efficiently using documented evidence.

In addition to the above-mentioned points, a critical activity for facilitating a Multi-Tiered Systems of Support team or transdisciplinary literacy leadership team is setting a mutually agreed-upon calendar of meetings. Many colleagues of ours will attest that the most productive study groups and transdisciplinary literacy leadership teams are the ones that have looked ahead and have literally blocked their calendar with future meeting dates. Setting calendars sends a clear and important message to all members of a study group or a transdisciplinary literacy leadership team. It confirms the seriousness of committing and communicates to all members that forward shifts take time. Without setting calendars upfront, meetings become haphazard social events, impeding sustainability and expanding success. Multiple supports at the macro, meso, and micro tiers can be implemented as supports for professional learning and will be described in the next sections of this chapter.

# Engaging in Transdisciplinary Literacy Coaching – Macro Tier of Professional Learning

Transdisciplinary literacy coaching is a professional learning macro tier of support to improve instruction throughout the school. Our premise for developing the concept of literacy coaching as a tier of support is based on years of firsthand experiences, the current literature, and literacy coaches at a school site where we coached and were coached by colleagues in a variety of contexts. This led us to conclude that transdisciplinary literacy coaching as a tier of professional learning was not just about a "coaching cycle" of pre-conference, observation, and post-conference. Although we do acknowledge that the pre-conference, observation, post-conference model of literacy coaching is a powerful model to promote forward shifts in professional learning and instruction, this is also powerful to enhance instructional techniques. Transdisciplinary literacy coaching is so much more than just a coaching cycle. As we learn more and more about the complex job of a literacy coach, the current literature published on literacy coaching confirms our original proposal that literacy coaching is multifaceted, recursive, and complex (Casey, 2006; Knight, 2007; Lyons & Pinnell, 2001; Puig & Froelich, 2011; Puig & Froelich, 2022; Toll, 2004; Walpole & McKenna, 2004).

Our experiences have shown us that for any initiative to be successful throughout a school, support systems need to be in place. Systems for timely assessment, curriculum content development, and professional learning opportunities increase the likelihood of successful implementation. Moreover, professional learning opportunities need to be job-embedded and provided in a timely manner. We have found that for professional learning opportunities to be job-embedded and timely, the support of a knowledgeable and credible literacy coach is critical for the implementation of a K-12 transdisciplinary literacy framework for instruction.

For smooth implementation of Multi-Tiered Systems of Support to occur, we propose that a transdisciplinary literacy coach serves as the conduit and catalyst for professional learning of teacher-colleagues and teacher leadership throughout the school at this macro tier. Although literacy coaching is used as a model for school reform, many districts and schools have not embraced the concept for a variety of reasons. For example, schools that use a highly scripted program for instruction may not need a literacy coach that is hired to encourage teacher-colleagues to take a critical stance where data are used to "inform" instruction rather than "guide" it. In schools where successful literacy coaching is implemented, the literacy coach is not viewed as an expert but rather as a lead learner with extensive expertise and experience, in addition to being respected and admired as an educator. As we continue to learn and our knowledge of transdisciplinary literacy coaching evolves, we have chosen the term lead learner instead of co-learner. "Lead learner" clearly addresses the behavior that effective and efficient literacy coaches are to model – lifelong learning. We have found that when transdisciplinary literacy coaches establish themselves as lead learners and approach transdisciplinary literacy coaching on a continuum of professional learning, resistance to coaching is diminished, and collaboration is increased.

Consequently, both transdisciplinary literacy coaches and transdisciplinary literacy leadership teams have a common ground to develop common goals in response to adaptive challenges and to ensure that conditions for learning (Crouch & Cambourne, 2020) are in place and are looked upon as necessary for learning and instruction. We encourage schools to adapt and rely on a knowledgeable coach to serve as a lead learner by serving as a conduit and catalyst to improve instruction throughout the school.

It is up to the principal and district/province teacher leadership personnel to ensure that a literacy coach's job is clearly defined if they are to serve as a professional learning support for an entire school to improve instruction and student learning over time. Once a literacy coach is selected, the question, which is still the question for an overabundance of research currently being conducted, is "What does a literacy coach do?" At the top of the list, we make the claim that effective and efficient literacy coaches work with students at least 40% of their work week to hone their own craft of teaching in order to be able to engage with teacher-colleagues on improving instruction. We also must clarify that we do not intend this to mean that the literacy coach is the teacher of record for a select group of students. When this occurs, the title and obligations of a literacy coach need to be reconsidered. A literacy coach must have the scheduling freedom to visit with colleagues and classrooms if they are truly to be coaching so that they can improve transdisciplinary literacy learning and instruction.

We argue that when literacy coaches are removed from students and are hired to work solely with adults, the job of the literacy coach becomes blurred. When this blurring occurs, literacy coaches are given an earbud and a walkie-talkie and are assigned to extensive data entry positions, hall duty, bus duty, cafeteria duty, and the proverbial "other duties as assigned" removing them from the reason their job exists – to directly support student/teacher interactions as they occur in a learning environment.

It cannot be stated clearly enough that principals, district/province teacher leadership personnel, and literacy coaches need to have a clear understanding of the job requirements of a literacy coach. An honest and open discussion is a critical step for administrators in teacher leadership positions that plan to utilize a literacy coach to guide a school as a lead learner. The operative word here is "guide." A literacy coach that serves as a lead learner never dictates a direction, but through research and evidence (formal and informal) guides teacher-colleagues and teacher leadership personnel to recognize and investigate adaptive challenges to learning and instruction. To realize the potential of the literacy coach when implementing a K-12 transdisciplinary literacy framework, we will review literacy coaching at the macro tier in a continuum of professional learning.

The literature is clear that the transmission model for professional learning has extraordinarily negligible impact on classroom instruction (Costa & Garmston, 2002; Joyce & Showers, 2003). We have read over and over that the best professional learning is on-going and job-embedded (Darling-Hammond, Wei, Andree, Richardson, & Orphanos, 2009; Killion, 2008). Hence, because of research we have, the current widely held belief of the importance of literacy coaching in education to improve learning and instruction. Yet, what is meant by on-going? What is meant by job-embedded? It is apparent that the research has been misinterpreted or ignored when so many literacy coaches report investing so little time where instruction takes place – the classroom.

To us, on-going implies that professional learning for teachers in K-12 never ceases, and professional learning opportunities are regularly scheduled and of consistent high-quality. We define regularly scheduled as at least 90 minutes once every two weeks to sustain and expand success over time. When sincere consideration is given to learning and instruction, this time should be non-negotiable. High-quality professional learning cannot occur in 15 minutes or during a teacher's planning period or while walking down a hall. If professional learning opportunities are scheduled for full days, we encourage you to schedule the day into 90 minutes sessions with 15 minutes break in between as downtime for processing information informally with colleagues or personal reflection. Professional learning opportunities that take place once every two to three months or last less than 90 minutes at a time seem to have the same impact as mass production in-service meetings. Mass production works when building automobiles, but it does not work well when supporting the multidimensional transdisciplinary development of human minds – especially when the goal is improving the complex acts of learning and instruction.

Job-embedded professional learning is generally accepted as relevant on-the-job learning. Effective and efficient literacy coaches provide job-embedded learning when they interact with colleagues at a school. True job-embedded learning does not burden literacy coaches, teachers, or students with finding time for learning since learning and instruction are addressed within the context of the learning environment during contractual school time. Job-embedded learning relies heavily on the Vygotskian concept of assisted performance (Tharp & Gallimore, 1988) and Cazden's (1988) performance before competence. The focus of job-embedded professional learning is on teaching with assistance rather than just seeing and hearing.

Although on-going job-embedded learning appears to be a more effective and efficient manner to improve learning and instruction, we do not dismiss the contributions that experienced consultants or attending workshops make to professional learning. Concerns arise when that is the only type of professional learning provided over time, and that these two approaches have no follow-up to determine whether they have been successful in their application into the learning environment. Attending workshops and hiring consultants is sometimes a necessity to infuse new language for thinking so that we can tackle adaptive challenges from a different level. Because of limited time, materials, and funds, the concept of on-going job-embedded learning forces literacy coaches to address professional learning as an adaptive challenge. With professional learning as an adaptive challenge in mind, the literature, as well as our personal experiences, beg for literacy coaching to be viewed on a broad-spectrum landscape of support. Furthermore, for the literacy leadership team and literacy coach to sustain and expand success, a broad-spectrum landscape of macro support means that literacy coaching must be viewed on a continuum where individuals fluctuate back and forth from face-to-face interactions to intra-action One size has never really fitted all.

The structure for understanding literacy coaching as a continuum opens a world of possibilities for literacy leadership teams to address adaptive challenges in learning and teaching throughout schools at the macro tier of supports. Literacy coaching as a continuum is a framework for thinking about the job requirements of the literacy coach and how the literacy coach can support teacher-colleagues and the literacy leadership team in tackling adaptive challenges. While the continuum of coaching has a limited number of professional learning opportunities, it is certainly not an exhaustive list of professional learning activities. Other professional learning activities can certainly be added to the continuum of coaching. The essential theme is that there is more than one way to coach or support teacher-colleagues and that investing too much time in one given area will be counterproductive over time. Although the continuum addresses literacy coaches specifically, both literacy leadership teams and literacy coaches must continually keep moving back and forth on the continuum if they are going to be constantly questioning, investigating, and growing. Borrowing from the Māori proverb, "You are either green and growing or ripe and rotting."

Even though a continuum of transdisciplinary literacy coaching may appear to be carried out in a very linear manner, it is not. There is no particular starting point or ending point for learning to begin or end. One thing is for certain, as stated previously, if too much time is invested in one area you will begin to metaphorically ripen and rot in others. The late Dr. Marie M. Clay has been described as always stirring the waters (Gaffney & Askew, 1999). When she accepted a lifetime achievement award at the National Reading Conference (now Literacy Research Association), she borrowed from the New Zealand poet Allen Curnow (1997) the line, "Simply by sailing in a different direction, you could enlarge the world." Our point is that a transdisciplinary literacy coach cannot enlarge their world if they do not sail in a different direction on what we propose as a continuum of coaching. In the next few pages, we will elaborate on each section of a continuum of transdisciplinary literacy coaching developed over time by Puig and Froelich (2011).

## Facilitating a Workshop as a Meso Tier of Professional Learning

When a literacy coach is charged with introducing a new instructional practice to a group of teacher-colleagues or new language needs to be introduced to promote alternative thinking, facilitating a workshop may be the venue. Facilitating a workshop is a highly supportive, subject-centered, and interactive endeavor to scaffold professional learning on a continuum of literacy coaching. Effective and efficient literacy coaches facilitate relevant and engaging workshops based on teachers' strengths and needs. Assessment and evaluation will make a workshop relevant while relationships and experiences make it engaging. Workshops facilitated by literacy coaches at the school level should always be based on formal and informal data analyzed. Data must be cross-checked or co-triangulated for a true adaptive challenge to be identified. In schools that have active literacy leadership teams, the literacy coach takes the lead to address an adaptive challenge after working collaboratively with the team.

The best decisions for addressing an adaptive challenge are made in collaboration with the team. Once a specific adaptive challenge has been identified and it can be addressed through professional learning, it then becomes the responsibility of the literacy coach to generate a "menu" for professional learning. We use the term menu rather than agenda since it implies that the responsibility for learning is on the learner. For example, when we go to a restaurant, we are given a menu, and the expectation is that we will select what we want to eat based on what we hunger for. When facilitating a workshop for adults, the expectation needs to be in place that the participants are ultimately responsible for their learning and what they select to learn is what they hunger to learn.

To begin, create a template for organizing a 90-minute workshop with colleagues at a school site. The template should be thought of as a menu of materials and activities to engage participants in the professional learning experience. Additionally, the menu must consider Cambourne's Conditions of Learning (Crouch & Cambourne, 2020) and utilized as conditions for learning. Founded on Cambourne's Conditions of Learning, these questions may be a springboard for a rich discussion between the literacy coach and the literacy leadership team in the development of a menu for professional learning:

- How will participants be immersed in the content?
- What kinds of demonstrations are needed based on data?
- What are the expectations before, during, and after the workshop?
- Who will be ultimately responsible for learning and instruction?
- What kinds of responses will be provided?
- How will approximations be honored in a failure-safe environment?
- What types of experience are necessary to promote engagement?
- How will the information be employed for future use?

A general outline for facilitating a workshop might include length of time, benefit, or benefits for participants as it relates to transdisciplinary learning and instruction based on assessment and evaluation, possible materials and activities, a closing activity, and an evaluation to gauge future in-service enterprises.

When facilitating a workshop think of yourself as an ethnographer constantly studying and responding to participants. You ground yourself in the climate and culture of the environment where learning takes place. In ethnographic research, data are triangulated by collecting participant observations, non-participant observations, and artifacts (Frank, 1999; Spradley, 1980). As a facilitator, be sure to balance your interactive discussion with firsthand experiences (participant observations), affirming remarks (based on non-participant observations), and the use of tangible items to make points. Think of a dynamic presenter or facilitator you have heard recently. Most dynamic presenters share personal stories and immediate observations from watching or listening to participants, and also use such artifacts as electronic presentations, books, or handouts. These dynamic facilitators triangulate and balance their presentations to engage participants. To create engaging and memorable presentations, you must balance the presentations with personal anecdotes, immediate observations, and artifacts. When a presentation is not balanced, participants tend to tune speakers out. Our top ten recommendations for facilitating a workshop are:

1. Start with an introduction that will attract your audience's attention by stating the benefits of the workshop to learning and instruction.
2. Present data selectively, clearly, and succinctly.
3. If you use an electronic visual presentation, print should never be smaller than 32 points.
4. When using quotations in a visual presentation, let the audience read it silently first before reading it yourself.
5. Make eye contact with different members of your audience in all locations of the room.
6. Write your talk, double-spaced, 14 points, and rehearse it.
7. If you use an electronic presentation application, learn how to use it well first.
8. Do not keep your audience hanging with "one more thing."
9. If time is limited, your introduction and closing are the most memorable information; eliminate from the middle.
10. Closing should have a personal and emotional hook.

## Providing an Observation Lesson – Meso Tier of Professional Learning

Providing an observation lesson is a reciprocal coaching model that ideally puts teacher-colleagues in the coaching seat. Observation lessons tend to be a little subject-centered in that a specific instruction practice is employed for a specific reason. It is quite a supportive endeavor in the process of learning and instruction, but not quite as supportive as facilitating a workshop. Here, the interaction is a bit more personal than the support provided in a workshop environment. We are purposefully avoiding the terms "model lesson or demonstration lesson" because we have seen so many model lessons that were not. Plus, labeling a lesson as a "model" implies perfection. In actuality, an observation lesson is a better descriptor of what we are trying to accomplish when working with colleagues. We are providing a professional learning opportunity to observe a lesson. An observation lesson is a time when the literacy coach works with students using a particular instructional practiced while a colleague or colleagues observe the lesson. Teacher-colleagues always appreciate colleagues that provide the opportunity to observe an instructional practice that they are curious about implementing. Think of how many times we have walked away from a workshop and used the phrase "I need to see it." Providing an observation lesson is the equivalent to "I need to see it."

Setting up an observation lesson starts with teacher-colleagues requesting this level of support. Although at times the literacy coach may request class time from a classroom teacher to provide an observation lesson for their own personal professional learning. When the request is made, regardless of who makes it, it is always a promising idea to set some ground rules for the experience to be a productive learning and instructional experience for the teacher, the students, and the literacy coach. Based on our experiences in providing observation lessons, we strongly recommend that the following ground rules be previewed and discussed with all involved in advance for observation lessons to be meaningful professional learning experiences:

- A specific and respectful time has to be scheduled for the observation lesson and the debriefing of the lesson afterwards.
- Prior to the observation lesson, the literacy coach is responsible for visiting the classroom numerous times to get to know the students and learn their strengths and needs.
- The classroom teacher clearly understands that she or he is to be observing and taking notes that will be used for discussion during the scheduled debriefing.
- The literacy coach must have a clear understanding of transdisciplinary literacy learning as a process in order to interact effectively and efficiently with students during the lesson.
- Some form of documented formal or informal assessment needs to be incorporated into the observation lesson.
- A plan for follow-up where the teacher employs the instructional practice that was demonstrated during the observation lesson needs to be established during the debriefing.

Providing observation lessons can be a double-edged sword for literacy coaches and literacy leadership teams to understand that. As we all know, any lesson has the potential to go awry. Yet, when literacy coaches provide observation lessons with the attitude and mentality that this is an opportunity for "learning and instruction," even the worst-case scenario can be productive. Our worst lessons have served us as rich experiences to prompt some breakthrough dialogue on what worked and what did not, and why. Furthermore, some of our worst lessons have leveled the playing field with colleagues, presenting us as a lead learner rather than an expert, and have served as a foundation for a long and trusting relationship which is essential in literacy coaching. We cannot stress enough, however, that in order to ensure a successful observation lesson, the literacy coach must know the students' strengths and needs. Without this working knowledge about the students, observation lessons become another dog and pony show with minimal impact on improving learning and instruction.

## Co-teaching in an Observation Classroom – Meso Tier of Professional Learning

In a co-teaching situation, the host teacher and the guest teacher (in this case, the literacy coach) share responsibility for learning and instruction with a consistent cohort of students. Ideally, over time the students see the host teacher and the guest teacher as simply their teachers. Co-teaching in an observation classroom is the ideal laboratory for literacy coaches to flourish in their pedagogical content knowledge of literacy learning and instruction. On the continuum of coaching, we place co-teaching in an observation classroom as a hybrid of support where the experience is still interactive, but somewhat subject-centered and solution seeking simultaneously. Literacy coaches that have adopted co-teaching in an observation classroom as a form of personal professional learning have found it to be a rewarding experience with many benefits. When involved in a co-teaching situation, literacy coaches are not viewed as an administrative position that is there to "fix" teachers. By placing themselves in a teaching position, literacy coaches will face the realities that classroom teachers face on a daily basis and provide a rich source of experiences to seek solutions with colleagues, not for colleagues. As in any relationship, co-teaching in an observation classroom must be nurtured with the understanding that a primary purpose is for new instructional practices to be employed. Since the literacy coach is responsible for providing professional learning opportunities for other colleagues, host teachers must accept a literacy coach's need for flexibility in scheduling their class time. Although a literacy coach may invest a great deal of time in the same classroom when co-teaching, there will be times when the literacy coach must provide professional learning opportunities for other colleagues in other classrooms.

In our experiences as literacy coaches and facilitators of courses for literacy coaches, we have found that during the first semester of a school year, more time is invested in co-teaching, with less time during the second semester. In some cases, elementary school literacy coaches have co-taught in a primary grade (K-2) during the first semester and then switch to co-teaching in an intermediate grade (3–5) to build up their knowledge of transdisciplinary literacy learning and instruction across grade levels. The advantage of this latter model is that elementary schools can have the luxury of a primary and an intermediate observation classroom for teacher-colleagues to visit. At the middle school and high school levels, a literacy coach may co-teach in a content area (language arts, mathematics, social studies, science, arts) classroom during the second semester for the same reason as their elementary counterpart – to build up their hebegogical content knowledge of transdisciplinary literacy learning and instruction across grade levels and disciplines. As with the elementary counterpart, the advantage of this model is that a reading/language arts and a specific content area observation classroom can be set up for teacher-colleagues to visit without ever having to leave their campus.

A big advantage to a school where literacy coaches co-teach with a host teacher is that it primes the school as a learning organization (Senge, 1990) and sets the stage for developing observation classrooms where other teachers on campus can visit to reflect, reenergize, and revitalize their own learning and instruction. Of course, setting up an observation classroom requires planning, time, and commitment from the host teacher, the principal, and the literacy coach. In setting up an observation classroom where the literacy coach is the co-teacher, the following considerations must be considered:

- A variety of genres and multi-leveled materials to accommodate the learning strengths and needs of the students.
- The furniture and its placement in the room.

- The number of students in the host classroom needs to be the same as in all the classrooms.
- The availability of technology.
- The focus should be on learning and instruction not on a published series of materials, although a published series of materials may be incorporated.
- It needs to be evident that instruction is informed by on-going formal and informal assessments.
- Age-appropriate instructional practices need to be in place.
- Release time for the host teacher to debrief with visiting colleagues must be considered.
- An age- and grade-level-appropriate transdisciplinary literacy framework is in place that supports and reflects students growing knowledge from kindergarten through grade 12.

We have found that successful observation classrooms are mindfully curated learning environments that are highly supported by literacy coaches who co-teach in them. Prevalent in observation classrooms is also a clear and succinct K-12 transdisciplinary literacy framework that considers where students are coming from and where they will be going. For example, working with the end in mind, ideally middle school (grades 6–8) and high school (grades 9–12) observation classrooms have a transdisciplinary literacy framework that builds upon the work started by their intermediate elementary school colleagues. In turn, an elementary intermediate (grades 3–5) observation classroom implements a transdisciplinary literacy framework that builds on the work that their primary (grades K-2) colleagues started. This highly buttressed comprehensive transdisciplinary literacy framework should inform the organizations (schools, districts, states, provinces) of observation classrooms at any grade level and support student learning as they mature through their K-12 academic career.

## Conferring, Observing, Debriefing – Meso Tier of Professional Learning

When most of us hear about any type of coaching (reading, literacy, instructional, cognitive, student centered, or evocative), conferring, observing, and debriefing appears to be the prevailing job description. Yet, for this elevated level of coaching to take place, a lot of trust must be established. Without a powerful sense of trust, this level of coaching can be counterproductive for improving learning and instruction. Some things to consider when developing trust is Tshannen-Moran's (2004) five facets of trust: kindness, trustworthiness, flexibility, dependability, and expertise. Once trust has been established, the literacy coach can proceed to this stage of level of coaching. This level of coaching has the potential to be the most productive to promote forward shifts in learning and instruction. It also has the most potential for backfiring since it involves a strong relationship between a teacher and a literacy coach. It has been our experience that this level of coaching is also the one that most literacy coaches have received the least in-service training on. Consequently, it is not surprising when many literacy coaches we have had conversations with do not engage in literacy coaching at this level, even though districts are constantly touting "the coaching cycle." Nonetheless, it is another level of coaching on a continuum of professional learning experiences to improve learning and instruction.

There are two routes to take when approaching coaching from the conferring, observing, debriefing model. Although both routes involve the same processes, adding another possible type of support, the nature of the conversations will be different. One conference or tier of support may be an introductory conversation with the literacy coach explaining that they will be in the classroom as an ethnographer collecting participant observations, nonparticipant observations, and artifacts to determine a possible coaching point or two based on student behaviors. Saying that the observation will focus on student performance is critical. Coaching is not about fixing a colleague. It is about improving learning and instruction. Call it what you would like, but literacy coaching is always "student-centered."

The second route may be an alternative conference that involves a dialogic conversation between the teacher and the literacy coach to seek a solution to an adaptive challenge the teacher may have. Both approaches have their advantages and disadvantages. We encourage literacy coaches and literacy leadership teams to investigate the advantages and disadvantages of one over the other in relation to the teachers at individual schools. With experienced teachers, engaging in a dialogic conversation may be a productive type of support to take, while, at the same time, adopting an ethnographic perspective with novice teachers may seem more appropriate.

This level of coaching on a continuum of professional experiences strikes a balance between interactive and intra-active. It is a sensitive transaction between a subject-centered orientation and a solution-seeking orientation with the focus always on student performance that is based on the students' strengths and needs. Consequently, observing is contingent on the type of conversation that took place prior to the observation. If the decision was made that the coach was entering the classroom from an ethnographic perspective, the observation will evolve as the lesson progresses, with one or two coaching points surfacing for discussion in the debriefing; always focused on student behavior. On the other hand, if the conversation revolved around a request for support and a concern the teacher had, the observation should focus on specific student behavior for solution seeking with the teacher during the debriefing addressing the teacher's concern. The challenge with always addressing the teacher's concern is that sometimes other issues that impede learning and instruction will be observed that were unintended or not discussed in the original conference. For this reason, effective and efficient literacy coaches need to be flexible with which tier of support to apply when supporting colleagues at this juncture on coaching on a continuum of professional learning. Although conferring, observing, and debriefing are listed on a continuum of coaching as one form of coaching, there are at least two tiers support to address coaching within this model. The decision to use one model over the other is dependent on the comfort level of the teacher and the coach along with the teacher's strengths and needs.

## Facilitating Collaborative Action Research – a Micro Tier of Professional Learning

On the opposite end of coaching on a continuum, we have placed collaborative action research as the micro tier of support for transdisciplinary literacy coaching that promotes reflection. Although the term "action research" was coined around 1944 by Kurt Lewin at MIT and appeared in a 1946 paper titled "Action Research and Minority Problems," it is now a common term in professional learning. Collaborative action research is a coherent and intentional, yet recursive and contingent, method of questioning, researching, curating, planning, executing, assessing, evaluating, and reflecting to improve instruction.

Facilitating and participating in collaborative action research promotes the acquisition of new knowledge, encourages, and executes change, and focuses on improving learning and instruction by individual teachers (Stinger, 1996). Research confirms that the reflective nature of the collaborative action research process empowers teacher-colleagues and teacher leadership personnel to improve learning and instruction (Bennett, 1994; Glanz, 2003; Hubbard & Powers, 1999). Kemmis and McTaggert (1988) describe essential components of collaborative action research that include: creating an action plan for improving learning and instruction; executing the plan; assessing and documenting change; and reflecting on the change to promote forward shifts. The experience of engaging in collaborative action research encourages forward shifts in instructional practices (Fullan, 2000).

Collaborative action research can be categorized into – deductive support and inductive support. The first focuses on executing an action plan, whereas the latter focuses on preparation for an action. The deductive support assists in executing an action plan, tracking implementation issues, and evaluating the final outcomes. The inductive support is to conduct collaborative action research to seek adaptive challenges or to find out what adaptive challenges need to be addressed in a specific learning and instruction situation. Mills (2003) created the following design for facilitating a deductive approach to collaborative action research:

- Identify an adaptive challenge.
- Highlight attributes of the adaptive challenge.
- Describe the novel practice to be executed.
- Create a schedule for implementation.
- Describe the necessary personnel to be involved in the collaboration.
- List resources to be used or investigated.
- Explain the vertical (grade levels) and horizontal (across grade level and disciplines) data needed.
- Create a plan for assessment and evaluation of the data.
- Decide on supportive material for investigating.
- Execute the plan to address the adaptive challenge.
- Share outcomes.

Burns (1999) proposes an inductive support to collaborative action research that utilizes the following interconnected practices:

- Explore an issue in learning and instruction.
- Identify adaptive challenges.
- Assess how the adaptive challenges relate in the context of the research.
- Collaboratively seek solutions to an adaptive challenge.
- Gather vertical and horizontal data to determine an action plan.
- Use a Design Thinking mindset to develop an action plan to address the adaptive challenge based on the data collected.

Both inductive and deductive support of collaborative action research involve collecting contextualized grade-level assessments and across grade-level/disciplinary assessments by individual teachers guided by other teacher-colleagues or coaches. A variety of relevant summative and formative assessments are used in both supportive approaches. Collaborative action research is coherent and intentional to specific adaptive challenges that teacher-colleagues and teacher leaders may face. It converts tacit understandings of learning and instruction into explicit and documented information that can be shared with district/state/provincial administration and communities. Generally, outcomes from collaborative action research leads to the confirmation or rejection of individual interpretations, observations, and dispositions based on mindfully curated data over time. More importantly, when transdisciplinary literacy coaches facilitate collaborative action research with individual teachers in their classrooms and school site, it promotes a collaborative culture of transformation (Fullan, 2000). Consequently, transdisciplinary literacy coaches, teacher colleagues, and teacher leadership personnel become more resourceful and less dependent on external sources for seeking solutions to learning and instruction that directly impacts their school and communities (Fullan, 2000).

## Unintended Consequences

Putting in place a Multi-Tiered System of Support for professional learning demands that certain policies, courtesies, and dispositions be acknowledged and accounted for. First and foremost, the right people need be placed in the right positions. At the macro tier, we are looking at putting in place a literacy leadership team. However, without knowledgeable and flexible colleagues on the team, little may be accomplished in an efficient and effective manner to improve instruction. Quality teacher leadership is paramount. Leadership at this level is about not just administration but also teacher leadership in a broad sense to make informed decisions that will positively impact teacher-colleagues and other stakeholders. When the wrong people are in place, misinterpretation and miscommunication, with the best of intentions, will occur.

At the meso tier, employing a literacy coach within the various roles and opportunities as described also comes with potential pitfalls. Literacy coaching has been around for decades. Yet, for all intents and purposes, has come into the education limelight since the mid-1990s to the present as a viable avenue to improve instruction. Although there are many positive attributes for employing a transdisciplinary literacy coach, there can also be some potential unintended consequences when a literacy coach is not seen as credible or trustworthy by teacher-colleagues. The lack of trust and credibility are two major factors that can potentially impact professional learning negatively at each of the tiers. If literacy coaching is not successful at the macro or meso tier, action research and additional coaching at the micro tier is less likely to take place. For these supports to occur as a micro tier, teacher colleagues and teacher leaders have to have trust, multiple positive experiences being coached over time.

# Emerging Understandings

Putting in place a Multi-Tiered System of Support for professional learning requires knowledgeable and trustworthy colleagues. We have observed that schools that have implemented Multi-Tiered Systems of Support for professional learning are successful by having a knowledgeable, credible, flexible, and trustworthy transdisciplinary literacy leadership team along with a transdisciplinary literacy coach and an intentional and coherent transdisciplinary literacy K-12 framework for instruction. Consequently, when putting in place multiple tiers (macro, meso, and micro) of support for professional learning, acknowledging that the job of a transdisciplinary literacy coach is multifaceted and complex like all learning and instruction is critical. To label anything in education as "simple" creates dangerous minefields that impede accelerating learning and improving instruction for all. Subsequently, a knowledgeable transdisciplinary literacy coach working in collaboration with teacher-colleagues, and literacy leadership team is a powerful combination to bring about positive transformations in a school. By carefully investigating and putting on the table the specific duties, dispositions, and obligations of the transdisciplinary literacy coach, teacher leaders, and teacher-colleagues, schools will be better equipped to rely on the transdisciplinary literacy coach as another rich resource to tackle adaptive challenges and improve instruction.

When a school thinks of transdisciplinary literacy coaching within a Multi-Tiered System of Support for professional learning opportunities, it unlocks the school to a safe culture of learning where productive failure becomes a learning opportunity for all. It is in this safe culture of learning that teacher leaders, transdisciplinary literacy coaches, teacher-colleagues, and students will grow. In this chapter, we presented coaching as a broad-spectrum professional learning opportunity on a continuum that includes a variety of approaches. We purposefully used the verbs to describe the variety of activities that coaches deal with to make the point that effective and efficient transdisciplinary literacy coaching is about taking action to improve K-12 learning and instruction across the disciplines. At any given point in our professional lives, we have both coached and been coached. Subsequently, each select activity in this chapter was given a brief section within a Multi-Tiered System of Support to describe points for professional discussion and helpful hints to assist transdisciplinary literacy leadership teams, teacher leaders, and teacher-colleagues in understanding transdisciplinary professional learning in a broader and more productive sense to support nurturing and magnifying achievement in a professional learning community of practice.

# References

Bennett, C. K. (1994). Promoting teacher reflection through action research: What do teachers think? *Journal of Staff Development, 15*(1), 34–38.

Burns, A. (1999). *Collaborative action research for English language teachers.* Cambridge: Cambridge University Press.

Casey, K. (2006). *Literacy coaching: The essentials.* Portsmouth, NH: Heinemann.

Cazden, C. (1988). *Classroom discourse: The language of teaching and learning.* Portsmouth, NH: Heinemann.

Costa, A. L., & Garmston, R. J. (2002). *Cognitive coaching: A foundation for renaissance schools* (2nd ed). Norwood, MA: Christopher-Gordon Publishers.

Crouch, D., & Cambourne, B. (2020). *Made for learning: How the conditions of learning guide teaching decisions.* Katonah, NY: Richard C. Owens.

Curnow, A. (1997). *Early days yet: New and collected poems 1941-1997.* Aukland University Press.

Darling-Hammond, L., Wei, R. C., Andree, A., Richardson, N., & Orphanos, S. (2009). *Professional learning in the learning profession*. Washington, DC: National Staff Development Council.

Frank, C. (1999). *Ethnographic eyes: A teacher's guide to classroom observation*. Portsmouth, NH: Heinemann.

Fullan, M. (2000). *Change force: The sequel*. Philadelphia, PA: Falmer Press.

Gaffney, J. S., & Askew, B. J. (1999). *Stirring the waters: The influence of Marie Clay*. Portsmouth, NH: Heinemann.

Glanz, J. (2003). *Action research: An educational leader's guide to school improvement*. Norwood, MA: Christopher-Gordon.

Hubbard, R., & Powers, B. (1999). *Living the questions: A guide for teacher researchers*. Portland, ME: Stenhouse.

Joyce, B., & Showers, B. (2003). *Student learning through staff development* (3rd ed.). Alexandria, VA: Association for Supervision and Curriculum Development.

Kemmis, S., & McTaggert, R. (1988). *The action research planner* (3rd ed.). Geelong, VIC: Deakin University Press.

Killion, J. (2008). *Assessing impact: Evaluating staff development*. Thousand Oaks, CA: Corwin Press.

Knight, J. (2007). *Instructional coaching: A partnership approach to improving instruction*. Thousand Oaks, CA: Corwin Press.

Lyons, C., & Pinnell, G. S. (2001). *Systems for change in literacy education: A guide to professional development*. Portsmouth, NH: Heinemann.

Mills, G. E. (2003). *Action research: A guide for the teacher researcher*. Upper Saddle River, NJ: Merrill/Prentice Hall.

Puig, E. A., & Froelich, K. S. (2011). *The literacy coach: Guiding in the right direction* (2nd ed.). Boston, MA: Allyn & Bacon/Pearson.

Puig, E. A., & Froelich, K. S. (2022). *Teaching K-12 transdisciplinary literacy: A comprehensive instructional framework for learning and leading*. Taylor & Francis/Routledge.

Senge, P. M. (1990). *The fifth discipline: The art & practice of the learning organization*. New York: Doubleday.

Spradley, J. P. (1980). *Participant observation*. Orlando, FL: Harcourt Brace Jovanovich College Publishers.

Stinger, E. T. (1996). *Action research: A handbook for practitioners*. Thousand Oaks, CA: Sage.

Tharp, R., & Gallimore, R. (1988). *Rousing minds to life: Teaching, learning, and schooling in social context*. Cambridge: Cambridge University Press.

Toll, C. A. (2004). *The literacy coach's survival guide: Essential questions and practical answers*. Newark, DE: International Literacy Association.

Tshannen-Moran, M. (2004). *Trust matters: Leadership for successful schools*. San Francisco. Jossey-Bass.

Walpole, S., & McKenna, M. C. (2004). *The literacy coaches handbook: A guide to research-based practice*. New York: Guilford.

# Multi-Tiered System for Family Engagement

> *Family not only need to consist of merely those whom we share blood, but also for those whom we'd give blood.*
> 
> –Charles Dickens

## Partnerships with Parents and Caregivers

Schools are multidimensional centers of activity in which parents, families, teachers, educational service providers, administrators, and students are challenged in numerous ways to prepare for the escalating demands of a complex future. Increasingly, families, caregivers, and legal guardians are recognizing that students can best be served if parents, families, and professionals work together as partners to share information, develop goals, and co-construct plans for academic achievement. Since these topics may range from the dissemination of information to the development of solutions for very complex issues, diverse engagement practices and expertise of multiple educational professionals may be needed to partner with the families. Engagement practices and partnerships are needed to address awareness, volunteer opportunities, and necessary involvement by parents and/or family members with decision-making to address topics of instruction, interventions, the assessment of student achievement, professional development, partnerships, and communication with multiple stakeholders within the community. Sharing expertise stimulates productivity, synergy, and solutions as team members collaborate.

The rationale to enhance the vision of partnerships within Multi-Tiered Systems of Support for family engagement in schools is to increase the understandings within both the school and family contexts. Students are part of families and communities with shared customs, values, and cultural norms. To effectively teach, educators must comprehend their students' contexts, including family dynamics and community influences (Christenson, 1995). Through partnerships and effective communications, bridges between educators and families are created and developed for the continuous sharing of information. By interacting directly with families and caregivers, educators can bridge the gap between home and school. These meaningful relationships benefit everyone involved, fostering a collaborative environment (Conoley, 1989). These meaningful relationships advance the goals for shared responsibilities for the academic and behavioral successes of the students. Home–school collaboration is a shared responsibility between schools and families for educational outcomes. When educators actively engage parents and families, student achievement improves (Milner, Flowers, & Moore, 2019). Developing a collaborative environment within schools for families and caregivers is critical to enhancing benefits for students.

## Collaboration with Families

The educational journey of students is enhanced by the collaborative efforts of their parents/families and school-based professionals, including teachers. These partnerships, woven with effective strategies, mutual understanding, and shared responsibility, unlock a world of possibilities for academic achievement, personal growth, and fulfilling school experiences. This chapter describes family–teacher collaboration, explores benefits, illuminates essential skills, and provides several examples of resources to nurture these crucial partnerships.

Families engage in their child's development and education in a variety of ways. Recognizing and respecting the many ways in which families support the learning and development of children and youth, both at home and in formal learning environments, is critical to the success of school-based family engagement practices. In fact, some would argue that this is an essential first step for schools looking to establish strong relationships with racially, linguistically, and culturally diverse families to benefit the students within the classrooms and schools (Baquedano-López, Alexander, & Hernandez, 2013).

# Benefits of Collaboration with Families

When building effective connections with families, collaboration emerges as the cornerstone of success, paving the way for increased academic performance, a more inclusive learning environment, and a shared commitment to nurturing every student's unique potential. The benefits of a productive parent–teacher partnership are numerous. Studies have shown that collaboration leads to:

- **Improved academic performance**: When parents and teachers work together to identify a child's strengths and challenges, they can tailor learning strategies and support systems that meet their individual needs, leading to significant academic progress (National Association of Special Education Teachers, n.d.).
- **Increased parental/family involvement**: Active parental and family participation in their child's education fosters a sense of ownership and responsibility, boosting engagement and motivation in both the child and the family (Collier, Keefe, & Hirrel, 2015).
- **Enhanced communication**: Open and honest communication forms the bedrock of this partnership. By sharing observations, concerns, and progress updates, parents and family members and teachers develop a deeper understanding of the child and can proactively address their evolving needs (Collier et al., 2015).
- **Increased understanding**: Collaboration allows both parents/caregivers and teachers to gain a holistic perspective of the child. Witnessing the child in different environments (home and school) provides valuable insights into their learning styles, social interactions, and emotional well-being, fostering a more comprehensive support system.
- **Increased trust and a more inclusive environment**: When parents and teachers collaborate effectively, they create a climate of mutual respect and shared responsibility. This trust translates into a more inclusive learning environment for all students, fostering empathy and acceptance (National Association of Special Education Teachers, n.d.).
- **Improved Student Learning**: Regular communication between teachers and families positively impacts student learning. It ensures alignment between home and school expectations, leading to better academic outcomes (Tanase, 2023).

- **Behavioral Improvements**: When families are informed about their child's progress, behavior, and challenges, they can provide necessary support. This involvement contributes to a conducive learning environment.
- **Teacher–Parent Alliance**: Effective communication turns families into allies. Teachers gain insights into students' lives, enabling personalized teaching strategies. Families, in turn, trust and support teachers.

# Necessary Collaboration and Communication

Collaboration is an ongoing process whereby educators with different expertise work together voluntarily to create solutions with parents and caregivers that are impacting student success, as well as to carefully monitor and refine the solutions based upon data-based decision-making within educational partnerships. Collaborators work jointly to cooperative interaction to achieve a shared vision or goal. In short, the major goal of collaboration is to improve instruction and interventions to students whose needs are not currently met. Collaboration is a way of being, not a set of isolated skills or a service. The collaborative process reframes how educators, parents, caregivers, and legal guardians interact in multiple school contexts, including interactions, data-driven decision-making, team meetings, problem-solving sessions, and educational services.

When considering the definition of collaboration, this is an ongoing process of parents, caregivers, and legal guardians with educators to address instructional and intervention responsibilities for student learning. Everyone connects and interacts in partnership. During the process of collaboration, each team member should be "all in" to problem solve, share knowledge and expertise, and develop plans to maximize the benefits of collaboration in any cooperative interactions to achieve the shared vision or goal.

Another critical component of collaboration requires parity among participants. Parity occurs when each person's contribution to the interaction within the team is equally valued, and each person has equal power in decision-making. If one or several individuals are perceived by others as having greater power with decisions, collaboration does not usually occur. It is important to realize that individuals may have parity of decision-making as they work together in one specific collaborative activity, even though they do not have parity in other situations or roles. For example, parents and caregivers have important knowledge of their children to share with educators when developing action and instructional plans. Collaboration is based upon mutual goals that are developed and shared by the members of the collaborative team. When the teams are first established, discussions about the shared goals set the expectations for collaboration among the team members.

The final component of collaboration depends on shared responsibility for participation and decision-making. During collaboration, each member of the collaborative team is responsible for actively engaging and carrying out continuous decision-making to assure that the goals for collaboration are achieved. Shared participation in specific collaborative teams (e.g., data teams, Multi-Tiered Systems for Support teams, etc.) does not imply that all members on the collaborative team share every task equally. However, each member of the collaborative team shares expertise, decision-making, and solutions equally. Successful collaboration requires family members, educators, and other stakeholders not only to voluntarily engage with other members on the team to accomplish the shared goals; it also requires the knowledge and commitment of collaborators with regard to interpersonal and communication skills.

## Skills for Collaboration with Parents throughout MTSS

Successful collaboration is difficult but rewarding. Each of the previously described components of collaboration must be practiced by the members of the team. Professionals who participate in collaborative teams must believe that collaboration will result in more powerful and significant outcomes than the results of individual efforts. Individuals who collaborate usually do not have the same expertise, backgrounds, or methods. For professionals who teach diverse groups of students with complex learning and behavioral needs, building collaborative relationships with others expands the diversity of solutions and opportunities. For example, the family members have knowledge of the student's interests and habits. The classroom teacher has a deeper understanding of the classroom dynamics, curriculum, and instruction. The social worker has deeper expertise in counseling and behavioral strategies. However, even if there is a strong belief in collaboration and the beneficial outcomes, collaboration does not occur simply through the formation of various team structures within the school. School professionals must feel relatively secure in fully exploring collaborative relationships with parents and family members. The goals, expectations, procedures, and responsibilities must be co-developed, co-shared, and co-implemented at the beginning of collaborative relationships within specific teams. At the outset, trust must be present for parents and educators to begin the work of the team, but with successful experiences, trust and collaboration grow as a sense of community develops. In effective collaborative teams, trust, rapport, and, subsequently, respect, are established and grow. As stated earlier, it is increasingly recognized that a sense of professional community through effective collaboration leads to better outcomes for students and increased satisfaction and support for educators through sustained and effective communication skills (Slanda et al., 2024).

# Effective Communication Skills

Given the vast amount of information that needs to be shared between parents and teachers, effective communication is vital. Utilizing clear and concise language, organizing information into manageable chunks, and providing multiple avenues for communication can help ensure everyone stays informed and engaged. Studies have shown that strong collaborative bridges between parents and teachers are built with specific communication skills, including:

- **Active listening**: This involves attentive engagement, asking clarifying questions, and demonstrating genuine interest in each other's perspectives. Empathetic listening fosters understanding and strengthens the trust needed for effective collaboration (Koch, n.d.).
- **Clear and concise communication**: Utilizing jargon-free language, explaining complex concepts in accessible ways, and providing consistent information across platforms ensures everyone feels informed and understood (National Association of Special Education Teachers, n.d.).
- **Flexibility and adaptability**: The educational landscape is dynamic, and the ability to adapt to changing circumstances, embrace different perspectives, and find creative solutions is crucial for navigating unexpected challenges (Collier et al., 2015).

- **Solution-seeking skills**: Working together to identify challenges, brainstorm alternative solutions, and implement strategies that benefit the child fosters a sense of shared responsibility and empowers all parties to contribute to the student's success (McKenna & Millen, 2013).
- **Cultural awareness**: Respecting and embracing diversity is key to building trust and rapport with families from different backgrounds. Teachers can actively learn about family values and practices, while parents/families share their cultural perspectives to create a more inclusive learning environment (Baquedano-López et al., 2013).

Communication skills are the initial building blocks for successful collaboration with all of the members on the teams, including parents, caregivers, and legal guardians. They form the foundation for productive collaborative relationships. For example, communication skills help to establish trust with other teachers, educators, and family members and facilitate the problem-solving processes. Effective communication sets the tone for learning about a situation, connect with others, indicate understandings, and sustain a conversation.

Enhancing communication skills can be learned. Although it may not be easy, enhancing our communication skills will improve the effectiveness of our collaboration with others. Communication skills include listening, reflecting, asking questions, and summarizing, as well as important non-verbal skills that include active engagement techniques. For example, good listeners communicate interest, involvement, and attentiveness through non-verbal behaviors such as posture, facial expression, and affirmations. Through our non-verbal interactions, we are establishing a context for effective communication within collaborative partnerships.

Listening is believed to be one of the most effective tools for influencing others. Almost half of our total communication is through listening. Effective listeners show interest in the other person and do not appear to be thinking ahead and preparing what they will say next. Other barriers to effective listening are the tendency for judge, criticize, contradict, or reject the message that is shared by others. Listening attentively and reflecting the content to the speaker through affirmations (e.g., "Interesting idea") and questioning (e.g., "Could you tell me more about it?") not only continue the open communication, but also encourage the sharing of important information for successful planning and problem-solving.

Another key skill for effective communication is paraphrasing. A paraphrase is a concise response to the speaker that states the essence of the speaker's content in the listener's words. In other words, the speaker's message is restated by the listener to both affirm the message and to assure that the content was understood as intended. Paraphrasing is not parroting back the words or statements. Rather, paraphrasing conveys that you are actively listening and greatly contributes to maintaining communication. A paraphrase checks accuracy of the message, as well (e.g., "Do I understand you to say that...").

Another key skill when communicating is reflection on emotions of the speaker and/or situation. Statements that reflect the other person's emotions are similar to paraphrases of the speaker's words. In other words, reflecting statements of emotions encourage the person to continue sharing, and they also serve as checks on understanding of the situation. There are numerous phrases that are effective, with one example, "As I understand you, this appears to be a frustrating situation."

Finally, asking questions when communicating with others gathers specific information that is a necessary prerequisite for solving a problem within effective collaboration. There are various types of questions that are needed within various collaborative teaming conversations. Regardless of the specific situation, the responsibility of the listener is to gather, share, and understand information directly related to the goal or problem. There are several types of questions, including:

- Open-Ended: exploratory questions to encourage the other person to provide extended answers of one phrase or sentence about a situation. Open-ended questions are designed to generate different types of information (e.g., facts, thoughts, feelings) about a situation and usually begin with words such as *what, why, and how*.
- Close-ended: questions requesting responses of *yes or no* to specific questions, especially when seeking specific facts or confirmation of understandings. Close-ended questions usually begin with words such as *when, where, are, do, have* or *can*.
- Indirect: questions that prompt responses without seeming to do so. Indirect questions are identified as such because they are statements that are accompanied by a questioning intonation. The use of indirect questions requests further information, but without asking too many direct questions, which can develop a more tense atmosphere.

- Clarifying: questions used to refine the information that has already been shared by the speaker. The purpose for the use of clarifying questions is to focus the speaker on the topic and on additional specifics in descriptions of the situation.

The communication skills presented form the foundation for effective teaming through collaboration. Effective communication among team members is important to successful collaboration. Communication skills continue to improve with awareness, practice, and feedback.

## Solution-seeking Processes

Parents, family members, teachers, and educational service providers are constantly engaged in the process of problem-solving and making decisions from multiple sources of assessment data to assist students to meet or exceed academic standards and behavioral expectations. The resulting solutions from problem-solving should be responsive to student needs, guided by the data collected, and provide information regarding the techniques necessary to assist students with acquiring new knowledge, building upon prior knowledge, developing critical thinking skills, and becoming engaged and motivated learners. When problem-solving, parents, caregivers, and educators should be purposeful, data-based, collaborative, and develop solutions directly aligned with students' needs. This dynamic and iterative problem-solving process is the foundation for collaborative solution-finding by educators within classrooms and schools.

As we implement problem-solving processes within complex educational systems to develop solutions, considerations about multiple variables of the parents, student, teacher, instruction, and curriculum need to be identified and addressed. Pedagogical content knowledge and deep understandings are needed to enhance and diversify instructional approaches, explanations, and supports to meet student's needs. Knowledge of students' interests, knowledge, strengths, and needs are best identified by the parents and family members to make decisions about the multiple curriculum and instructional variables of learning and teaching. During the instructional process of assessing, planning, teaching, and re-assessing student learning, strategic use of evidence-based instructional practices, interventions, and various cognitive and meta-cognitive systems are important to meet instructional needs of students. Often, the diverse expertise of other educational service providers is needed to develop solutions to unique situations.

Although educators are skilled at the collection of assessment data through formal and informal assessment procedures, instructional decision-making requires "sensemaking" of the data (Mandinach, 2012) to determine necessary evidence-based instructional methods and resources by all of the members of the educational teams. Further, educators need not only to know how to interpret data, but also how to intensify instruction using various strategies that meet the unique learning needs of the student for the collaborative problem-solving process to be successful that parents and family members provide. These problem-solving steps as described by Little, Slanda, and Cramer (2024) include:

1. Identify a classroom problem to solve.
2. Develop and implement a plan to solve the problem.
3. Collect and analyze data; and
4. Use and share results.

As described, problem-solving is enhanced when done in collaboration with parents, family members, and other educators within the school (Little et al., 2024). It facilitates families, teachers and other school personnel to share ideas, interpretations, and conclusions so colleagues address unique situations by sharing diverse expertise (Bradley-Levine et al., 2009). In this way, collaboration using skillful communication within the problem-solving process enhances solutions through the use of data as part of their discussion with their colleagues during data meetings, Professional Learning Communities, lesson studies, and professional development to address instructional concerns.

# Multi-Tiered Systems to Support Macro, Meso, and Micro Tiers

To develop and enhance collaboration with parents and family members within schools to maximize the benefits described, three tiers of family engagement are needed. The overall **macro-tier** of MTSS for family engagement strengthens the overall, school-wide communication and interactions to develop trusting relationships and shared goals for students within the schools. Consistent, positive communication skills of active listening, clear and open discussions of important issues, and communication structures (e.g., team meetings of solution-finding and problem-solving) are critical to the development of home and school communications. These communications provide the foundation for building a comprehensive system of collaboration for family engagement. Using expert and sustained communication at the macro-tier level, the goal is to develop a shared understanding and initial trust relationships through dissemination of information to notify and build awareness of school-related activities, resources, and opportunities. Specific examples of dissemination activities for families include:

1 **Newsletters and Emails**:
   a Regular communication through newsletters and emails keeps families informed about classroom activities, curriculum updates, and upcoming events.
   b Teachers can share important announcements, project details, and educational resources.
   c Families appreciate timely information that helps them stay engaged in their child's education.
2 **Homework and Assignments**:
   a Clear communication about homework assignments, due dates, and expectations is crucial.
   b Teachers can provide detailed instructions, and parents can support their child's completion of assignments.
   c When parents understand the purpose of homework, they can reinforce learning at home.
3 **School Websites and Portals**:
   a Many schools have online platforms where parents can access information.
   b Parents can check grades, attendance records, and school policies.
   c Teachers can post resources, study guides, and project guidelines.
4 **Social Media Groups**:
   a Closed groups on platforms like Facebook or WhatsApp allow parents to connect.

b Parents can share tips, ask questions, and discuss school-related matters.
c Teachers can use these groups to share photos, celebrate achievements, and build a sense of community.

Within the **meso-tier** for family engagement within the MTSS framework in schools, parent and family support and engagement opportunities are provided, with requests for attendance, but not required. Given multiple and various parent and family responsibilities, school-related educational opportunities are disseminated, and volunteers are requested, but not required, to be sensitive to the variety of family needs and contexts. During planning, it is important for educators to consider the diversity responsibilities of their parents and families to provide the greatest access for family engagement, such as language, web-based accessibility, scheduling, childcare, etc. Several examples of engagement opportunities at the meso-tier include:

1 **Volunteer Opportunities**:
   a Schools often invite parents to volunteer during events, field trips, or in the classroom.
   b Parent volunteers contribute to a positive school environment.
   c They may assist with reading programs, art projects, or organizing school fundraisers.
2 **Parent Workshops**:
   a Workshops cover various topics, such as study skills, parenting strategies, and understanding curriculum changes.
   b Parents gain insights into effective ways to support their child's learning.
   c Teachers can collaborate with experts to lead these workshops.

The **micro-tier** of family engagement and involvement includes school–parent meetings, planning sessions, and discussions where attendance is required with individual family members. With so many instructional decisions to be made to actualize the full benefits of engagement and partnerships with parents and families, active participation by educators and family members as members of a team produce improved educational outcomes for students, as described earlier as an important benefit. Among the examples of family engagement at the micro-tier are:

1. **Home Visits**:
    a. Teachers visiting students' homes to understand their environment and build stronger relationships.
2. **Parent–Teacher Conferences**:
    a. These scheduled meetings allow parents or guardians to discuss their child's progress, strengths, and areas for improvement with teachers and other educators, as decided.
    b. Teachers and other educators share insights into academic performance, behavior, and social development.
    c. Parents can ask questions, seek clarification, and collaborate with teachers on strategies to support their child's learning.

Collaboration within various team structures were centerpieces in education, special education, and related services for many years before federal and state laws mentioned them. Similarly, a rich tradition exists of professional team meetings to discuss and plan for students. A team approach for family participation at the micro-tier is centered on the individual student.

The composition of student-centered teams varies according to the team's purpose and the students' needs. The members of the student-centered team could include grade-level teachers, special education teachers, school psychologists, social workers, administrators, nurses, ABA therapists, speech language pathologists, and other educational service providers. The development of student-centered problem-solving teams continued to address students' academic and behavioral needs. Educators are often organized within schools on grade-level teams, data teams, co-teaching teams, and student success teams. States, school districts, and schools often use various team names, but with the purpose to address and achieve student success. The goal of each of these teams continues to focus on collaboration and problem-solving with multiple sources of assessment data among teachers and other educational service providers to address student needs. Integral members on each of these educational teams are parents, caregivers, and legal guardians. Collaboration and effective communication skills not only develop and enhance trusting relationship and honest communications, but also build the needed bridges to improve outcomes for each and all students in the school.

# Continued Learning to Enhance Family Engagement

There is a need for effective and continuing professional learning for teachers and school-based educators that includes hands-on guidelines for actively engaging families with diverse backgrounds, needs, and roles. The following resources are available to enhance to family engagement and nurture parent–teacher collaboration:

- **National Parent–Teacher Association (PTA)**: The PTA provides resources and training programs to help parents advocate for their children's education and participate actively in school activities.
- **National Education Association (NEA)**: The NEA offers professional development resources and guidance for educators for collaborating effectively with parents, including those from diverse backgrounds.
- **Parent Teacher Home Visits**: This non-profit organization helps schools and families build relationships through home visits, fostering trust and understanding, and promoting communication.
- **Individualized Education Programs (IEPs)**: IEPs are developed collaboratively between parents and teachers, outlining the student's specific needs and the support services they require. This shared document can serve as a foundation for ongoing communication and collaboration.
- **Online resources**: Online platforms like the National Center for Learning Disabilities and Understood.org offer comprehensive information and practical strategies for parents and educators supporting children with disabilities.

Collaboration between families and teachers is not merely an option; it is the bedrock of inclusive and nurturing educational experiences for students within our schools.

# Unintended Consequences

Although collaboration holds immense potential, it is not without its challenges and potential side effects. Language barriers, cultural differences, and socioeconomic factors can sometimes create roadblocks to effective communication and understanding. Consequently, it is crucial that teachers and school-based educators recognize these challenges and develop strategies to overcome them. While collaborating with family members to address challenges, it is critical for the student to be involved in the discussions and solutions. One possible side effect may lead to enabling the child to disengage with the issues and solutions, if parents, family members, and/or caregivers develop possible solutions to issues. Being overly involved can lead to stepping in too frequently to deal with issues the child should handle. Also, not all teachers are comfortable with a parent volunteer in class. Some students are too distracted by the presence of their parents, which can cause a lack of focus or behavior problems.

The obstacles and potential side effects among families and school personnel might seem insurmountable, but when parents/families and teachers join forces, a bridge of support and understanding empowers them to reach new heights. Positive relationships with teachers are associated with enhanced academic and social outcomes for students with and without disabilities. To attain enhanced learning outcomes, however, continued open and honest communication is necessary. For example, not all teachers are comfortable with a parent volunteer in class. Also, some students are too distracted by the presence of their parents. Therefore, effective communication and collaboration skills to build and discuss roles and relationships within the classroom and school are needed when considering increased family involvement in classrooms and schools. Relationship building is especially important when working with vulnerable populations such as students with disabilities and their families.

Respecting and embracing cultural differences are key to building trust and rapport. When parents are encouraged to share their perspectives and insights, teachers can actively learn about the family's cultural background and values. This mutual understanding fosters a more inclusive and supportive learning environment for all. When language becomes a barrier, creative solutions are needed. Utilizing interpreters, providing translated materials, and encouraging open communication through gestures and visuals can help bridge the gap and ensure everyone feels heard and understood. Time constraints and lack of familiarity with the education system can also hinder family involvement. Recognizing these challenges, educators within schools can offer flexible meeting times, provide resources and support in navigating the system, and ensure information is readily accessible in various formats.

# Emerging Understandings

Teachers and educational service providers face unique challenges and educational opportunities daily to collaborate with and engage parents and caregivers within their classrooms and schools. Family engagement is enhanced through a continuum of strategies, from dissemination of information to active members on school teams. The members of school teams engage in a myriad of problem-solving situations to address issues with curriculum, instruction, professional development, and school policies to assure student learning. Multiple team structures are in place within schools and classrooms to develop, implement, and evaluate solutions in educational services that meet the academic and behavioral needs of students. Teachers, other school professionals, and parents participate as members of various teams within their schools. Within each of these teams, collaboration, communication, and partnership skills enhance the solutions and action plans developed through the diverse expertise of the team members. Educational team structures merely provide teachers with opportunities to enhance their professional learning and expert solution finding. Collaboration and effective communication are the keys to unlocking the potential benefits in each of the team structures. As members of these important teams, teachers can employ collaborative skills, to build rapport and work effectively with others, sharing a common purpose to support students' academic and behavioral needs with parents, caregivers, and family members.

# Professional Reflection Questions

Whether you seek parent support or involvement, the following illustrative questions may serve as guideposts for in-depth critical and professional discussions:

a  How do we communicate and collaborate with parent or legal guardian external school support or internal school involvement?
b  How are we going to keep parents or legal guardians informed of students' academic progress?
c  What are the benefits for parents or legal guardians?
d  How are behavioral and academic expectations clearly defined for parents or legal guardians?

e How are school and district policies inclusive of all parents and legal guardian regardless of gender identification, socio-economic status, religious affiliations, political affiliations, sexual orientation, and race?

f How can teacher leaders buttress a positive teacher–parent/guardian relationship?

# References

Baquedano-López, P., Alexander, R. A., & Hernandez, S. J. (2013). Equity issues in parental and community involvement in schools: What teacher educators need to know. *Review of Research in Education, 37*(1), 149–182.

Bradley-Levine, J., Smith, J., & Carr, K. (2009). The role of action research in empowering teachers to change their practice. *Journal of Ethnographic & Qualitative Research, 3*(3).

Christenson, S. L. (1995). Home-school collaboration: Establishing meaningful and collaborative relationships. *School Psychology Quarterly, 10*(4), 376–393.

Collier, M., Keefe, E. B., & Hirrel, L. A. (2015). Preparing special education teachers to collaborate with families. *School Community Journal, 25*(1), 117–138.

Conoley, J. C. (1989). The school psychologist as family systems expert. *School Psychology Review, 18*(4), 556–562.

Koch, K. (n.d.). *IEP: Students benefit when we collaborate.*

Little, M., Slanda, D., & Cramer, E. (2024). *The educator's guide to action research.* New York: Rowman and Littlefield.

Mandinach, E. B. (2012). A perfect time for data use: Using data-driven decision making to inform practice. *Educational Psychologist, 47*(2), 71–85.

McKenna, M. K., & Millen, J. (2013). Look! Listen! Learn! Parent narratives and grounded theory. Models of parent voice, presence, and engagement in K-12 education. *School Community Journal, 23*(1), 9–48.

Milner, H. R., Flowers, T. J., & Moore, J. L. (2019). Family engagement in urban schools: A multilevel examination of teacher practices. *Urban Education, 54*(1), 120–144.

National Association of Special Education Teachers. (n.d.). Positive communication strategies for collaborating with parents of students with disabilities. Retrieved May 1, 2024 from https://www.naset.org/publications/the-practical-teacher/positive-communication-strategies-for-collaborating-with-parents-of-students-with-disabilities/

Slanda, D. D., Pike, L., & Little, M. (2024). *The general educator's guide to inclusive education: essential knowledge, skills, and dispositions.* New York: Rowman & Littlefield.

Tanase, M. (2023). The benefits and challenges of home-school communication in urban settings. *Contemporary School Psychology, 27*, 426–441.

# 6 Multi-Tiered System for Transdisciplinary Curriculum Content

*Let the questions be the curriculum.*

–Socrates

Another key multi-tiered system that needs to be in place accounts for transdisciplinary curriculum content. Curriculum in education is one of those ubiquitous terms that has multiple meaning for multiple people (Pinar et al., 1996). As we have stated before, many times instructional practices are not effectively implemented because of a lack of a succinct definition to inform professional conversations. For many teacher-colleagues and teacher leaders, curriculum is synonymous with content. We define curriculum as the coherent and intentional interaction among teacher-colleagues, teacher leaders, and students with disciplinary content, materials, resources, and processes for assessing, evaluating learning, and leading. It is a broad-spectrum pathway for learning and leading that accounts for all stakeholders. Curriculum, broadly speaking, encompasses many facets involved in transdisciplinary learning of disciplinary content.

A narrow definition of curriculum is problematic when schools are implementing Multi-Tiered Systems of Support to improve instructional services. From a Universal Design for Learning lens, we consider "curriculum" to have four components: (1) Goals, objectives, and standards, (2) Research-validated instructional practices and professional learning opportunities, (3) Resources to be employed, and (4) Static and dynamic assessments and evaluation. The curriculum should provide intentional and coherent direction for teachers and teacher leaders to convey content. It is a blueprint for instruction over time. Unfortunately, the word "curriculum" is currently tossed about by many vendors selling a published series of "teacher-proof" materials or printed scripted programs. Consequently, teacher-colleagues and teacher leaders are adopting a pre-packaged, so called, curriculum that is simply defined as a published series of materials or program.

For Multi-Tiered Systems of Support to function and sustain transdisciplinary learning and leading for all over time, we need to adopt a broad-spectrum, harmonic perspective of curriculum that does not just address curriculum content with the goal of putting in place a pre-packaged program or published series of "teacher-proof" materials, if such a thing exists. From a design thinking mindset, for this to occur, teachers and teacher leaders should consider the curriculum as overlapping perspectives from a humanistic viewpoint, a social angle, a systemic outlook, and an academic vista (McNeil, 2006). We have found that in schools where Multi-Tiered Systems of Support is superficially implemented, or synonymous with Response to Intervention/Instruction, implementation was only put in place from an academic perspective involving many schools with a test-prep survivalist mentality to address "achievement" rather than lifelong transdisciplinary learning.

Within a humanistic perspective, teachers and teacher leaders create a warm and nurturing transdisciplinary learning environment while continuing to operate as a learning resource and facilitator across all content areas. Albert Einstein's statement, "The supreme act of the teacher is to awaken joy in creative expression and knowledge," grounds a humanistic mindset within a Multi-Tiered Systems of Support transdisciplinary framework for instruction that serves students, families, communities, teachers, and teacher leaders. Humanistic teachers and teacher leaders motivate through trust. Operative words to inform professional curriculum conversations from a humanistic perspective are participation, integration, relevance, intention, and coherence.

From a social perspective, teachers and teacher leaders are political people, who relate intentionally and unintentionally state, national, and international academic standards along with social protocols to student learning. A social mindset in curriculum development means that teachers and teacher leaders accept the concept that schools are designed for social reproduction, and this occurs by nurturing critical thinkers that tackle social issues sensitively and respectfully to create a better society and world. Borrowing from Paulo Freire, a social perspective of curriculum development is about educating people to learn to read the world and not just the word. A social perspective is about inclusivity to solve such world problems as education, inflation, global warming, and universal health care. None of those issues can be approached from within a single discipline. Future solution-seeking students have to be nurtured in a well-curated transdisciplinary learning environment.

Accounting for a systemic perspective in curriculum development means that we have a primary focus on effectiveness and efficiency in delivering content. A systemic perspective looks at standards, goals, benchmarks, test results, and other indicators to monitor progress over time. Keeping in mind that standards, regardless of their quality, are all minimum standards identified for specific age groups or grade levels. Standards should not be the end goal for a particular group of students. Rather, standards should be targets to meet and exceed to foster critical transdisciplinary thinking global citizens. All these indicators are ideally seen as instruments of empowerment for students, teachers, and teacher leaders through highlighting strengths and identifying areas of needs. A systemic mindset for curriculum content is grounded in looking at learning tasks from simple to complex, complex to simple, parts to wholes, wholes to parts, and going beyond systematic and explicit to intentional and coherent instruction in a harmonic manner.

The academic curriculum mindset places content knowledge and the acquisition of content knowledge at the forefront of learning. Traditionally, the academic curriculum contradicts the idea of transdisciplinary literacy with a focus on the disciplines as separate sources of information that students acquire and eventually draw upon to seek solutions to tackle personal issues. Over time, the academic curriculum is shifting to a more transdisciplinary approach where learners are being taught from the start that they will need to draw from different disciplinary sources of information to solve real-world problems.

What we have found is that no single curricular perspective will serve a school well if Multi-Tiered Systems of Support are not considered to improve instruction. *Grounded in design thinking, effective implementation of Multi-Tiered Systems of Support occurs at the intersection of the humanistic, social, systemic, and academic curriculum.*

## Macro tier – State/Province K-12 Standards

At a macro tier within a Multi-Tiered System of Support for curriculum content, meeting and exceeding standards becomes a primary focus to foster student learning, along with a simultaneous focus on essential professional learning opportunities for teachers and teacher leaders to improve instruction. At this macro tier, it is not an issue of "unpacking" standards but rather "unfolding" standards so they can be thoroughly investigated within the context of a transformational professional dialogue. This process addresses timetables and resources. We have to note here that most standards are minimum requirements for grade-level content knowledge. Consequently, professional conversations among teachers and teacher leaders have to address meeting and exceeding standards to produce independent lifelong transdisciplinary critical thinkers.

## Meso tier – Employing a Comprehensive K-12 Transdisciplinary Literacy Framework for Instruction

To date, most schools are reminiscent of the Industrial Age, with schedules, physical facilities, and rigid margins among administration, grade levels, content areas, classrooms, and student–teacher relationships. Curating a transdisciplinary, multisensory learning environment goes beyond rigor and relevance, and requires vigor and vigilance to develop an intentional and coherent K-12 framework to support the professional learning of teacher-colleagues to improve literacy learning and instruction (Puig & Froelich, 2021). Currently, society demands multisensory learning environments that support people, places, and ideas, and are fluid in their organization of space, time, and technologies. A positive relationship among these factors promotes robust professional learning communities of practice grounded in respect, trust, and collaboration among students, teacher-colleagues, teacher leaders, and families. In constructing such learning environments, we come closer to the vision John Dewey (1980) expressed years ago:

> ...to make each one of our schools an embryonic community life, active with the types of occupations that reflect the life of the larger society, and permeated throughout with the spirit of art, history, and science is the goal. When the school introduces and trains each child of society into membership within such a little community saturating him with spirit of service and providing him with the instruments of effective self-direction, we shall have the deepest and best guarantee of a larger society which is worthy, lovely, and harmonious.

With his words, Dewey has set the standard for families and school systems.

When we say learning environment, most people imagine a classroom, a library – everything in perfect rows facing a focal area and a teacher. Although learning may take place in such physical locations, we need to consider that a learning environment can be a blended space with face-to-face or virtual and online interactions. One useful way to think about transdisciplinary literacy learning environments is as elegant and graceful structures that facilitate conditions for learning – structures that buttress individual learning needs based on strengths and scaffolds positive social-emotional interaction for effective and efficient learning. Learning environments are the structures, mechanisms, and communities that arouse curiosity and wonder, and instill awe among students and teacher-colleagues. In other words, these structures serve to motivate, address interest, and engage all learners. We use the term "learners" broadly to include all educators and the students they impact. We use "great educators are great students first" as our guiding mantra throughout this text and have strong beliefs that schools have to be a place of learning for ALL who are in it if positive forward shifts are to occur (Tharp & Gallimore, 1991).

Learning must be grounded in social collaboration to promote formal and informal learning. This is what Vygotsky (1978) has called scientific and spontaneous learning. Although we are addressing the need to curate a multisensory learning environment in this chapter, we do not want to lose sight of the importance of such multi-tiered systems of support as: understanding literacy learning as a process; using static and dynamic assessments to inform practice; using narrative (literature) and non-narrative (informational) texts; investigating instructional practices; and putting in place systems for ongoing professional learning. While understanding that these multi-tiered systems of support will be discussed separately, it is important to remember that each topic or issue is a critical component for curating a multisensory learning environment and a coherent K-12 transdisciplinary literacy framework for instruction.

Intentional and coherent learning occurs when these structures are aesthetically and seamlessly integrated into a consistent whole in which each structure is dependent on and supports the other. It is worth emphasizing, too, that these support structures are valuable not as ends, but as a means to sustain a greater goal – to nurture students, and the teacher-colleagues that teach them, emotionally, socially, physically, and academically. Transdisciplinary literacy learning and instruction have to be intimately intertwined with social, emotional, and physical health. Therefore, a multisensory learning environment must deal with the multifaceted and interconnected learning needs of students, while at the same time, capitalizing on their strengths.

Our experiences have taught us that if real acceleration in learning is to occur, we have to take the learners' strengths into account (Dweck, 2009). The prevalent viewpoint of assessing needs, remediating deficits, and solution-seeking as the best routes to learning and teaching is no longer adequate for current learners (Csikszentmihalyi & Schneider, 2000; Schreiner & Anderson, 2005). Acceleration in learning will be hindered if we only look at students' needs or deficits. A multisensory learning environment may seem to be one of several support structures in a coherent K-12 transdisciplinary literacy frameworkn In fact, however, it takes multi-tiered systems of support to ensure coherent transdisciplinary instruction and learning over time. We have learned from the popular systematic and explicit approach to instruction. We now need to move on to an intentional and coherent approach to instruction. Curating a transdisciplinary multisensory learning environment is an aligned and synergistic model of overlapping scaffolds that:

- Produces professional learning opportunities, where teacher support and the physical environment is employed to scaffold literacy learning and instruction.
- Facilitates professional learning communities of practice, RtI/I, and lesson study that enable teacher-colleagues to collaborate, construct, and execute an array of lessons that coherently support student learning across disciplines as they progress through grade levels.
- Inspires and engages students to learn across disciplines in relevant contexts with vigor and vigilance.
- Affords access to quality culturally sensitive and age-appropriate offline and online resources.
- Incorporates designated areas for large-group, small-group, and individual learning.
- Supports extended local, national, and international involvement in learning, both face-to-face and online; and
- Is founded on implementing conditions for learning.

Informed by research and grounded in common-sense lifelong learning, this transdisciplinary multisensory environment promotes learning specifically aimed at the strengths, needs, interests, and desires of the student and the teacher-colleagues that facilitate the learning. It is designed to promote intentional and coherent, rather than just systematic and explicit, learning and instruction. Such learning and instruction offer literacy learning and instruction across core disciplines (language arts, mathematics, science, social studies, and the arts). Most effective learning environments today are more flexible, colorful, purposeful, and engaging than their 20th-century counterparts; they are differentiated, personalized, and targeted to students' sensual learning (visual, auditory, kinesthetic, or tactile).

Although we are addressing a coherent K-12 transdisciplinary literacy framework to improve literacy learning and instruction, the physical environment in which learning takes place cannot be ignored. Students may no longer sit in rows of chairs bolted to the floor. Students' work may be on display. Technologies may be present, such as an interactive whiteboard, electronic tablets, or a few computers, not to mention other personal electronic devices. While the building alone does not constitute a school, the qualities of where we learn affect the quality of how we learn. Learning spaces are changing and will not all look the same. The industrial era's assembly line approach to school design does not complement today's multifaceted educational needs. Schools and other places of learning need to reflect our current understanding of how people learn in preparation for career, college, global citizenship, and a productive life.

Designing for flexibility is key. Learning spaces must adapt to whatever changes the future may hold since no one can predict accurately how educational technologies and teaching modalities will evolve. To achieve this flexibility, multisensory learning environments need to be designed with furniture that can easily be reconfigured for different learning opportunities. From furniture arrangement to curriculum content, the school of the future has to nurture the imagination by inspiring wonder, awe, and curiosity with an intentional focus promoting culturally responsive, socio-emotional interactions.

Students today need to be immersed in an information-intensive multisensory learning environment that will help them imagine, create, experiment, comprehend, estimate, calculate, and communicate. For a while now, a print-rich learning environment has been insufficient since the internet opened our eyes to a world beyond our immediate lived experiences. Teacher-colleagues need to critically access tools and resources to share and create knowledge and instructional practices with other professionals and interact with colleagues with expertise in their field. Teacher leaders need access to these same tools and resources to manage the complexities of coherent K-12 transdisciplinary literacy learning and instruction – from student records and performance data to personnel management and facilities operations.

An infrastructure designed for flexibility and growth can facilitate these connections. The essential goal of technologies, as it is with all systems for learning, is to support learners' relationships to each other and their work. In planning any complex task, infrastructure design must be approached with one eye on today's practical realities; the other on tomorrow's opportunities; and an imagination for what is possible. No longer is thinking creatively sufficient. Our learning and teaching have to focus on supporting learners in designing and creating boxes that will serve as springboards for curiosity and the imagination to create what is possible.

A transdisciplinary multisensory learning environment combines physical and technological infrastructures to seamlessly support learning within a coherent K-12 literacy framework to support all learners over time. Combining face-to-face with online learning is essential for schools today, but savvy educators know achieving such a goal takes vigor and vigilance over time. It is definitely a planner's project rather than a quick fix with all the bells and whistles of available electronic technologies and games.

The flexible spaces that enable effective learning and shared opportunities, creative scheduling that promotes continuous learning, and technologies that support collaboration among the school community and the outside world are the scaffolds within a system of learning that are valuable as long as they effectively support culturally responsive human interactions on which learning depends. John Dewey long ago conceived of schools as "miniature communities" that imitated the social relations and activities of the larger society in which they were set. However, schools have been separated by disciplinary silos where classrooms are separated from other classrooms, teacher-colleagues are separated from other teacher-colleagues, and schools are separated from the outside world.

Constructive and productive associations within and outside a school enable it to carry out the work more effectively and efficiently. When people are engaged through collaborative arrangements, their effect is multiplied. We believe that knowledge is socially constructed (Vygotsky, 1978). A true professional learning community of practice within a positive culture is more likely to nurture innovation and excellence. Furthermore, a true professional learning community of practice cannot be scheduled or given a label. Keep in mind that professional learning communities of practice evolve over time and involve ALL stakeholders in an environment where learners are free to take risks and productive failures are learning opportunities. If we are to move forward, we have to realize that a regularly scheduled and mandated "meeting" DOES NOT constitute a professional learning community – never has!

There is no single model that will fit all schools. Each school must create its own matrix of teaching talents, instructional approaches, and effective distributive leadership to meet the unique learning strengths and needs of its students and teacher-colleagues. One common element, though, unites all effective professional learning communities of practice: a commitment on the part of every member to the learning of everyone; students, families, teacher-colleagues, and teacher leaders alike (Tharp & Gallimore, 1991). A climate of respect and trust among students, teacher-colleagues, teacher leaders, and families is essential to an effective school. Trust and respect also imply a commitment to the idea that every student, family, teacher, and teacher leader deserves and wants to learn, and that every member of the school community is dedicated to the success of everyone (students, teacher-colleagues, parents, and teacher leaders).

Career- or college-minded global citizens need to think critically and creatively, embrace diversity and ambiguity, and construct (as well as consume) information. They need to be resourceful and self-reliant, while also skilled at collaboration. Collaboration is a skill learned in kindergarten. We know that tools are only as effective as the tool users. In addition to sophisticated physical structures and technologies, there has to be support for literacy learning and instruction for teacher-colleagues as well as students. Schools need to be redesigned to reach beyond the traditional classrooms many of us experienced when we were young. The transdisciplinary multisensory learning environments must incorporate a productive mix of technologies, learning orientations, and virtual and real-life relationships. Making all this happen requires vigor and vigilance; no longer is rigor and relevance sufficient.

Schools, like teacher-colleagues and students, need both supports and challenges to thrive and grow. For schools, adaptive challenges are plentiful through accountabilities and responsibilities. The quality of student learning in any educational setting depends on the quality of learning among the teacher-colleagues themselves (Hattie, 2009; Darling-Hammond, Chung Wei, Andree, Richardson & Orphanos, 2009). Teacher-colleagues and teacher leaders must be given access to the knowledge and tools that support professional learning over time. They must also be offered time to learn, ownership of their learning, and respectful generative responses to nurture the collegial conversations that foster professional learning communities of practice. Ongoing professional learning demands revising our language. We have learned to update our language away from the term "feedback" and prefer to use the term "response." Usually, the term feedback has mechanistic and behaviorist connotations that always positions one person over another.

At the helm, of course and we believe this wholeheartedly, is effective teacher leadership at all levels Leadership must provide opportunities to share expertise and emerging promising practices with colleagues inside and outside their professional learning community. Again, in our ongoing learning we said, "emerging promising practices" not "best practices." Experienced teacher-colleagues are well aware that best practices are relevant to a particular group of students and seldom apply to all. What may be "best" for one may not be best for another. Leadership among educators make decisions about curriculum to determine solutions within their classrooms and schools.

# Micro tier – Instructional Resources (Print, Non-Print, Technology)

The micro tier of a multi-tiered system for transdisciplinary curriculum content should have teachers and teacher leaders taking a close look at available instructional materials, such as assessments, leveled texts, decodable texts, and a variety of online resources. When the intent is to create independent, flexible, and strategic critical thinkers, a singular assessment is insufficient. Co-triangulating and evaluating assessments provide a truer picture of students' strengths and needs to inform instruction. To teach for strategic activities, a variety of reading and writing assessments across disciplines need to be in place that highlight students' strengths and indicate needs.

Literacy experts and teacher leaders consistently tell us that assessment should inform instruction. Yet, seldom do we hear what type of assessment we should rely on to ensure that we employ powerful research-validated instructional practices that are a good match for students. Teachers that teach for strategic activity rely on both static and dynamic assessments (Dixon-Krauss, 1996). Static assessments are summative assessments that tell us in general terms what students are learning in relation to other students or what students are learning in a specific content area. They are assessments of learning. This is vital information for teacher-colleagues to gauge their instruction and curricular content. Static assessments are state tests, chapter tests, and the like. Dynamic assessments refer to formative assessments that focus on students' strengths and needs. They are assessments for learning. Static assessments potentially reveal what students have learned and dynamic assessments potentially reveal how students learn and what they need to learn. One focuses on outcomes while the other focuses on process. Consequently, teaching for strategic activity means relying on static and dynamic assessment to make informed decisions that support student learning.

Experienced teachers understand that learning occurs and changes over time. Monitoring and documenting those changes are critical when teaching for strategic activity. A teacher's classroom is packed with split-second decision-making throughout the day. Unfortunately, our human memory can only hold so much for so long before information is replaced with more current information. Therefore, when our intention is to teach powerfully, our students' learning must be monitored and documented for assessment to truly inform instruction. Thus, to teach for strategic activity means on-going monitoring and documenting our students' strengths and needs.

We want to support and nurture students in becoming transdisciplinary strategic critical thinkers. The goal is not to make it easy. Rather, the goal is to make it easy to learn. Only by teaching students how to learn can we ensure that we are supporting students in becoming self-extending learners that will be career and/or college ready. The language we use and the instructional practices we employ certainly impacts whether we accomplish that goal.

A quick glance into any school catalog reveals a variety of books labeled within a specific leveling system, usually from kindergarten to eighth grade. The levels are there to serve as a tool to support teachers in selecting texts that are considerate to promote students' literacy learning over time. Unfortunately, we have seen leveled texts misused as a technology of domination to control what students read and reward students' reading habits or abilities. Within a K-12 integrated transdisciplinary literacy framework for instruction across core content areas, leveled texts are never intended to be used to level classroom libraries, designate book boxes from which students can choose a text to read, create intimidating classroom multi-colored data walls where students are labeled with a text level, or used to label students. Additionally, leveled texts were never meant to be used as a reporting system of student progress to families. They were designed to inform instruction based on students' strengths and needs as students' progress toward more complex texts and provide an opportunity for teachers to report to families' students' strengths and needs sans the levels.

Leveled texts should be used as a tool by highly vigilant teachers during guided instructional practice while keeping students on the outer edge of their learning, where literacy learning is most likely to occur. Highly vigilant teachers and teacher leaders are colleagues who make informed decisions for instruction based on static summative assessments and dynamic formative assessments that highlight students' strengths and needs over time with the pedagogical/hebegogical content knowledge that we are always learning to read. Highly vigilant teachers and teacher leaders reject the limiting and dichotomous view of learning to read and reading to learn. Leveled texts, like decodable texts, are another scaffold for instruction to support students' growth over time from where they are and what they know, to where they need to be and what they need to know. Instructional scaffolds are only as good as the foundation they rest upon. Understanding students' strengths and using it to scaffold new learning is a definition of good instruction.

Instructional scaffolds are ineffective when used within a deficit model of instruction that relies solely on static summative assessments (e.g., standardized state tests, end of course exams) to inform instruction discounting critical teacher decision-making beyond a recommended curricular decision tree. When matched to students' strengths and needs, leveled texts, decodable or not, are building blocks to support teachers in constructing, deconstructing, and reconstructing instructional scaffolds. We also need to remember that all scaffolds are temporary. They go up when needed and come down when they are not. A scaffold that remains in place too long may become an impediment to future learning and potentially disabling learners (Clay, 2015). Only an informed and responsive teacher can make the decision.

Within a K-12 comprehensive transdisciplinary literacy framework for language arts, mathematics, sciences, social studies, and arts, decodable texts are relative to the learner. A decodable text for a learner in first grade is completely different from a decodable text for a tenth grader. For example, as you are reading and comprehending this text, it is decodable for you. More than likely, this text will not be decodable to a learner in the primary grades or someone with no pedagogical/hebegogical content knowledge. When we define decodable through the lens of comprehensive transdisciplinary literacy instruction, it means that students are taught to use various sources of information (graphophonic, syntactic, semantic, lexical, pragmatic, and schematic) to decode a text and make meaning. In a K-12 comprehensive transdisciplinary framework for instruction. A decodable text goes beyond simply matching sounds to letters. *There is no room for the overuse of decodable texts in a K-12 comprehensive transdisciplinary literacy framework.* In fact, we have observed many students where the overuse of decodable texts has disabled a learner by narrowing their view of "reading" to simply matching sounds to letters or word patterns and ignore making sense of the text.

Decodable texts are a type of leveled text used primarily in beginning literacy instruction which are judiciously sequenced to gradually include words that are consistent with the letter–sound relationships that a student has been explicitly taught. A small number of high-frequency words that have more challenging or unexpected spellings, such as "the" and "was," are also used. In a structured, not comprehensive, literacy program, some colleagues with literacy instruction expertise believe that decodable texts should closely match the sequence of phonics instruction, especially for low-progress learners. Decodable texts are leveled readers that utilize contrived vocabulary based primarily on the letter–sound relationship or predictable onsets and rimes matched to synthetic programmatic phonics instruction (Puig & Froelich, 2021).

As in all issues about instruction, appropriately using decodable texts for instruction relies heavily on a vigilant teacher's understanding of literacy learning as a process in addition to recognizing students' strengths and needs. Some colleagues with expertise in literacy instruction feel that decodable texts should be utilized during the beginning stages of literacy learning with all students. Yet, there are also other colleagues with literacy expertise who will respectfully add that it depends on the strengths and needs of the individual learner. Due to a strong focus on word-level reading, we have found that relying heavily on decodable texts for instruction in the earlier stages of literacy learning does not ensure that students, including low-progress learners, will have the necessary foundational skills to become strategic transdisciplinary learners and critical thinkers.

According to the National Reading Panel Report, "very little research has attempted to determine whether the use of decodable books in systematic phonics programs has any influence on the progress that some or all children make in learning to read" (NICHD, 2000, pp. 2–137). Furthermore, many literacy experts in the field have argued that there is no empirical evidence supporting the use of decodable texts for beginning readers (Allington & Woodside-Jiron, 1998; Hoffman, Sailors, & Patterson, 2002). Consequently, depending on the student, decodable texts can be considerate or inconsiderate to the learner.

## Unintended Consequences

Although a standardized curriculum has many pedagogical/hebegogical, political and economic benefits, one drawback of having a standardized curriculum is its inflexible design, which can limit adaptability to individual student strengths and needs. This lack of flexibility can hamper the general usefulness of the educational system by failing to accommodate for the diverse learning orientation and trends of students. Moreover, the interests and motivation of students may not be considered. Additionally, they may not reflect specific strengths which students possess that could be essential for successful functioning in school and society.

To safeguard that teachers cover everything stipulated by their state's curriculum content standards, teachers must often limit auxiliary activities, students' questions, and inquiry as they scurry through curricular content. There is little extra time for exposure to new transdisciplinary literacy experiences, or for the necessary deep coverage for understanding and thinking critically about a vital subject. Many standards-based assessment tests not only emphasize facts and definitions, but also require that students show a mastery of those facts and definitions on multiple choice online tests. This narrow approach to assessment refutes efforts that use numerous ways of learning and leading to enlarge the groups of students who succeed, and leaves behind students who are better able to show what they know and can do with an essay, presentation, or other project (Falk, 2002). As noted by Darling-Hammond and Falk (1997), in the name of ambitious-sounding reforms, such standards-based initiatives are exacerbating differences between students from different backgrounds and placing constraints on education that undermine effective teaching.

## Emerging Understandings

When considering tiers of support within a system for transdisciplinary curriculum content, we look at standards at the macro tier, a framework for instruction at the meso tier, and available resources at the micro tier. In this text, we are taking a unique perspective on Multi-Tiered Systems of Support and are arguing that for Multi-Tiered Systems of Support to be implemented effectively and efficiently, it has to be distinguished from a Response to Intervention/Instruction model. Yet, we do acknowledge that a Response to Intervention/Instruction model has to be one of the systems within a Multi-Tiered Systems of Support framework.

## Professional Conversation Prompts

It takes many drivers to move successful schools forward. Developing a system that accounts for transdisciplinary curriculum content over time is one of those vital drivers that assists in promoting forward shifts for all involved. The following professional reflection questions serve as a springboard to create a blueprint for developing an intentional and coherent multi-tiered system for developing transdisciplinary curriculum content

- When will teacher-colleagues and teacher leaders have the opportunity to collaboratively unfold core standards for instruction across disciplines?
- What types of formative and summative assessments will we use to monitor progress over time?
- Where will materials be housed?
- How will materials be shared or distributed for classroom use across grade levels and disciplines?
- How will materials be matched to students' strengths and needs?
- What additional professional learning opportunities will be needed to implement curriculum content effectively and efficiently?
- What will intentional and coherent Conditions of Learning (Crouch & Cambourne, 2020) look like across disciplines and grade levels?

In the next chapter, we will share another vital driver for forward shifts by investigating the role of community engagement within a Multi-Tiered Systems of Support framework. We will look at a macro tier with a focus on developing a leadership team, followed by rethinking the role of community services off-campus as a meso tier, and employing community services on campus as a micro tier. As in any of the systems mentioned up to this point, the macro, meso, and micro tiers are conceptual third spaces that increase in intensity to improve support for all involved in a school by highlighting necessary next steps that promote forward shifts over time.

# References

Allington, R. L., & Woodside-Jiron, H. (1998). Decodable text in beginning reading: Are mandates and policy based on research? *ERS Spectrum, 16*(2), 3–11.

Clay, M. M. (2015). *Change over time in children's literacy development.* Portsmouth, NH: Heinemann.

Crouch, D., & Cambourne, B. (2020). *Made for learning: How the conditions for learning guide teaching decisions.* Katonah, NY: Richard C. Owens, Publishers.

Csikszentmihalyi, M., & Schneider, B. (Eds.). (2000). *Becoming adult: How teenagers prepare for the world of work.* New York: Basic Books.

Darling-Hammond, L., & Falk, B. (1997). Supporting teaching and learning for all students: Policies for authentic assessment systems. In *Assessment for equity and inclusion: Embracing all our children* (pp. 51–76). New York: Routledge.

Dewey, J. (1980). *Democracy and education,* 1916, rpt. *The middle works,* vol. 9. Carbondale: Southern Illinois University Press.

Dixon-Krauss, L. (1996). *Vygotsky in the classroom: Mediated literacy instruction and assessment.* Ann Arbor, MI: Longman Publishers.

Dweck, C. S. (2009). Mindsets: Developing talent through a growth mindset. *Olympic Coach,* 21(1), 4–7.

Falk, J. H. (2002). The contribution of free-choice learning to public understanding of science. *Interciencia, 27*(2), 62–65.

Hattie, J. (2009). The black box of tertiary assessment: An impending revolution. Tertiary assessment & higher education student outcomes. *Policy, Practice & Research, 1,* 259–275

Hoffman, J. V., Sailors, M., & Patterson, E. U. (2002). *Decodable texts for beginning reading instruction: The year 2000 basals.* CIERA Report.

McNeil, J. D. (2006). *Contemporary curriculum in thought and action.* Hoboken, NJ: John Wiley & Sons, Inc.

National Reading Panel (US), National Institute of Child Health, & Human Development (US). (2000). *Report of the national reading panel: Teaching children to read: An evidence-based assessment of the scientific research literature on reading and its implications for reading instruction: Reports of the subgroups.* National Institute of Child Health and Human Development, National Institutes of Health.

Pinar, W. F., Reynolds, W. M., Slattery, P., & Taubman, P. M. (1996). *Understanding curriculum*. New York: Peter Lang Publishing, Inc.

Puig, E. A., & Froelich, K. S. (2021). *Teaching K–12 transdisciplinary literacy: A comprehensive instructional framework for learning and leading*. Routledge.

Schreiner, L. A., & "Chip" Anderson, E. (2005). Strengths-based advising: A new lens for higher education. *NACADA Journal, 25*(2), 20–29.

Tharp, R. G., & Gallimore, R. (1991). *Rousing minds to life: Teaching, learning, and schooling in social context*. Cambridge: Cambridge University Press.

Vygotsky, L. S. (1978). Mind in society. In *The development of higher psychological processes*.Cambridge, MA: Harvard University Press.

Wei, R. C., Darling-Hammond, L., Andree, A., Richardson, N., & Orphanos, S. (2009). *Professional learning in the learning profession. A status report on teacher development in the United States and Abroad*. Dallas, TX: National Staff Development Council.

# Multi-Tiered System for Community Engagement

*We are all connected to each other, in a circle, in a hoop that never ends.*

*—Pocahontas*

## Community Engagement and Partnerships

In recent years, community engagement and partnerships have emerged as a priority in education. Community partnerships are now considered a critical aspect of educational reforms and improvements. This importance is underscored by decades of research suggesting that partnerships among schools, families, and communities improve student learning outcomes (Jeynes, 2022; McWayne et al., 2008). Partnerships among school personnel, families, and community members have proven to be especially important as it pertains to serving students from underserved communities (Durand, 2011). Yet members from the communities are often an untapped resource when it comes to improving student learning in schools (Jeynes, 2018). How do we develop and enhance a comprehensive framework of multi-tiered systems of support? The focus of this chapter is the development, implementation, and sustainability of community partnerships to improve student outcomes through a comprehensive, multi-tiered systems framework of actions and supports.

As a starting point, educators should promote interactions and communications that connect home, school, and the community (Alvarez, 2014), build trusting relationships (Shiffman, 2019), and learn about each other

DOI: 10.4324/9781032707976-7

(Durand, 2011). Educators should strive to establish common understandings with families and community members. A shared definition of community engagement is needed to develop shared understandings and trusting relationships as a foundation. Community engagement is a process used to build positive, goal-oriented relationships within local communities among multiple stakeholders, including students, parents, seniors/grandparents, and local businesses. To lift up and raise our schools to a place that suits all 21st-century learners, understandings, communications, and connections need to come from many parts of the community. The term "engagement" indicates active participation through shared power and opportunity balanced among the members of the community, school, and parents (Epstein, 2010). The leading roles should be alternated according to the need and focus of the particular goals of the transformational project. Effective community engagement is mutually respectful, sustains and embraces cultures and languages, and includes genuine efforts to understand diverse beliefs, values, and priorities. If we respect each other and acknowledge our unique contributions, we can move forward quickly in a positive environment where we can all be teachers and learners (Epstein et al., 2019).

Home, school, and community contexts represent overlapping spheres of influence. The stakeholders in each of these spheres of influence may have different beliefs, experiences, and goals. However, the families, school personnel, and community members that are most effective at supporting student learning have a shared mission and goals focused on student learning and development (Epstein & Sanders, 2000). In addition, these spheres can be influenced by external factors from additional community, state, and national sources such as educational policies, practices, and unique community factors, as well as internal factors such as communications and social interactions among the stakeholders (see Figure 7.1). To address external factors, decision-making through sustained communication within shared governance structures among members of the school, families, and community develops innovative solutions and extends collaboration.

While identifying and describing the mutual goals within the local communities, sources of resources and assets to address goals for developing and enhancing community relations and engagement need to be identified. These discussions and decisions determine, develop, and sustain the social capital that exist among the educational partners within communities that will ultimately serve to support student learning (Wood et al., 2017). Yosso

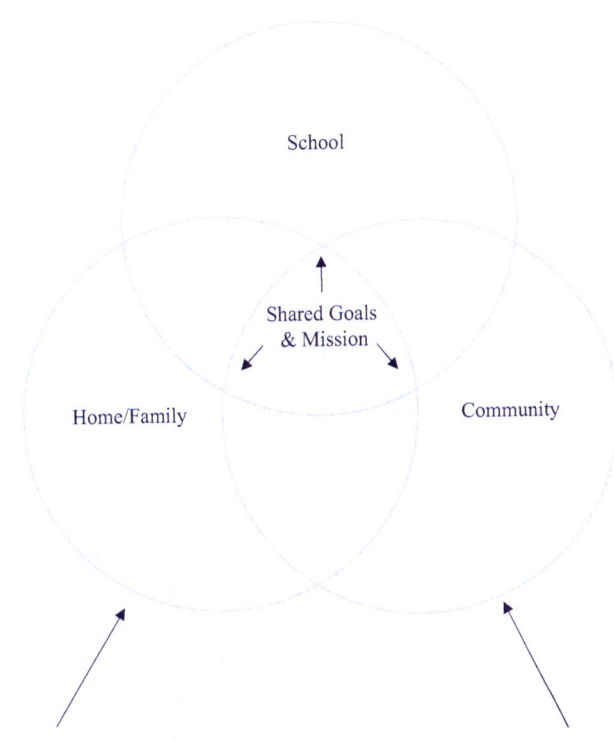

Influenced by external factors such as educational policies, practices, & unique community factors

*Figure 7.1* Spheres of Influence in Schools, Community, & Families

(2013) expands the notion of leveraging social capital within our communities to improve student learning and outcomes by including additional capital termed "community cultural wealth". These resources are developed and nurtured in communities that include social capital of aspiration, linguistic, family, social, and resistant capital. While forms of capital are acquired by individuals, cultural wealth is meant to be shared within a community (Yosso, 2013).

Therefore, a comprehensive framework of multi-tiered systems of support within the overlapping spheres of influence among community members, parents, and school personnel creates a structure in which stakeholders communicate, collaborate, and plan to facilitate and deepen the development of "community" within schools. As stakeholders share the combined school and community "wealth", relationships are developed, communication and collaboration are deepened, and there is advocacy to achieve the shared mission of improved student learning. Within this comprehensive framework of the various spheres of influence within multi-tiered systems of support for community relations and engagement, collaboration and communication facilitate the processes for developing trusting relationships (McCauley et al., 2023). From these trusting, sustained communications, specific principles provide the foundation of the community "wealth". These components are described in the next sections of this chapter.

## Communication and Collaboration to Build and Enhance Community Relations

Effective communication is essential to building and enhancing partnerships and relationships among the multiple stakeholders in schools and the local communities. This is especially critical within communities with diverse cultures and languages (Alvarez, 2014). Communication describes the sharing and exchanging of information regularly among families, educators, and community members to address the shared vision for student learning using culturally sensitive and transdisciplinary practices. Establishing personal communications with students, families, and community members should be the basis of a school's and a district's communication strategy (Breiseth et al., 2011). Educators should endeavor to establish rapport in a welcoming environment and make sure communication includes culturally sensitive practices. In addition, communication in multiple languages is a realistic requirement in many schools, so educators must consider and use translation services, employ multilingual personnel, and investigate and utilize technology-based, multilingual accessibility features and tools. However, effective communication among diverse stakeholders must not only address *access* to messages and information through translation resources and services. It is also critical that sustained communication and relationships must include effective opportunities for *engagement* in discussions and decision-making processes among the stakeholders to impact the common vision, goals, and activities (Garcia et al., 2016).

Establishing relationships among educators, parents, and community members through effective and honest communication and collaboration are critical to student learning. School, family, and community relationships require establishing connections to build trust and support to accomplish the shared vision and goals within the school and local communities. To identify and leverage the social capital and the community cultural wealth (Yosso, 2013) within each community, stakeholders should understand and value the language, backgrounds, and cultural traditions of the diverse members within their school and local communities. Teachers and administrators should create a school environment and climate which welcome diverse stakeholders within an open and trusting environment. Trusting relationships positively impact community relationships and engagement in student learning and outcomes.

With open and effective communication and trusting relationships among school personnel, families, and local community members, more meaningful collaboration beyond the traditional roles and relationships to enhance advocacy and creativity are developed and sustained (Shiffman, 2019). Advocacy among the stakeholders for identified, shared goals is a process of engaging stakeholders as key decision-makers in shaping activities and programs that promote student learning across and within the various contexts of the community. One key aspect of community relations and engagement is the inclusion and empowerment of families and community members in the planning process of school decisions. Identifying types of educational decisions and processes for decision-making will provide opportunities for input and engagement by multiple stakeholders. When family and community stakeholders contribute with school personnel, all are invested in positive results from the co-developed events, programs, and activities to support student learning, (Breiseth et al., 2011).

## Principles and Steps to Build and Enhance Community Relations

Based upon sustained communication, collaboration, and trust, specific steps to build upon and enhance community relations and development impact school change within both the school and the local communities. This continuous school improvement process transforms schools into interactive communities of educators, local community members, families, and students who collaborate to develop, implement, and strengthen conditions for student learning. This continuous model to enhance community engagement in schools establishes the processes for change to engage communities within schools (see Figure 7.2). Members of the school community collaboratively identify, track, and make progress toward local goals and outcomes for both the school and the larger community. Quality, actionable data are collected and easily accessible to all members of the school community. The community sees the results of its efforts and feels a sense of collective efficacy. Continuous improvement cycles show progress on locally determined outcomes. Each school community contains unique assets and resources, specific needs, vision, and goals (Scott et al., 2020). School planning within a community begins by convening a diverse leadership team of families, educators, youth, and community members with a lead coordinator.

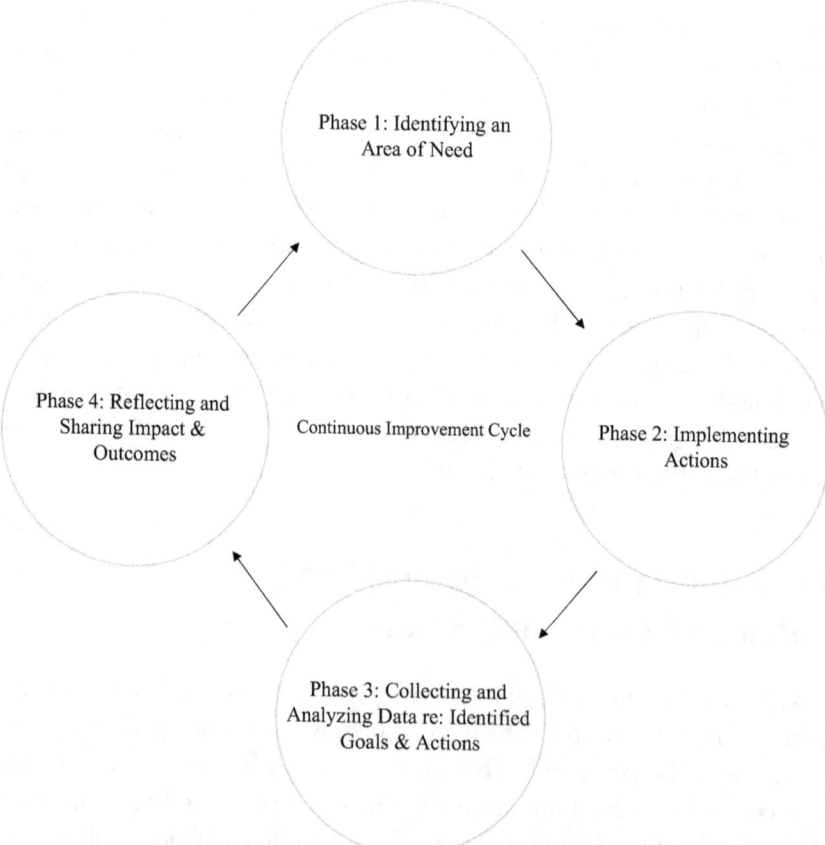

Figure 7.2 Collaborative Problem-Solving/Data-Driven Decision-Making Process for Community Engagement

The leadership team conducts an asset and needs assessment that includes baseline measures to determine the status of goals and outcomes, while also identifying areas to address. Then the process of collaborative problem-solving is implemented to develop and sustain a shared vision, goals, and solutions for each unique school setting (Cramer et al., 2015). The next section briefly describes the phases of the collaborative solution-seeking process.

# Phase 1: Identifying an Area of Need

To begin the collaborative solution-seeking process for continuous improvement, community stakeholders on the leadership team (e.g., the School Improvement Team (SIT), the School Advisory Committee, etc.) must first observe, question, and reflect on current goals and information to investigate a concern and develop goals. They evaluate the current situation and compare it to the expectations and standards for the students. The additional, specific data helps to identify the problem or issue to address. At the beginning of this process, it is important to consider curricular standards, behavioral expectations, and community goals for the students. This process may take time. Teachers, administrators, family members, and community members observe and consider current situations to identify an area of need for classroom and/or school improvement, facilitated by the lead coordinator. It can also be helpful to collaborate with other members of the school and community teams, especially knowledgeable colleagues who may have suggestions and/or resources that may address the issue.

After reflecting on current concerns and addressing the questions, the stakeholders may identify several different concerns to target for the identified needs of students that are related to the identified issues, such as medical, health, and nutritional factors. The leadership team members focus on a problem statement that is a priority need, which, when addressed, can produce positive results for the students within the school community.

The problem statement needs to answer these five questions:

- *Who is affected by the problem?*
- *What might be causing the problem?*
- *What is the goal for improvement?*
- *What might be done about the problem?*
- *Who can contribute to the solution and action plan?*

## Phase 2: Implementing Actions

This phase of the collaborative solution-seeking process focuses on the implementation of the specific action plan to address the needs and concerns identified from data review and reflection. The plan is a blueprint or actions for immediate changes within the school community. Before writing the specifics of the action plan, it is helpful to outline actions by answering the *"What?"*, the *"How?"*, and the *"When?"* with the members of the leadership team.

Once the priority needs are identified and outlined by the members of the school leadership team, specific action plans, including personnel, resources, and engagement strategies, are identified, developed, and committed by family, school and/or community stakeholders with expertise and resources to address the issue.

There are three important and inter-related components during this phase of this collaborative solution-seeking process to engage educators, families, and community members: community-connected instructional activities; enriched learning; and comprehensive systems of support. These three components are critical to the development and implementation of an action plan for improved student achievement. As educators identify the curricular and behavioral goals with family and community members on the leadership team, the curriculum can be clearly connected with the local community and students' identities, cultures, and previous experiences. The learning opportunities then can be enhanced to include before- or after-school, weekend, and summer programs for students to further explore their interests, expertise, and content. (Please see specific examples in the following sections.) By identifying multiple family and community resources to address the identified goals and/or concerns, the members of this team intentionally and systematically coordinate services, supports, and opportunities to improve both individual and team growth and achievement. To do this, a comprehensive support structure needs to be developed, implemented, and sustained.

## Phase 3: Analyzing Data re: Identified Goals and Actions

To develop and sustain community-based innovative solutions to identified needs and concerns, a comprehensive and supportive infrastructure, including clear roles and responsibilities, must be articulated and implemented. Shared governance of schools must be expanded to include diverse members of families and community members. Specific roles and responsibilities for school functioning, once seen as only within the purview of school personnel, now can be enhanced and supported by families and members of the community as identified through asset-mapping processes (Scott et al., 2020), data collection and analyses. Various assets, including resources, funding, technical assistance, and policies, should be identified during the development of shared governance in general and applied to the specifically developed action plans and data collection during the collaborative solution-seeking processes. It is critical to the success of the shared vision and developed action plans of the school communities that clearly identified resources and supports are identified, shared and completed by members of the school community within timeframes, as identified (Morris & Shockley, 2023).

# Phase 4: Sharing Impact and Outcomes

To align and maximize the collaborative solution-seeking process within continuous school improvement among multiple stakeholders in the school community, purposeful, sustained professional learning to reflect and share evaluation data aligned with identified goals and outcomes is necessary. Coordination and communication among each of the educational partners provides valuable input for continuous improvement (Little, 2006). Once data have been collected and reviewed by the members of the school community leadership team, plans for the next steps based upon those data are needed. If the results show improvement and mastery of the established goals, the team can decide to continue the action plans as developed. However, if the results do not evidence improvements, the collaborative solution-seeking process would need to be initiated again to identify the concerns more specifically and adjust the initial plan. This process may require additional professional learning, community support, and additional resources to address the academic and/or behavioral issues more accurately. In this way, the cyclical nature of the problem-solving process is also a source of continuous learning for all the stakeholders (Ishimaru, 2020).

Continuous improvement through learning assures high-quality implementation of the collaborative, solution-seeking process by community stakeholders within schools. There are multiple, collaborative professional development structures that provide opportunities to engage in discussions and learning about resources and actions to improve student learning. Data team meetings, professional learning communities (PLCs), lesson studies, and curriculum committees and meetings have been instituted as sources of continued learning among educators and community members within schools. Through ongoing professional learning and collaboration with colleagues, knowledge and skills to improve, use, and enhance services and results for students occurs.

## Multi-Tiered Systems of Support (Macro, Meso, and Micro)

To develop and enhance collaboration and engagement with parents and community members with school personnel to maximize the processes as described, three tiers of community engagement are needed. At the outset, a well-articulated vision, shared beliefs, knowledge, and respect for community cultural wealth set the foundation for developing and enhancing community relations and engagement. Effective and honest communication among diverse community members invites multiple stakeholders into the collaborative problem-solving sessions to address co-constructed goals and strategies continuous school improvement. Shared governance structures and procedures establish a way of work among members of the advisory committee to address adaptive challenges within a comprehensive and coordinated Multi-Tiered Systems of Support framework to enhance and support community relations and engagement.

The overall **macro-tier** of Multi-Tiered System of Support for community relations and engagement strengthens the overall, school-wide communication and interactions with the multiple stakeholders within the local school community. Members of the communities may represent local churches, community centers, organizations, small businesses, and health providers. The goal is to develop trusting relationships and shared goals for students within the schools, especially if the goals for the students include services and resources not typically considered within the realm of services schools can provide. For example, to understand the potential benefits of community partnerships with schools, members of the school community must ask what is needed for the students in the school. A focus on academic excellence? A safe environment? Medical and therapeutic services? A community gathering place? Access to food, clothes, and other necessities?

When school community leadership teams meet to determine specific goals and needs during collaborative problem-solving, the answer to these questions might be "all of the above" as priority needs. But the next question is, "How do we deliver all of these services and resources?" Addressing these needs requires community partnerships. This is especially critical for children and families within communities with economic challenges. Community members, in collaboration with school personnel and families, need to figure out how to blend resources to address the complexities that may hinder students from being fully able to participate and achieve at schools.

The idea is that when schools and communities provide more resources, such as health care and counseling services, students experience fewer barriers to learning and have more reasons, opportunities, and supports to attend school. When students can go to school and get on-site medical care, they don't have to miss important lessons in their classes because of illnesses or appointments. When parents have access to food pantries and healthy eating recipes, the students are less likely to feel hungry and distracted in classes.

Community and school collaboration can lead to major benefits for students and their families, particularly for students in high-poverty schools. Students who receive medical care, dental services, counseling, and social services as part of the total services offered within a comprehensive, tiered service delivery framework often show improved attendance, social skills, behavior, and academic achievement (Ishimaru, 2020).

The services offered through a tiered, comprehensive system are also effective in improving family connections and trust within the school and local community. Consistent, positive communication skills of clear and open discussions of important issues, and communication structures (e.g., team meetings of collaborative problem-solving) are critical to the development of communications. These communications provide the foundation for building and sustaining a comprehensive system of collaboration for enhanced community relations and engagement (Ross, 2023). Using expert and sustained communication at the macro-tier level, the goal is to notify and build awareness of school-related activities, resources, and opportunities within the local communities. Specific examples of community activities that involve multiple community partners include:

1. **Medical and dental services offered at school sites with community engagement**.
   a. Regular check-ups and availability for medical and dental care provided on-site increases attendance and the completion of routine medical and dental care (e.g., prevention, vaccinations, cleanings, etc.)
   b. School personnel can refer students evidencing specific symptoms to increase efficiency and resolution of medical issues.
   c. Families appreciate timely services that helps students stay engaged in their classes.
2. **Enriched, community-integrated learning opportunities.**
   a. Curricular standards and instructional lessons connect with real-world community opportunities (e.g., library, museums, parks, etc.).
   b. Learning includes cultural capital and resources from local communities to connect with student interests, cultures, and experiences. Family members and local community members can share about local community assets.
   c. Multiple inquiry-based, authentic learning experiences and projects connect and engage students in meaningful learning and problem-solving.
3. **Expanded learning opportunities**.
   a. Many school-based and community groups, such as the YMCA, 4-H, Scouts, etc., connect directly with school extra-curricular clubs and activities.
   b. School group and/or individual counseling can occur on-site.
   c. Before- and after-school, weekend, and summer programs can be co-planned and implemented to address identified student needs within the community (e.g., sports, interactive games, tutoring, etc.)
4. **Community-Based Social Media Groups**.
   a. Closed groups on platforms like Facebook or WhatsApp allow community members, parents, and school personnel to connect.
   b. Community members can relate and extend learning on school-related matters.
   c. Teachers, community members, and families can use social media to share photos, celebrate achievements, and build a sense of community.

The **meso-tier** for community relations and engagement within the Multi-Tiered System of Support framework in schools provides for engagement opportunities with a focus on governance structures of program development opportunities within the schools such as the Parent–Teacher Organization, the School Advisory Committee, and other opportunities for collaboration and problem-solving. Given the multiple and diverse backgrounds and experiences of families and community members, school personnel need to not only invite community members to these panning meetings, but also communicate to empower the diverse members. During planning, it is important for educators to consider not only *access* to the meetings for engagement (e.g., language, web-based accessibility, scheduling, childcare, etc.), but also communication skills *to empower* the family and community members to partner and engage in decision-making and planning. As mentioned earlier, it is our responsibility to continuously enhance the participation and engagement of community members to maximize collaboration to synergize and create innovative solutions. A continuum of participation (Vogel et al., 2014) has been described as:

1. Inform – to provide balanced and objective information to understand the problem, alternatives, and/or solutions.
2. Consult – to obtain feedback or analyses.
3. Involve – to work directly with stakeholders to ensure concerns and aspirations are consistently understood and considered.
4. Collaborate – to partner with stakeholders in each aspect of planning and decision-making for preferred solutions.
5. Empower – to place the decision-making in the hands of the stakeholders.

Throughout the discussions by community stakeholders within the various governance structures and leadership teams (PTO, PTA, etc.), clear parameters re: decision-making needs to be clarified as the spectrum of participation is enhanced to assure maximum collaboration and empowerment. Several examples of engagement opportunities at the meso-tier include:

1. **School Advisory Committee (SAC) Opportunities**.
    a. Annually, goals, strategies, and assessments are identified based upon student assessment data as instructional targets for the school year.

Community member involvement could enrich and connect instructional goals with community resources.

  b Local experts could provide historical and cultural contexts related to state and district instructional goals to be met in the annual School Improvement Plan (SIP).

  c Enhanced learning opportunities for groups (e.g., tutoring, volunteers, etc.) and individuals (e.g., cross-age peers from local high schools, community libraries, etc.) could be planned and implemented to support student learning.

2 **Parent–Teacher Organization/Community Workshops**.

  a Workshops cover various topics, such as curriculum and instruction, parent connections to SIP, instructional goals, etc.

  b Community members and parents gain insights into effective ways to support their child's learning.

  c Teachers can collaborate with community members to lead these workshops.

The **micro-tier** of community relations, engagement, and involvement includes establishing systems to support and sustain the community connections. With so many decisions to be made to actualize the full benefits of engagement and partnerships within local communities by members of teams to produce improved educational outcomes for students, considerations, and actions to sustain the shared vision need to be addressed. Several examples of community engagement at the micro-tier include:

1 **Funding Appropriations**.

  a Develop and sustain innovative programs to address more comprehensive educational, physical, medical, and social needs of the broader community, a representative team of stakeholders must be developed to identify funding mechanisms, both in-kind and actual, to sustain innovations and action plans.

  b Identify additional sources of funding (e.g., federal and state grants, donations, benefactors, etc.) must be developed and maintained.

2 **Program Evaluations**.

  a Determine specific data to address innovative solutions must be identified to both share impacts of changes for continuous improvements,

and also demonstrate efficacy and results to current stakeholders as well as future, potential funders.
b  Identify teachers and other educators to share insights into academic performance, behavior, and social development.
c  Encourage Community members to ask questions, seek clarification, and collaborate with others on strategies to support accomplishment of action items.

Collaboration within various team structures is critical to developing and sustaining community relations and engagement. A team approach for community participation at the micro-tier is centered on the continued support for community engagement by multiple, diverse stakeholders. There will be various teams within the multi-tiered systems of supports, determined by the goals and objectives of each of the teams. An overall leadership team is needed to comprehensively develop the vision and overall activities of community engagement within the school. Continued communication of action planning and innovations in alignment with the overall mission and vision of the SIT in each school is vital. The composition of additional teams varies according to the team's purpose to address school's needs. For example, a community liaison team, a budget team, an enhanced curriculum team, and ad hoc collaborative problem-solving teams may all be needed to address various functions of community engagement. All teams and members must work in concert with each other with the overall school mission and goals as their foundation.

## Getting Started with Community Engagement

There are so many opportunities to enhance community relations and engagement with the school personnel and families. By reviewing the structures and suggestions listed above, what are current structures in your school that can be enhanced by connecting with local community members? What local community leaders are already involved within your school who can connect with local community members? What data, structures, and processes will enhance the collaboration among an expanded community?

As you move forward, consider some of the following suggestions and examples listed below.

## Reach Out to Community Stakeholders

One of the best ways to connect and create an authentic bond is to go to the people who matter most and meet them right in the community. A series of community walks are a great way to start. Ask the teachers and some local businesses leaders to visit local businesses, churches, and senior homes to connect with others in the community. Host several Open Houses at the school site. Try the same approach with groups of students. This time, let the students communicate what they hope and wish for their school and encourage them to ask for mentoring and support. Deliver an open invitation to reconnect, collaborate, and share various experiences, skills and time to make a difference.

## Create a Community Asset Map

A visual representation of your community and the various skills people have to offer provides information about available community resources. If you build one, also point out the materials people can supply at cost or for free, the time they can invest in projects, and how they can connect to curriculum and classroom activities. Include the networks they can utilize to raise awareness of the needs of local children and families, and always promote and foster resource-sharing and collaboration. For example, libraries are important hubs and can provide meaningful connection points outside the school gates. In addition, consider the largely untapped wealth of experience and knowledge that resides with retirees, grandparents, and millions of socially isolated senior citizens in care facilities.

## Connect with Curriculum

Much of what we learn as children and adults happens outside the classroom through real-world experiences and from our peers, mentors or on the job. How might we connect today's core curriculum with the real world? That is an important question that is in urgent need of answers. Community members can identify ways to partner with local businesses and subject matter experts to connect core curriculum to the outside world and design engaging learning experiences in and out of the classroom.

## Continued Conversations with the Community

Educators and local community members, including policymakers, system leaders, and funders, expect their schools to increase young people's engagement at school, boost their learning, and improve their overall well-being to prepare them for productive lives as adults. They also expect schools to enhance the well-being of engaged families and communities. At the outset, it is important to identify common goals to support implementers and evaluators in assessing and informing progress toward these goals and outcomes by establishing measurable indicators of these outcomes. These outcomes and indicators can be used to monitor short- and medium-term progress toward locally determined goals. They also can provide data to guide continuous improvement of the local community school strategy.

## Unintended Consequences

Given the multiple perspectives and previous experiences among the community members with school personnel, one potential unintended consequence may be difficult relationships from past interactions. Barriers to communication can be both perceived and real. Previous negative experiences, a lack of time, and diverse cultural expectations and languages may be perceived as resistance to collaboration and change. This is critical to address at the outset by developing trusting, honest, and open relationships through effective and honest communication. Although communication seems to be a simple component, it can also be one of the greatest challenges. As mentioned early in this chapter, communication to develop, strengthen, and enhance trusting relationships is critical. Open, honest, and sustained communication develops partnerships within the community to enhance engagement. Therefore, awareness, development, and sustained efforts to enhance communication and collaboration by community members are essential to maximizing the outcomes and benefits when implementing community engagement within the multi-tiered systems of support in the school and local communities. The sincere use of numerous processes to develop connections with community members will enhance and nurture all within the school community.

## Emerging Understandings

An African proverb says, "It takes a village to raise a child." One could imagine that it would take a community to raise a school. We can't rely on local, state, or federal governments to take ownership of the issues we face locally. We need to work as a community to nurture our schools for our school and community needs.

We believe the answer to school transformation is strong, authentic community connections and actions among community members, families, and educators. When families, community groups, businesses, and schools join together to support learning, young people achieve more in school, stay in school longer, and connect within their communities. Creating and implementing comprehensive frameworks of multi-tiered systems of support not only expands community-based experiences but also enhances and connects students, families, educators, and community members. As community members, families, and educators work toward a common vision and outcomes, they are encouraged to think in terms of key areas to address with community and family stakeholders through continuous, collaborative problem-solving approaches to seeking solutions. Implementing continuous improvement strategies with families and community members focus to achieve important educational goals:

Enhanced communication and trust: Schools that engage families and members of the community strive to offer a safe and welcoming culture for students, families, and educators that promotes collective well-being. In doing so, the school creates the conditions for community stakeholders to feel safe and empowered. Examples of outcomes include trusting relationships, perceptions of safety and belonging, and increased engagement.

Local capacity for collaborative solution seeking: Members of the school community collaboratively identify, develop action plans, and make progress toward local goals and outcomes for both the school and the larger community. Quality, actionable data are collected and easily accessible to all members of the school community. The community sees the results of its efforts and feels a sense of collective efficacy as continuous improvement cycles show progress on locally determined outcomes that result in various outcomes.

## Multi-Tiered System for Community Engagement

Transformed schools: Through a common vision and identified outcomes and activities, schools transform into community hubs – developed by and for students, educators, families, and neighbors – that provide "whole-child" learning environments, spaces for civic engagement, and access to resources and services. Students, families, educators, and community members feel welcomed at the school and hold a shared responsibility for student success. As described, families, educators, students, and community members are involved in meaningful decision-making processes at the school. Resources, services, and instruction align around a comprehensive whole child vision of learning and support for students and families.

Engaged, healthy, empowered students and families: Avenues for collaborative problem-solving, a supportive school community, and access to resources, such as physical and mental health care, all prioritize the well-being of students and families. Students' and families' physical, mental, and emotional needs are identified and can be met through continuous, collaborative problem-solving. Families and community members feel that they are safe and valued and that their cultures and languages are respected and engaged as equals in important decision-making. As members of collaborative problem-solving teams within schools, critical issues are identified, and action plans are developed with positive, continuously improving schools.

Student enrollment and teacher retention: To build a strong and supportive community and create an optimal learning environment, a focus needs to be on the retention of both teachers and students. The engagement and support by the entire school community should make the school a place where students, families, and educators want to be. Research clearly demonstrates the positive academic improvements by students when taught be knowledgeable, certified, and caring teachers.

Academic growth and deeper learning: The well-being of students through the access to multiple services and a positive school climate create the foundation for learning and achievement of rigorous curriculum. In addition, curriculum and instruction that is rigorous, community-connected, and meaningful to students engage students, families, and community members with learning.

Students are engaged in learning within schools, at home, and in the community.

<u>Confident, well-prepared students:</u> Students excel academically, confidently navigate the in- and out-of-school pursuits and have the resources and skills to pursue their postsecondary goals. Students demonstrate content mastery and develop 21st-century skills, habits, and mindsets. Students take increased ownership over their learning and enrichment and develop a sense of agency in their school and community. Students learn, pursue their passions and interests, and find a sense of purpose within engaged schools. When school personnel enlist community members, families, and students as key partners in shaping the environment, priorities, and programs, the school becomes a place of learning, sharing, leadership, and participatory dialogue and decision-making for both adults and students.

## Professional Conversation Prompts:

As you and your team develop and enhance support and engagement by community members, the following illustrative questions may serve as guideposts for in-depth critical and professional discussions:

- What medical, psychological, and academic social services are available for students in the community?
- What extra-curricular activities are available for students in the community beyond the school day?
- How does the school tap into or interact with community services to support student learning?
- What do the students need from the community to support their learning?
- How can the school be viewed as the center of community events?
- What kind of support does the community expect from the school?

# References

Alvarez, S. (2014). Translanguaging *tareas*: Emergent bilingual youth as language brokers for homework in immigrant families. *Language Arts, 91*(5), 326–339.

Breiseth, L., Robertson, K., & Lafond, S. (2011). *A guide for engaging ELL families: Twenty strategies for school leaders.* http://www.colorincolorado.org/sites/default/files/Engaging_ELL_Families_FINAL.pdf

Cramer, E., Little, M., & McHatton, P. (2015). *Demystifying the data-based decision-making process.* Manassas Park, VA: Teacher Education Yearbook XIX, Association of Teacher Educators.

Durand, T. M. (2011). Latina parental involvement in kindergarten: Findings from the early childhood longitudinal study. *Hispanic Journal of Behavioral Sciences, 33*(4), 469–489.

Epstein, J. L. (2010). School/family/community partnerships: Caring for the children we share. *Phi Delta Kappan, 92*(3), 81–96.

Epstein, J. L., & Sanders, M. G. (2000). Connecting home, school, and community. In M. T. Hallinan (Ed.), *Handbook of the sociology of education.* Springer. https://doi.org/10/1007/0-387-36424-2_13

Epstein, J. L., Sanders M. G., Sheldon, S., Simon, B. S., Salinas, K. C., Janson, N. R., Van-Voorhis, F. L., Martin, C. S., Thomas, B. G., Greenfield, M. D., Hutchins, D. J., & Williams, K. (2019). *School, family, and community partnerships: Your handbook for action* (4th ed.). Thousand Oaks, CA: Corwin.

Garcia, M. E., Frunzi, K., Dean, C. B., Flores, N., & Miller, K. B. (2016). *Toolkit of resources for engaging families and the community as partners in education.* Regional Educational Laboratory Pacific. https://files.eric.ed.gov/fulltext/ED569110.pdf

Ishimaru, A. M. (2020). Reimagining American education: Possible futures: Youth, families, and communities as educational leaders. *Phi Delta Kappan, 103*(6), 52–55. https://doi.org/10.1177/00317217221082811

Jeynes, W. (2022). *Relational aspects of parental involvement to support educational outcomes: Parental communication, expectations, and participation for student success.* Oxfordshire: Routledge.

Jeynes, W. H. (2018). A practical model for school leaders to encourage parental involvement and parental engagement. *School Leadership & Management, 38*(2), 147–163. https://doi.org/10.1080/13632434.2018.1434767

Little, M. (2006). Schools for all students: Issues and solutions for school leaders. *Educational Forum, 21*(2), 35–43.

McCauley, C., Webb, J., Abdelrahim, S., & Mahmoud-Tabana, S. (2023). A community engaged framing: Building successful community engagement for schools and families of bilingual students through inquiry. *School Community Journal, 33*(1), 11–36. http://www.schoolcommunitynetwork.org/SCJ.aspx

McWayne, C., Campos, R., & Owsianik, M. (2008). A multidimmensional, multilevel examination of mother and father involvement among culturally diverse Head Start families. *Journal of School Psychology, 46*(5), 551–573. https://doi.org/10.1016/j.jsp.2008.06.001

Morris, R. V., & Shockley, D. (2023). Building community-school engagement. *Childhood Education, 99*(4), 76–79. https://doi.org/10.1080/00094056.2023.2232287

Ross, E. M. (2023, March 21). *The case for strong family and community engagement in schools.* Harvad Graduate School of Education. https://www.gse.harvard.edu/ideas/usable-knowledge/23/03/case-strong-family-and-community-engagement-schools

Scott, D. L., Sharma, R., Godwyll, F., Johnson, J., & Putman, T. (2020). Building on strengths to address challenges: An asset-based approach to planning and implementing a community partnership school. *Journal of Higher Education Outreach and Engagement, 24*(2), 69–84. https://openjournals.libs.uga.edu/jheoe/article/view/2070

Shiffman, C. (2019). Learning to communicate across language and culture: Demographic change, schools, and parents in adult ESL classes. *School Community Journal, 29*(1), 9–38. https://www.adi.org/journal/2019ss/ShiffmanSS2019.pdf

Vogel, R., Moulder, E., & Huggins, M. (2014). The extent of public participation. *Public Management, 96*(2), 6–10.

Wood, L., Bauman, E., Rudo, Z., & Dimock, V. (2017). *How family, school, and community engagement can improve student achievement and influence school reform.* Quincy, MA: Nellie Mae Education Foundation.

Yosso, T. J. (2013). *Critical race counterstories along the Chicana/Chicano education pipeline.* Oxfordshire: Routledge.

# Multi-Tiered System for Developing Distributive Teacher Leadership

*If your actions inspire others to dream more, learn more, do more and become more, you are a leader.*

–John Quincy Adams

Transformational distributive teacher leadership is a professional communal approach in which solution seeking is a collaborative effort among teacher colleagues within a school to enhance individual abilities and contributions by each individual. Not only does it empower multiple voices, but it also focuses forward shifts toward the school's mission and needed adaptive challenges. Distributive teacher leadership centers on how a professional learning community of practice collaborates by sharing pedagogical content knowledge and expertise to improve learning and instruction. As members of a professional learning community of practice share pedagogical knowledge and expertise, new knowledge and solutions are developed. Consequently, when administrators, teacher colleagues, and other educators within school teams learn and create solutions to unique situations and understandings, learning and instruction improves for all students.

Creating opportunities for developing leadership among school professionals always merits serious considerations within multi-tiered systems of support frameworks. We have found that distributive teacher leadership within a school has a positive impact on learning for all. Developing distributive teacher leadership creates a professional learning environment where nurturing human and professional capital is seen as vital to the continuous improvement of a school (Hord, 2004). Teacher leadership can be formal with titles such as director, principal, or assistant principal or informal (without titles) with conscientious, goal-oriented individuals. All teacher colleagues have the potential for leadership within schools. Developing distributive teacher leadership needs time and support for self-directed professional learning and ongoing generative professional responses from colleagues to realize self-selected goals for improvement.

## Impacts of Distributive Teacher Leadership

The literature is clear on the positive impact of distributive teacher leadership (Harris, 2013; Leithwood, Mascall, & Strauss, 2009). The research describes a relationship among distributive teacher leadership, school improvement, and student learning outcomes (Hallinger & Heck, 2009; Leithwood & Mascall, 2008). Some studies show that the difference between high-progress and low-progress schools can be attributed to varying levels of leadership distribution (Leithwood et al., 2009). Although differences exist in the quality and nature of distributive teacher leadership from school to school, it is still to be considered in a network of factors contributing to high progress and the impact on student learning over time (Leithwood & Mascall, 2008). Specifically, successful distributive leadership driven by the constructs of school leadership for learning is second only to teachers' instruction as one of the greatest significant factors that impact student learning and school improvement (Hallinger, 2011).

## Facing Adaptive Challenges

Within schools, distributive teacher leadership is most effective when groups of individuals are assembled that possess a variety of skillsets and transdisciplinary experiences with a shared intentional and coherent mission to promote and sustain a culture that cultivates lifelong learning for all. To realize positive change from distributive teacher leadership requires reflection about current practices and structures to set goals for communal planning and solution seeking. We should be asking about the kinds of distributive teacher leadership that should be employed to ensure forward shifts will occur to improve professional and student learning over time. Grounded in our work with administrators and teacher colleagues within districts, we acknowledge upfront that change can be arduous and unsettling and comes with no assurance that it is going to work positively.

We clearly understand that distributive teacher leadership is not a cure for top-down panoptic leadership for compliance nor is it a confusing, skewed, or distorted substitute. Distributive teacher leadership cannot be thought of as a short-term, quick-fix remedy for leadership. It is a comprehensive system of engagement, responsibilities, and solution seeking among members of a broader school community. Developing and enhancing a system of leadership requires dealing with adaptive challenges. A few of the adaptive challenges will be issues of time, funding, trust, positional threat, and authentic responsibilities by administrators, teachers, educational colleagues, students, families, and community members. When distributive teacher leadership is implemented successfully, all stakeholders are responsible and accountable for their leadership actions and results from the novel roles, responsibilities, and structures generated. The collaborative work is defined by the symbiotic relationship and roles among stakeholders within the school community. Distributive teacher leadership is about communal inspiration and encouragement to improve a learning environment. It is not a haphazard by-product of high-progress schools but, as the research shows, it can be a major factor in school improvement (Hargreaves, Boyle, & Harris, 2014).

Time must be recognized as necessary to institute adaptive changes to nurture leadership endeavors that are confined by multifaceted, communal, and professional environments (Leithwood et al., 2009). Time for discussions and decisions must address structures such as current systems of role positionality while enacting professional learning communities of practice (Daly e al., 2010; Lee, Hallinger, & Walker, 2012). Accentuating the importance of communities of practice creates the conditions, artifacts, and connections of their leadership activity (Harris, 2013; Spillane et al., 2001). Relationships and their consequential influences on Professional Learning Communities of practice may be regarded as products of the environments in which distributive teacher leadership is applied (Forsyth, Adams & Hoy, 2011). A primary benefit of positive professional learning communities of practice and beliefs is an increase in the quality of professional connections among school administrators, teacher colleagues, and teacher leaders at the state, province, and district levels. At this point, we must note that a genuine professional learning community of practice cannot be scheduled or headed by a hierarchical position with a specific topic to review. *Genuine Professional Learning*

*Communities of practice develop over time with self-monitoring, self-regulating, and self-accountable individuals that acknowledge and balance productive struggles and failures along with non-productive successes to improve transdisciplinary literacy instruction.* In other words, when a professional learning community of practice is scheduled and led by a hierarchically positioned individual to review a specific topic IT IS A MEETING, not a community.

## Nurturing Generative Professional Dialogue

We wholeheartedly believe that language is a tool for critical thinking (Vygotsky, 1978). Consequently, the role of language during professional learning opportunities cannot be underscored enough. We have observed that developing a common language is a critical first step toward enhancing positive relationships, trust, and professional connections within Professional Learning Communities. Generative professional dialogue fosters trust among school administrators and teacher colleagues that is critical for distributive teacher leadership to flourish and impact instruction. Generative professional dialogues promote forward shifts in professional learning which will impact student learning in the classroom (Darling-Hammond, 2005; Fullan, 2004; Hattie, 2009). Improving generative professional dialogue is one of the goals for the work to empower teacher colleagues and collaborate in improving learning for all stakeholders (Fairman & MacKenzie, 2015; Portin et al., 2013). Robust generative professional dialogue and productive communications are vital for boosting distributive teacher leadership in schools (Brezicha, Bergmark, & Mitra, 2015; Holloway et al., 2018). Distributive teacher leadership is about:

- coordinating transdisciplinary literacy instruction;
- promoting professional learning opportunities across the disciplines;
- addressing transdisciplinary adaptive challenges;
- solution seeking cooperatively; and
- discussing transdisciplinary pedagogical content knowledge.

Communications in distributive teacher leadership incorporate respectful and humane professional conversations with colleagues about reflection and progresses by listening, sharing, demonstrating, and modeling to facilitate a positive culture where approximations and productive failures are viewed as learning opportunities (Weiner & Woulfin, 2018). There is a mutual respect and understanding among teacher colleagues and administrators at all levels. Distributive teacher leadership facilitates and increases productive interactions between students and faculty. The nature of teacher leaders' positions in hybridized configurations structures their work in both formal and informal ways. Distributive teacher leadership is the keystone of high-functioning schools where everyone holds themselves accountable for improving instruction.

## Factors that Contribute to Forward Shifts

There are three major factors that contribute to effective teacher distributive leadership to promote forward shifts in learning for all stakeholders. The three factors include:

1 Creating and utilizing transdisciplinary literacy leadership teams where each member contributes their pedagogical content knowledge and expertise.
    a  Support research-validated instruction through the development of Professional learning Communities of practice where collaborative planning schedules have a priority.
    b  Engage teacher colleagues through cycles of peer observations, professional responses, and reflection to adapt and improve instruction grounded on students' strengths and needs.
    c  Lead and demonstrate how to apply a growth mindset with an expectation that school is a place of learning for all, and approximations are viewed as part of the process of learning.
    d  Promote ongoing formative dynamic and summative static assessments and evaluation of student strengths and needs over time to ensure school-wide learning.
    e  Provide intentional, consistent, and coherent ongoing, job-embedded professional learning opportunities in a timely manner respectful of the individual adult learner.
2 Engaging school administrators to empower and sustain the work of the transdisciplinary literacy leadership teams. This is accomplished by

augmenting leadership capacity and by creating conditions where pedagogical content knowledge can be distributive throughout the school for educators to work individually and collaboratively with the goal of improving instruction and learning.
3. Promoting effective distributive leadership focused on interactions among professionals to improve learning and instruction within a humane, respectful, and collaborative school culture.

If we think about leadership as being restricted to only those in positions of power, then we are knowingly discounting the leadership talent and aptitude of many others in school. If leadership is primarily about influence, then within any school there are many sources of knowledge and expertise, both formal and informal. Distributive teacher leadership concentrates on developing leadership qualities that is shared, collaborative, and constructive with a focus on transformational change and improvement.

## Multiple Tiers of Support to Enhance Distributed Teacher Leadership

Focused on leadership as a source of collaborative influence and shaped by Bronfenbrenner's bioecological framework for human development (Bronfenbrenner, 1979; Bronfenbrenner, 1994; Bronfenbrenner & Morris, 2007), we re-envisioned three pragmatic, mutually interdependent tiers of support for distributive teacher leadership to improve transdisciplinary lifelong learning for all stakeholders. At the core, more universal, implementation broad-spectrum phase, we describe the macro tier to support the development of transdisciplinary literacy leadership teams. Once a team is established, we proceed with a more connective and targeted effort into a meso tier where utilizing a transdisciplinary literacy coach becomes essential toward distributive teacher leadership for forward shifts to occur in instruction. Over time, we have found that after a few years of transdisciplinary literacy coaching, many teachers may also engage in the role of peer coaches. Hence, peer coaching becomes a more personalized and micro tier that supports and establishes colleagues as ongoing reflective practitioners. In the next few sections, we will go into more detail for each tier within a system of support for distributive leadership to empower colleagues and improve instruction.

# Macro Tier – Transdisciplinary Literacy Leadership Teams

Transdisciplinary literacy leadership teams are school-embedded teams and are the most common forms of teacher distributive leadership. Charged primarily with implementing research-validated instructional practices to improve learning, transdisciplinary literacy leadership teams usually include administrators (principals, assistant principals, and deans) and grade-level teacher colleagues (language arts, mathematics, sciences, social sciences, arts, special education) representatives. Media specialists, school psychologists, school counselors, or social workers are often members as well, supporting teacher colleagues and administrators to better understand and address behavioral and academic strengths and needs of students. Professional learning opportunities, data discussions, and curriculum planning meetings led by teacher colleagues are all examples of distributive teacher leadership that develop and enhance the impact of teacher leaders. Distributive teacher leadership may look different from school to school, district to district, and province to province. Yet, regardless of the context, these processes and structures are envisioned and supported by school administrators who cultivate trust, support collaboration, focus on lifelong learning, and create leadership opportunities for all team members.

With a shared vision for distributed teacher leadership and a positive professional learning environment, teacher distributive leadership enhances a school community to be more connected, open to a variety of perspectives, and engaged with solution-seeking endeavors. Teacher leadership development focuses on solution seeking to improve instruction with research-validated practices to ensure lifelong learning for all. When transdisciplinary literacy leadership teams are employed, the work at hand is experienced differently. We have observed that a forward shift occurs from mechanistic compliance to collaborative solution seeking that ensures genuine engagement by all stakeholders with a common investment that benefits all. With equal parts of engagement and trust, stakeholders are more likely to generate and sustain impactful positive change in productive professional learning communities of practice.

Within a productive framework of Multi-Tiered Systems of Support, teacher colleagues will accomplish the work successfully and resistance and burnout will be reduced. At a time when large numbers of teachers leave the field within five years, distributive teacher leadership might be the solution to teacher retention. It is much easier to tackle adaptive challenges and feel hopeful about the result when a group of colleagues learn from and lean on each other with mutual goals.

The idea of transdisciplinary literacy leadership teams is certainly not a new concept in education. We have found that, over time, many school literacy initiatives fall short because there was never a long-term ongoing, job-embedded plan, implemented and supported by a knowledgeable transdisciplinary literacy leadership team. Our experience has taught us that a pivotal starting point for a transdisciplinary literacy leadership team is to develop a common language and understanding about transdisciplinary literacy processing and adult learners (Puig & Froelich, 2022). Without this critical knowledge, it is unlikely that a transdisciplinary literacy leadership team will recognize vital data that will influence learning and instruction in a positive manner. The team has to have this understanding to formulate a theory or rationale for what is occurring and how to interact with what is occurring by utilizing both distributed and collective knowledge. Each team member will bring a wealth of personalized knowledge and experiences that is needed to acknowledge and use for thinking in different directions so that they are better able to support the school as a place of learning for everyone.

Everyone comes to the metaphoric table with what Gonzalez et al. (2005) call "funds of knowledge." If we want schools to be places of learning and instruction for all (Craig, 2006; Froelich & Puig, 2010; Tharp & Gallimore, 1988), we must put in place Multi-Tier Systems of Support. Lyons and Pinnell (2001) tell us that forward shifts rarely occur because of one person or a few people (including the principal and the literacy coach). Forward shifts have to occur on-site and at the whole-school level to sustain and expand success (Darling-Hammond, 2005, Knight & Stallings, 1995, Hill & Crévola, 1999, Maden & Hillman, 1996, Langer, 2000; Maden, 2001). To create forward shifts in schools, the creation of transdisciplinary literacy leadership teams is essential for implementing on-site Multi-Tier Systems of Support to successfully sustain and expand a K-12 transdisciplinary framework for coherent instruction. Furthermore, for these Multi-Tier Systems of Support to be in place, a dynamic transdisciplinary literacy leadership team with distributed experiences and knowledge guided by a highly qualified literacy coach as a lead learner is paramount (Craig, 2006; Ross, 1992; Booth & Rowsell, 2002; Pennell, 2020; Puig & Froelich, 2022; Veenman & Denessen, 2001).

In his journal, Leonardo DaVinci (1510) wrote,

> Those who are in love with practice without theoretical knowledge are like the sailor who goes onto a ship without rudder or compass and who never can be certain whither he is going. Practice must always be founded on sound theory.
>
> (Isaacson, 2017)

We have found that without a strong theoretical foundation, most literacy initiatives waiver and wane over time in a school setting. Likewise, for transdisciplinary literacy leadership teams to sustain success, they need to have a strong theoretical understanding. In other words, understanding the compelling "why's" is foundational for rationale and solution-seeking. Some key challenges that transdisciplinary literacy leadership teams encounter when implementing change are dealing with adult colleagues in a professional, respectful, and sensitive manner; supporting and replicating multisensory transdisciplinary literate environments; communicating with a common language; and understanding how students process information to improve learning and instruction. With a strong theoretical foundation, most of those challenges can be discussed and adapted to fulfill a school's need for improving learning and instruction.

In working with many transdisciplinary literacy leadership teams, it has been our experience that in order to make a start, the team, or any genuine Professional Learning Community of practice, must develop a common language. Overall, language can be ambiguous and vague due to the variety of experiences of the stakeholders. Consequently, we cannot overstate the importance of developing a common language as a first step to minimize misinterpretation among team members.

To assist transdisciplinary literacy leadership teams in developing a common language, honest discussion about understandings is a critical step. It will be the responsibility of the transdisciplinary literacy leadership team to share and clarify the faculty's language to promote forward shifts. In particular, understanding the benefits of any enterprise, such as developing a common language, is one of the principles Cambourne (1988) describes as essential to increase the likelihood of engagement. Additionally, a prime conduit and catalyst for the team to develop a common language is the literacy coach (Puig & Froelich, 2011). The significant role of a knowledgeable literacy coach in supporting the transdisciplinary literacy leadership is essential.

When assembling a transdisciplinary literacy leadership team, numbers are important. For elementary or primary schools with 400 students or fewer, we have found that a primary grade (K-2) teacher representative and an intermediate grade (3–5/6) representative is sufficient teacher representation on a team. In schools with more than 400 students, the teachers that need to be a part of the transdisciplinary literacy leadership team should be one from each grade level. In addition, to be highly effective and to work for the maximum long-term transformational change, the team should have an administrator (ideally the principal), a counselor, a special education teacher/interventionist, a media specialist, as well as representatives from music, arts, and physical education. If the school has an assigned speech pathologist/audiologist and school nurse, it would also be advisable to have them on the team. The literacy coach should anchor this team as a conduit of information and a catalyst for improving instruction.

At the secondary level (middle and high school), the team needs to have the principal, the literacy coach, as well as a member from each content area. In middle and high school, we have found that grade-level representation is not as critical as content area representation. A counselor, a representative from the vocational department and special education, as well as the technology department, should also be included. The goal is to have as many people as possible understand the importance of transdisciplinary literacy learning and instruction. With some exceptions, most academic disciplines do not see the necessity to understand why we all need to be knowledgeable about literacy learning and instruction. Many teachers still hold to the theory that literacy instruction is the purview of either the language arts teacher or a reading specialist. They see reading as a "subject" that someone else teaches instead of a "tool" to access information in all content areas. But to make real and lasting changes, so that students are afforded the best possible chance to succeed, all teachers must believe that reading and writing are the underpinnings of all academic success (Craig, 2006; Froelich & Puig, 2010). If the students cannot read or write at a certain level of proficiency, they are less likely to be successful in any core content area classroom. The common understanding that the language arts is THE common denominator among all disciplines has to be emphasized.

To assure productivity and solution seeking among members of the transdisciplinary literacy leadership team, several norms should be promoted. Members of the team should be invited to participate and recognized for their contributions. It should be a place that helps team members build not only a community of learners but also a place that challenges the members to think about literacy and instruction in innovative ways. The team members realize that studying an adaptive challenge is critical to their learning, and for the learning of their students. Describing and understanding a sound theoretical understanding of transdisciplinary literacy learning as a process has to occur; otherwise, literacy instruction will be haphazard (Clay, 2015; Puig & Froelich, 2011).

Once a foundation of norms has been decided, we usually see scaffolds raised to support workers in the construction of a building. Just like any construction project, the literacy leadership team has to raise scaffolds to ensure sustaining and expanding success. When completed, just like a building, the scaffolds are put away until new work needs to be done. By recognizing and utilizing these scaffolds, transdisciplinary literacy leadership teams can continue to tackle adaptive challenges to improve learning and instruction. The scaffolds that support the construction of a building are made of metal and wood. The scaffolds that support the work of a literacy leadership team are made with a knowledgeable literacy coach, passionate teacher colleagues, supportive teacher leaders, a long-term school-wide plan, and district and state or provincial support. The transdisciplinary literacy leadership team will be better equipped to tackle adaptive challenges with these scaffolds in place.

Because literacy coaches' primary responsibility is the professional learning of teacher colleagues, they are in a prime position to serve as a scaffold for a transdisciplinary literacy leadership team. Through the literacy coach, the team has a built-in mechanism for providing and supporting ongoing professional learning opportunities. The team and the literacy coach are a catalyst to sustain and expand success. Coupled with a long-term school-wide plan and a sound framework for instruction in place, the transdisciplinary literacy leadership team focuses on improving learning and instruction for all stakeholders. Transdisciplinary literacy leadership teams assist their school in making forward shifts in learning by highlighting what works with determination and support and investigating potential side effects.

The best professional learning opportunities we have encountered are intentional and coherent, and have always taken place over time. When professional learning occurs over time, participants are given the opportunities to process information and experiment with implementing and refining new practices to support learning and instruction (Fullan, Hill, & Crévola, 2006). If forward shifts in learning and instruction are to be accomplished, time must be allocated for professional learning. Without dedicated, genuine professional learning time set aside, teacher leaders become business managers rather than instructional leaders. With the support of the administrators, an effective literacy coach and an efficient transdisciplinary literacy leadership team, sustained professional learning addresses identified issues. "Without someone with an informed vision of what good literacy instruction entails leading the charge, instructional change is likely to be beset with problems" (Biancarosa and Snow, 2004, p. 21). The collaboration between teachers and teacher leaders "with an informed vision of what good literacy instruction entails" play a crucial role in ensuring the success of school level transdisciplinary literacy reforms.

The transdisciplinary literacy leadership team provides provinces, states, and local districts a strong return on investment due to its strength in building capacity to incorporate research-validated practices throughout the school. The ability to deliver coherent transdisciplinary instruction and a shared sense of responsibility and efficacy across the school site cannot be underestimated as a means of serving to the individual learning strengths and needs of students. The literacy leadership team provides the ongoing, job-embedded professional learning supported in the research literature. While some may argue that teacher leadership initiatives pull our best teachers from their important classroom duties, Scherer (2007) prefers to view it as "expanding their reach." They continue to work within the classroom's multisensory learning environment so that the students can enjoy continued success, while sharing this success with their colleagues.

## Meso Tier – Utilizing a Transdisciplinary Literacy Coach for Distributive Teacher Leadership

The meso tier is the connective tier. Our experiences have shown us that for any distributive teacher leadership initiative to be successful in a school, support systems need to be in place. Systems for timely assessment, curriculum content development, and professional learning opportunities increases the likelihood of successful implementation. Moreover, professional learning opportunities need to be job-embedded and provided in a timely manner. We have found that for professional learning opportunities to be job-embedded and timely, the support of a knowledgeable, flexible, and credible literacy coach that embraces transdisciplinarity is critical for the implementation of a K-12 transdisciplinary literacy framework for instruction (Puig & Froelich, 2022).

Although this text is not about literacy coaching, we felt it necessary to dedicate a section to emphasize the importance of an on-campus support system that empowers teacher colleagues and teacher leaders while implementing Multi-Tiered Systems of Support (MTSS) within a K-12 transdisciplinary literacy framework. Hence, in this section we will define literacy coaching from a broad-spectrum perspective to support K-12 teacher colleagues as they scaffold instruction for student learning across core content areas.

Transdisciplinary literacy coaching, as with all coaching, is professional learning on a continuum of varying support, carried out face to face and online. On that continuum of coaching, we propose supporting lesson study, study groups, and transdisciplinary literacy leadership teams as a type of transdisciplinary literacy coaching. It is part of the job. Our premise for developing the concept of literacy coaching as continuum is based on years of firsthand experiences, the current literature and as literacy coaches at a school site where we coached and were coached by peers in a variety of contexts. This led us to conclude that literacy coaching was not just about a "coaching cycle" of pre-conference, observation, and post-conference, although we do acknowledge that the pre-conference, observation, post-conference model of literacy coaching is a powerful model to promote transformational forward shifts. Although, on the flip side, we found that when coaching cycles are overemphasized, its impact on improving instruction diminishes as it becomes something else to check off. Literacy coaching is so much more than just a coaching cycle. *A narrow definition of literacy coaching can become an impediment and counterproductive.* As we learn increasingly about the complex job of a literacy coach, the current literature published on literacy coaching confirms our original claim that literacy coaching is multidimensional, recursive, and complex (Walpole & McKenna, 2004; Lyons & Pinnell, 2001; Casey, 2006; Toll, 2004; Knight, 2007; Puig & Froelich, 2011).

For fluid implementation of a K-12 transdisciplinary literacy coaching process to occur within Multi-Tiered Systems of Support, we recommend that a literacy coach serve as the conduit for professional learning and as a catalyst for classroom implementation of research-validated practices. Although literacy coaching is used as a model for school reform, many districts and schools have not embraced the concept for a variety of reasons. In schools where successful transdisciplinary literacy coaching is implemented, the literacy coach is viewed not as an expert but rather as a "lead learner" with extensive expertise and experience. As we continue to learn and our knowledge of transdisciplinary literacy coaching evolves, we have chosen the term "lead learner." "Lead learner" clearly addresses the behavior that is modeled by effective and efficient literacy coaches, which is lifelong learning. We have found that when transdisciplinary literacy coaches establish themselves as lead learners and approach transdisciplinary literacy coaching on a continuum of professional learning, resistance to coaching is diminished, and collaboration is increased.

We argue that when literacy coaches are removed from students and are hired to work solely with adults, the job of the literacy coach becomes blurred. When this blurring occurs, literacy coaches are given an earbud and a walkie-talkie and are assigned to extensive data entry positions, hall duty, bus duty, cafeteria duty and the proverbial "other duties as assigned" removing them from the reason their job exists – to directly support student/teacher interactions as they occur in a transdisciplinary learning environment.

It cannot be stated clearly enough that principals, district/province teacher leadership personnel, and literacy coaches need to have a clear understanding of the job requirements of a literacy coach. An honest and open discussion is a critical initial step for administrators in teacher leadership positions that plan to utilize a literacy coach to influence a school as a lead learner. The operative word here is "influence." A literacy coach that serves as a lead learner never dictates a direction; rather, they rely on research and evidence (formal and informal). However, a literacy coach influences teacher colleagues and teacher leadership personnel to recognize and investigate adaptive challenges to learning and instruction. Consequently, both transdisciplinary literacy coaches and transdisciplinary literacy leadership teams have a common ground to develop common goals in response to adaptive challenges and to ensure that conditions for learning (Crouch & Cambourne, 2020) are in place. They are looked upon as indispensable for learning and instruction. We encourage schools to adapt and rely on a knowledgeable coach to serve as a "lead learner."

It is up to the principal and district/province teacher leadership personnel to ensure that a literacy coach's toles and responsibilities are clearly defined to include professional learning support to improve instruction and student learning. In fact, clearly defining roles and responsibilities are critical. At the top of the list, we make the claim that effective and efficient literacy coaches work with students at least 40% of their workweek to enhance their own craft of teaching in order to be able to engage with teacher colleagues on improving instruction through professional knowledge and credibility. We also must clarify that we DO NOT intend for this to mean that the literacy coach be the teacher of record for a select group of students. When this occurs, the title and obligations of a literacy coach need to be reexamined. A literacy coach must have the scheduling freedom to visit with colleagues and classrooms if they are truly to be coaching so that they can improve transdisciplinary literacy learning and instruction.

The literature informs us that the transmission model for professional learning has an extraordinarily negligible impact on classroom instruction (Joyce & Showers, 1982; Costa & Garmston, 2002). We have read over and over that the best professional learning is ongoing and job-embedded (Darling-Hammond, 2005; Killion, 2016). Hence, because of research, we have the current widespread belief of the importance of literacy coaching in education to improve learning and instruction. Yet, what is meant by ongoing? What is meant by job-embedded? It is apparent that the research has been misinterpreted or ignored when so many literacy coaches report investing so little time where instruction takes place – the classroom.

To us, ongoing implies that professional learning for teachers in K-12 never ceases and that professional learning opportunities are regularly scheduled, intentional, and of consistently high quality. We define regularly scheduled as meaning at least 90 minutes once every two weeks in order to sustain and expand success over time. When thoughtful consideration is given to learning and instruction, this time should be non-negotiable. High-quality professional learning cannot occur in 15 minutes or during a teacher's planning period or walking down a hall. If professional learning opportunities are scheduled for full days, we encourage you to schedule the day into 90-minute sessions, with a 15-minute break in between as downtime, either for processing information informally with colleagues or through personal reflection. Professional learning opportunities that take place once every two to three months or last less than an hour and a half at a time seem to have the same impact as a mass-production in-service meeting. Mass production works when building automobiles, but it does not work well when supporting multifaceted development of human minds; especially when the goal is improving the complex acts of learning and instruction.

Job-embedded professional learning is accepted as relevant on-the-job learning. Effective and efficient literacy coaches provide job-embedded learning when they interact with colleagues at a school either formally or informally. True job-embedded learning does not burden literacy coaches, teacher colleagues, administrators, or students with finding time for learning since learning and instruction are intertwined and addressed within the context of the learning environment during contractual school time. Job-embedded learning relies heavily on the Vygotskian concept of assisted performance (Tharp & Gallimore, 1988) and Cazden's (1988) performance before competence. The focus of job-embedded professional learning is on doing with assistance rather than just seeing and hearing.

Although ongoing job-embedded learning appears to be a more effective and efficient manner to improve learning and instruction, we do not dismiss the contributions that experienced consultants or workshop attendance make to professional learning. The concerns arise when that is the only type of professional learning provided, and that these two approaches have no follow-up to determine whether they have been successful in their application into the learning environment. Attending workshops and hiring consultants is sometimes a necessity to infuse new language for thinking so that we can tackle adaptive challenges from a different level.

Because of limited time, materials, and funds, the concept of ongoing, job-embedded learning forces literacy coaches to address professional learning as an adaptive challenge. With professional learning as an adaptive challenge in mind, the literature, as well as our immediate experiences, describe literacy coaching as comprehensive support. Furthermore, for the transdisciplinary literacy leadership team and literacy coach to sustain and expand success, comprehensive support means that literacy coaching must be viewed on a continuum where individuals fluctuate back and forth from face-to-face interactions to intra-action (personal reflection).

The structure for understanding literacy coaching as a continuum within Multi-Tiered Systems of Support opens a world of possibilities for

# Multi-Tiered System for Developing Distributive Teacher Leadership

transdisciplinary literacy leadership teams to address adaptive challenges in learning and leading. Literacy coaching as a process and system of thinking about the requirements of the literacy coach to support teacher colleagues to address adaptive challenges. While a continuum of coaching addresses the needs of adaptive challenges, other professional learning activities, such as lesson studies and book studies, can certainly be added to any continuum of coaching. The essential theme is that there is more than one way to coach or support teacher-colleagues within schools. Although a continuum addresses literacy coaches specifically, both transdisciplinary literacy leadership teams and literacy coaches must continually support teachers' leaning by constantly questioning, investigating, and growing. Borrowing from the Māori proverb, "You are either green and growing or ripe and rotting."

Even though a continuum of coaching may be viewed in a very linear manner, it is not. There is no particular starting point or ending point for learning. The late Dr. Marie M. Clay has been described as always stirring the waters (Gaffney & Askew, 1999). When she accepted a lifetime achievement award at the National Reading Conference (now Literacy Research Association), she borrowed from the New Zealand poet Allen Curnow and stated, "simply by sailing in a different direction, you could enlarge the world." Our point is that a literacy coach, and for that matter a transdisciplinary literacy leadership team, cannot enlarge the world if they do not sail in a different direction within a continuum of coaching.

The job of a transdisciplinary literacy coach is multifaceted and complex like all learning and instruction. To label anything in education as "the simple view" creates dangerous minefields that impede accelerating learning and improving instruction. A transdisciplinary literacy coach working in collaboration with teacher leadership personnel and teacher colleagues is a powerful combination to bring about positive change in a school. By carefully investigating and putting on the table the specific duties, dispositions, and obligations of the transdisciplinary literacy coach, teacher leaders, and teacher colleagues, schools will be better equipped to rely on the transdisciplinary literacy coach as another rich resource to tackle adaptive challenges.

When a school thinks of transdisciplinary literacy coaching on a continuum of professional learning opportunities, it opens the school to a safe culture of learning where productive failure is becomes a learning opportunity for all. It is in this safe culture of learning that teacher leaders, transdisciplinary literacy coaches, teacher-colleagues, and students will grow. In this chapter, we presented coaching as broad-spectrum professional learning on a continuum that includes a variety of approaches. We purposefully used the verbs to describe the variety of activities that coaches deal with to make the point that effective and efficient transdisciplinary literacy coaching is about taking action to improve K-12 learning and instruction across the disciplines. Each activity listed on the continuum of coaching was given a brief section to describe points for discussion and helpful hints to assist teacher leaders and teacher colleagues in understanding transdisciplinary literacy coaching in a broader and more productive sense to support sustaining and expanding success in a professional learning community of practice.

## Micro Tier – Employing Peer Coaching for Distributive Teacher Leadership

Peer coaching in education has been around for quite some time, grounded in research in the 1980s from Bruce Joyce and Beverley Showers (Joyce & Showers, 1982; Showers & Joyce, 1996). Peer coaching is commonly recognized as teacher colleagues working shoulder to shoulder and coaching each other to empower each other in their practice (Donegan, Ostrosky, & Fowler, 2000; Lu, 2010). It is a learning relationship, where teacher colleagues hypothesize and investigate research-validated classroom practices as professionals committed to facilitating each other's leadership learning development.

As with any transdisciplinary literacy coaching setting, unrestricted and uncluttered communication is essential for peer coaching to occur. Peer coaching conversations are non-evaluative and must be cultivated over time by teacher-colleagues (Ladyshewsky, 2006; Showers & Joyce, 1996). A common language is one characteristic of teacher colleagues engaged in peer coaching. Consequently, developing a common language is vital to peer coaching and improving instruction and student results.

Showers and Joyce (1996) eliminated the word "feedback" from their peer-coaching model as they realized over time that when the teachers in their research attempted to provide each other feedback, the collaboration among peers disintegrated. In addition, the word implies positioning one colleague over another. Consequently, we find that the word "response" is a better fit, when we are actually talking about a collaborative relationship among peers.

The non-evaluative quality of peer coaching is a distinguishing aspect of the model. Trust and reflection are essential to the construct of peer coaching conceptualized by Joyce and Showers (1982) and common within peer-coaching relationships. The criticality of grounding a peer-coaching relationship on trust is distinctly acknowledged in the literature (Jackson, 2004; Ladyshewsky, 2006; Robertson, 2005a; Slater & Simmons, 2001). As with any professional learning community of practice, trust increases as colleagues develop a common language and understanding (Wenger, McDermott, & Snyder, 2002). Trust becomes stronger over time in peer coaching (Wenger et al., 2002). It is imperative that time is dedicated to institute trust when starting peer coaching.

Another significant attribute of peer coaching is reflection. Jackson (2004) suggests that peer coaching is inherently a reflective enterprise where peer colleagues need to be experienced in reflection (Loughran, 2002; O'Connor & Diggins, 2002). Reflective practice consequently needs to be present in any peer coaching in-service. Doneganet et al. (2000) suggest that the development of reflection comes through active and engaged participation in a peer coaching relationship. Additionally, we must acknowledge that reflection is necessary for any teacher-colleague or teacher leader to improve instruction, regardless of expertise, credentials, or experience. By employing questioning, peer coaches question colleagues to facilitate reflection on various instructional issues. Integral to productive reflective coaching conversations is committed and enthusiastic listening skills (J. Robertson, 2005a; Robertson, 2005b). Void of this ability, peer coaches are incapable of communicating the reflective questions essential to embolden peers to seek solutions. When engaging in professional dialogues, peer coaches sometimes are too eager to communicate their ideas and classroom experiences, which does not always enhance reflection.

Trust, reflection, dedicated time, and a common language are recognized as essential elements necessary for positive forward shifts to occur in peer coaching (Robertson, 2005a; Wenger et al., 2002). It is critical that these elements are appreciated, fostered, and nurtured over time if peer coaching is to have a sustainable impact on improving instruction. Zwart, Wubbels, Bergen, and Bolhuis (2009) tell us that peers should acquire these needed attributes for productive peer coaching. In our experiences with coaching, we have found that after teacher-colleagues have been coached over time (usually 3 to 5 years), many feel comfortable taking on the role of a peer coach. In addition, time has to be allocated at the school level for teacher-colleagues as peer coaches to form trusting relationships. It is important that peer coaching is preceded with many opportunities to be coached first as a model for teacher colleagues to emulate.

Consistent benefits of peer coaching, such as encouragement, support, and learning from each other, are evident and well-documented in the literature (Anderson, Barksdale, & Hite, 2005; Donegan et al., 2000). By building strong peer coaching relationships within Multi-Tiered Systems of Support, teacher colleagues are empowered to seek solutions to improve transdisciplinary literacy instruction with research-validated practices. Another one of the strengths of peer coaching is that being a peer coach means that the coach must reflect on their own practices and those of their coaching partner.

Peer coaching can be utilized as a professional learning mechanism across the content areas. The current literature confirms that peer coaching can be an effective model that can be used to promote classroom implementation of research-validated practices to improve instruction. We also must acknowledge that there are limitations to what peer coaching can accomplish and its impact on improving instruction. Factors such as time, commitment, and varying levels of content knowledge can all influence the success or failure of peer coaching within Multi-Tiered Systems of Support frameworks to improve instruction and learning. If peer coaching is to be successful within Multi-Tiered Systems of Support, teacher-colleagues need to commit to the relationship and must be prepared to overcome hurdles, such as time or work commitments. However, if the right support is given by the literacy coach and if the peer coaches themselves have the necessary attributes and disposition, then peer coaching could be a worthwhile support mechanism within Multi-Tiered Systems of Support to ensure success.

## Application within Multi-Tiered Systems of Support

Fundamentally, due to the diverse culture among schools, districts, and provinces, there is no specific organized and detailed plan for employing distributive teacher leadership that will work for everyone everywhere. Schools and the communities are uniquely different. Additionally, while there may be specific publications on distributive teacher leadership, there are no specific infographics, decision trees, prescriptions, or recipes for implementation. But there are certain actions that can be taken to ensure that distributive teacher leadership is implemented authentically to serve a given school and community. Taking a pragmatic perspective, begin by recruiting a robust collaborative group of colleagues where leadership can be organically and genuinely distributive. Intentional and consistent collaboration is a competence that has to be procured, recurrent, and experienced with such a professional learning community of practice.

If genuine consideration is given to embracing distributive teacher leadership, then the actions taken to ensure transdisciplinary collaboration are critical. Leadership cannot be shared if teacher colleagues cannot work together across disciplines. Transdisciplinary collaboration is the primary groundwork for distributive teacher leadership, but it has to be intentional, mindful, and consistent. Collaboration has to extend beyond cooperation when sustainability and solution-seeking is the goal for improving instruction. The call to action is vigor and vigilance beyond rigor and relevance. It needs to be focused and disciplined to ensure forward shifts in learning outcomes (Jones & Harris, 2013). Moreover, outstanding group performance is accomplished through vigilant preparation, development, and self-regulation (Collins & Hansen, 2011). It demands structural alignment, a common language, and a growth mindset (Dweck & Yeager, 2019). For school, district, and province administrators pursuing school improvement, the adaptive challenge demands creating professional conditions of learning to enhance pedagogical/hebegogical content knowledge to cultivate a broad-spectrum learning environment redefining "school" as a place where learning takes place for ALL stakeholders.

## Emerging Understandings

Although we acknowledge that the principal of a school is the keystone, experience has taught us that schools, as a nuclear organization, are too multifaceted and complex for one individual to be solely responsible for forward shifts to occur. Forward shifts occur when knowledge is socially and collaboratively constructed. In other words, *distributive teacher leadership is not about holding people accountable; instead, it is about supporting people as they learn to hold themselves accountable*. As a side note, holding ourselves accountable is certainly a positive behavior and a good life skill to pass on to students as they transition from childhood through adolescence and into adulthood.

## Professional Conversation Prompts

The concept of distributive teacher leadership is grounded in the fact that no single individual can be everywhere, always, nor realistically and legally, be responsible for everything that occurs in schools on any given day. We reiterate that we acknowledge the significant roles of district, province, and school administrators, but we add the caveat that *productive leadership is about distributing decision-making power without abdicating responsibility*. Subsequently, we encourage designing a complex Multi-Tiered System of Support for developing distributive teacher leadership by revisiting the following questions as professional conversation starters. These reflective questions are offered to serve as a springboard for discussion and reflection to sustain the ongoing process:

a   What opportunities for distributive teacher leadership are available at the school level?
b   What opportunities for distributive teacher leadership are available at the district or province level?
c   What professional learning opportunities or pathways are available to develop distributive teacher leadership?
d   What are some common understandings or norms that need to be in place for distributive teacher leadership to occur?
e   What is a clear and succinct pathway for professional growth leading to distributive teacher leadership?
f   How will you deal with resistance to distributive teacher leadership at the school level and the district level?

## References

Anderson, N. A., Barksdale, M. A., & Hite, C. E. (2005). Preservice teachers' observations of cooperating teachers and peers while participating in an early field experience. *Teacher Education Quarterly, 32*(4), 97–117.

Biancarosa, G., & Snow, C. E. (2004). *Reading next: A vision for action and research in middle and high school literacy: A report from Carnegie Corporation of New York*. Alliance for Excellent Education.

Booth, D., & Rowsell, J. (2002). *The literacy principal: Leading, supporting and assessing reading and writing initiatives*. Portland, Maine: Stenhouse Publishers.

Brezicha, K., Bergmark, U., & Mitra, D. L. (2015). One size does not fit all: Differentiating leadership to support teachers in school reform. *Educational Administration Quarterly, 51*(1), 96–132.

Bronfenbrenner, U. (1979). Beyond the deficit model in child and family policy. *Teachers College Record, 81*(1), 1–6.

Bronfenbrenner, U. (1994). Ecological models of human development. In *International Encyclopedia of education*, 2nd ed. Oxford: Elsevier.

Bronfenbrenner, U., & Morris, P. A. (2007). The bioecological model of human development. In *Handbook of child psychology, 1*. Hoboken, NJ: John Wiley & Sons, Inc.

Cambourne, B. (1988). *The whole story: Natural learning and the acquisition of literacy in the classroom*. Australia: Ashton Scholastic.

Casey, K. (2006). *Literacy coaching: The essentials*. Portsmouth, NH: Heinemann.

Cazden, C. B. (1988). *Classroom discourse: The language of teaching and learning*. Portsmouth, NH: Heinemann.

Clay, M. M. (2015). *Change over time in children's literacy development*. Portsmouth, NH: Heinemann

Collins, J., & Hansen, M. (2011) *Great by choice*. New York: Harper Business Press.

Costa, A. L., & Garmston, R. J. (2002). *Cognitive coaching: A foundation for renaissance schools*. Norwood, MA: Christopher-Gordon Publishers, Inc.

Craig, P. (2006). *Literacy leadership teams: Collaborative leadership for improving and sustaining student achievement*. Routledge.

Daly, A. J., Moolenaar, N. M., Bolivar, J. M., & Burke, P. (2010). Relationships in reform: The role of teachers' social networks. *Journal of Educational Administration, 48*(3), 359–391.

Darling-Hammond, L. (2005). Teaching as a profession: Lessons in teacher preparation and professional development. *Phi delta kappan, 87*(3), 237–240.

Donegan, M. M., Ostrosky, M. M., & Fowler, S. A. (2000). Peer coaching: Teachers supporting teachers. *Young Exceptional Children, 3*(9), 9–16.

Dweck, C. S., & Yeager, D. S. (2019). Mindsets: A view from two eras. *Perspectives on Psychological Science, 14*(3), 481–496.

Fairman, J. C., & Mackenzie, S. V. (2015). How teacher leaders influence others and understand their leadership. *International Journal of Leadership in Education, 18*(1), 61–87.

Forsyth, P. B., Adams, C. M., & Hoy, W. K. (2011). Collective trust. *Why schools can't improve*, 101–171.

Froelich, K. S., & Puig, E. A. (2010). *The literacy leadership team: Sustaining and expanding success*. Boston, MA: Allyn & Bacon.

Fullan, M. (2004). *Leadership & sustainability: System thinkers in action*. Corwin Press.

Fullan, M., Hill, P., & Crévola, C. (Eds.). (2006). *Breakthrough*. Corwin Press.

Gaffney, J. S., & Askew, B. J. (1999). *Stirring the Waters: The Influence of Marie Clay*. Portsmouth, NH: Heinemann.

González, N., Moll, L., & Amanti, C. (2005). *Funds of knowledge: Theorizing practices in households, communities, and classrooms*. New York: Routledge

Hallinger, P. (2011). Leadership for learning: Lessons from 40 years of empirical research. *Journal of Educational Administration, 49*(2), 125–142.

Hallinger, P., & Heck, R. H. (2009). Distributed leadership in schools: Does system policy make a difference? In *Distributed leadership: Different perspectives* (pp. 101–117). Dordrecht: Springer Netherlands.

Hargreaves, A., Boyle, A., & Harris, A. (2014) *Uplifting leadership*. Hoboken, NJ: Jossey Bass.

Harris, A. (2013) *Distributive leadership matters*. Thousand Oaks, CA: Corwin Press.

Hattie, J. (2009). *Visible learning: A synthesis of over 800 meta-analyses relating to achievement*. Oxford: Routledge.

Hill, P. W., & Crévola, C. A. (1999). Key Features of a whole-school, design approach to literacy teaching in schools. *Australian Journal of Learning Difficulties, 4*(3), 5–11.

Holloway, J., Nielsen, A., & Saltmarsh, S. (2018). Prescribed distributed leadership in the era of accountability: The experiences of mentor teachers. *Educational Management Administration & Leadership, 46*(4), 538–555.

Hord, S. (2004). *Learning together, leading together: Changing schools through professional learning communities*. Teachers College Press.

Isaacson, S. (2017). Instruction that helps students meet state standards in writing. In *Students who are exceptional and writing disabilities* (pp. 39–54). Routledge

Jackson, P. (2004). Understanding the experience of experience: A practical model of reflective practice for coaching. *International Journal of Evidence Based Coaching and Mentoring,2*(1), 57–67.

Jones, M., & Harris, A. (2013) Disciplined collaboration: Professional learning with impact. *Professional Development Today, 15*(4), 13–23.

Joyce, B., & Showers, B. (1982). The coaching of teaching. *Educational Leadership, 40*(1), 4.

Killion, J. (2016). Changes in coaching study design shed light on how features impact teacher practice. *The Learning Professional, 37*(2), 58.

Knight, J. (2007). *Instructional coaching: A partnership approach to improving instruction*. Thousand Oaks, CA: Corwin Press.

Knight, S. L., & Stallings, J. A. (1995). The implementation of the Accelerated School model in an urban elementary school. In *No quick fix: Rethinking literacy programs in America's elementary schools*, 236–252.

Ladyshewsky, R. K. (2006). Peer coaching: A constructivist methodology for enhancing critical thinking in postgraduate business education. *Higher Education Research & Development, 25*(1), 67–84.

Langer, J. A. (2000). Excellence in English in middle and high school: How teachers' professional lives support student achievement. *American Educational Research Journal, 37*(2), 397–439.

Lee, M., Hallinger, P., & Walker, A. (2012). A distributed perspective on instructional leadership in International Baccalaureate (IB) schools. *Educational Administration Quarterly, 48*(4), 664–698.

Leithwood, K., & Mascall, B. (2008). Collective leadership effects on student achievement. *Educational Administration Quarterly, 44*(4), 529–561.

Leithwood, K., Mascall, B., & Strauss, T. (2009). *Distributive leadership according to the evidence.* London: Routledge.

Loughran, J. J. (2002). Effective reflective practice: In search of meaning in learning about teaching. *Journal of Teacher Education, 53*(1), 33–43.

Lu, H. (2010). Research on peer coaching in preservice teacher education—A review of literature. *Teaching and Teacher Education, 26*, 748–753.

Lyons, C. A., & Pinnell, G. S. (2001). *Systems for change in literacy education: A guide to professional development.* Heinemann, Portsmouth, NH.

Maden, M. (2001). *Success against the odds: Five years on.* London: Routledge

Maden, M., & Hillman, J. (1996). Lessons in success. *National Commission on Education, Success Against the Odds.* London: Routledge.

Pennell, C. (2020). *Evaluating the K–12 literacy curriculum: A step by step guide for auditing programs, materials, and instructional approaches.* Routledge.

Portin, B. S., Russell, F. A., Samuelson, C., & Knapp, M. S. (2013). Leading learning-focused teacher leadership in urban high schools. *Journal of School Leadership, 23*(2), 220–252.

Puig, E. A., & Froelich, K. S. (2011). *The literacy coach: Guiding in the right direction,* 2nd ed. Boston: Pearson/Allyn and Bacon.

Puig, E. A., & Froelich, K. S. (2022). *Teaching K–12 transdisciplinary literacy: A comprehensive instructional framework for learning and leading.* New York: Routledge.

Robertson, J. (2005a). *Coaching leadership: Building educational leadership capacity through coaching partnerships.* Wellington: New Zealand: NZCER Press.

Robertson, K. (2005b). Active listening: More than just paying attention. *Australian Family Physician, 34*(12), 1053–1055.

Ross, J. A. (1992). Teacher efficacy and the effects of coaching on student achievement. *Canadian Journal of Education/Revue canadienne de l'education,* 51–65.

Showers, B., & Joyce, B. (1996). The evolution of peer coaching. *Educational Leadership, 53*(6), 12–16.

Slater, C. L., & Simmons, D. L. (2001). The design and implementation of a peer coaching program. *American Secondary Education, 29*(3), 67–76.

Spillane, J. P., Halverson, R., & Diamond, J. B. (2001). Investigating school leadership practice: A distributed perspective. *Educational Researcher, 30*(3), 23–28.

Tharp, R. G., & Gallimore, R. (1988). *Rousing minds to life: Teaching and learning in social context.* New York: Cambridge University Press.

Toll, C. A. (2004). *The literacy coach's survival guide: Essential questions and practical answers*. Newark, DE: International Reading Association.

Veenman, S., & Denessen, E. (2001). The coaching of teachers: Results of five training studies. *Educational Research and Evaluation, 7*(4), 385–417.

Walpole, S., & McKenna, M. C. (2004). *The literacy coach's handbook: A guide to research-based practice*. New York: Guilford.

Weiner, J., & Woulfin, S. L. (2018). Sailing across the divide: Challenges to the transfer of teacher leadership. *Journal of Research on Leadership Education, 13*(3), 210–234.

Wenger, E., McDermott, R., & Snyder, W. M. (2002). *Managing organizational knowledge through communities of practice*. Boston, MA: Harvard Business School Press.

Zwart, R. C., Wubbels, T., Bergen, T., & Bolhuis, S. (2009). Which characteristics of a reciprocal peer coaching context affect teacher learning as perceived by teachers and their students? *Journal of Teacher Education, 60*(3), 243–257.

# Multi-Tiered System for Response to Intervention/Instruction

*Education is not preparation for life; education is life itself.*
—John Dewey

## RtI/I within Multi-Tiered Systems of Support

Historically, public schools have not been successful in providing instruction, interventions, and sufficient supports and enhancements to all students, specifically students from diverse backgrounds, leading to lower academic performance, higher dropout rates, negative behavioral and social outcomes, and limited prospects for higher education (Jackson, 2021). This is particularly worrisome, considering that more than 55% of students come from diverse backgrounds (Office of Special Education Programs, 2021). Federal legislation and policies were enacted as comprehensive approaches that emphasized equity and instructional approaches to improve educational opportunities and results for every student, including those who have faced historical disadvantages and marginalization (IDEA, 1997). Multiple policies were enacted separately during the last 45 years to address this goal. Currently, Multi-Tiered Systems of Support (MTSS) presents a comprehensive framework for schools, districts, and provinces, to integrate fundamental educational practices to address equity and support the academic, behavioral, and social-emotional learning of all students through data-informed decision-making and research-validated, tiered instruction and supports (Jackson, 2021). Response to Intervention/Instruction (RtI/I) is a component, a system, for developing a harmonic and comprehensive

DOI: 10.4324/9781032707976-9

MTSS for improving the academic and behavioral outcomes for all students through legislation, policies, and implementation.

Daily, teachers and other educators strive to improve learning and outcomes for students. This goal is achieved through the continuous use of multiple assessments, research-validated practices, and interventions by teachers and other school professionals within a solution-seeking process. Screening measures, diagnostic assessments, and the continuous progress monitoring of students' learning over time provide data and ongoing response to teachers, who, in turn, utilize data collected from assessments to inform instruction. This data-informed decision-making process is used for many purposes including classroom instruction, accountability, and continuous progress monitoring as part of the RtI/I system within MTSS in classrooms and schools. This process of data-informed decision-making is central to the interpretation and use of assessment data for classroom instruction and intervention. But how are all these processes, terms, procedures, and frameworks connected? More importantly, how do these processes appropriately contribute to meeting the instructional strengths and needs of students by their teachers and other school personnel?

All students require access to general education curriculum content. However, some students may require additional support to fully access and master the curriculum content. RtI/I is a comprehensive, systemic continuum of the use of research-validated instructional practices that facilitates an immediate response to students' needs by leveraging student strengths through data-informed decision-making (Little et al., 2024a). RtI/I has evolved over time to encompass a comprehensive data-informed decision-making approach that addresses academics, behavior, and social-emotional learning.

The conceptualization and implementation of an RtI/I builds upon previous United States federal legislation, such as the Individuals with Disabilities Education Act (1997) in special education and the Every Student Succeeds Act, 2015. RtI was described in the special education policy and procedures to provide early intervention approaches and services prior to identification of students with a disability. MTSS, however, is a promising general education initiative (Batsche, 2014; Stoiber, 2014) which has the potential to prevent learning issues through proactive, solution-seeking approaches to instruction by differentiating and intensifying pedagogical and hebegogical research-validated instructional practices (Miciak et al., 2020). Additionally, we include hebegogical and andragogical practices. Subsequent research has supported its implementation and results (e.g., Hoover & Soltero-González, 2018; Lemons et al., 2017). In addition to systematic and explicit instruction, the overall goal of RtI/I is to promote and implement a coherent and intentional system of instruction and intervention by connecting multiple factors to enhance teacher and student learning.

Ideally, RtI/I within MTSS provides and matches high-quality research-validated instructional practices and curricular resources to students' strengths and needs academically, behaviorally, and socially (Leonard et al., 2019). The main components of an RtI/I model include: (a) high-quality, differentiated classroom instruction for all students; (b) systemic and sustainable change; (c) integrated data system; and (d) positive behavioral support (CEEDAR, n.d.). Furthermore, the critical features of these components include universal screening, data-informed decision-making and solution seeking, continuous progress monitoring, focus on successful outcomes, and continuum of research-validated interventions. These components have evolved over time and build upon previous legislation in special education to enhance educational policies and initiatives for all students.

# Response to Intervention/Instruction (RtI/I)

Within the proposed MTSS framework is Response to Intervention/Instruction (RtI/I), a tiered approach to identifying strengths and supporting students with academic and behavioral needs. The purpose of RtI/I is to address holistic educational concerns to improve academic and behavioral outcomes. RtI/I was originally designed to detect potential learning disabilities with students, enhance the intensity of instruction, and offer academic opportunities to students (Little, 2009; Little, 2012; Pullen et al., 2018). RtI/I involves varying high-leverage practices (Council for Exceptional Children, 2017) and levels of progressively intensive, research-validated interventions. RtI/I is characterized by cultural and linguistic responsiveness, use of static and dynamic assessments, and employing research-validated intervention practices. According to the National Center on Intensive Interventions (n.d.), RtI/I consists of four components: (a) universal broad-spectrum screening; (b) research-validated practices and instruction; (c) progress monitoring; and (d) tiered instruction (broad-spectrum, targeted, and intensive).

# Positive Behavioral Interventions and Supports (PBIS)

Positive Behavioral Interventions and Supports (PBIS) is a research-validated, tiered framework for supporting *students'* behavioral, social, emotional, and mental health needs. When implemented with fidelity, improved social emotional competence, classroom behavior, and school climate can be achieved. It also improves teacher health and well-being. It is a way to create positive, predictable, equitable and safe learning environments where everyone thrives (PBIS, n.d.). According to the Center on Positive Behavioral Interventions and Supports, PBIS has been adopted by over 25,000 schools and can create an equitable and responsive school environment where all students have an opportunity to flourish.

Supported within a tiered model, students receive proactive and preventative universal supports delivered schoolwide during Tier 1 instruction. Teacher-colleagues and teacher leaders focus on assisting students to develop the necessary social skills to meet and exceed state standards. During Tier 2 and Tier 3, students receive targeted and intensive behavioral supports designed to meet their individual strengths and needs. An effective PBIS system prioritizes equity, student center outcomes, utilizes data, emphasizes research-validated equitable behavioral practices, and invests in systems that support fidelity of implementation (PBIS, n.d.). PBIS has been linked to improved behavior and academic outcomes (Kittelman et al., 2019).

# Social Emotional Learning Supports

Incorporating Social Emotional Learning (SEL) supports into a harmonic and comprehensive RtI/I model provides a solid foundation for addressing the diverse strengths and needs of students (Lane, 2007). RtI/I with embedded SEL serves as a catalyst and conduit for an equity-focused school revitalization that addresses the strengths and needs of students who require additional supports that can address both behavior and academic needs. Similar to PBIS, Tier 1 of SEL within an RtI/I model allows for schoolwide adoption of social emotional intervention strategic practices and professional learning opportunities teacher-colleagues of research-validated practices for students (Steed & Shapland, 2020). At Tiers 2 and 3, educators can implement targeted and intensive SEL supports for students who require individualized supports if they are experiencing trauma or show signs of aggression or anxiety. As SEL continues to be embedded within an RtI/I model and research continues to be developed in this area, culturally responsive practices are being more intentionally addressed (Steed & Shapland, 2020).

# Implementing RtI/I within MTSS

An RtI/I model within a MTSS framework provides a harmonic, comprehensive, flexible, asset-based structure to assure students receive quality instruction and interventions within a continuum of tiers through ongoing, solution-seeking processes to address academic, behavioral, social, emotional, and mental health needs grounded on students' strengths. Within analogous tiered instructional harmonic networks of RtI/I, PBIS, and SEL, teacher-colleagues and teacher leaders provide supports and interventions with increasing intensity over time. The proposed harmonic and comprehensive MTSS framework, in this text, promotes proactive solution seeking to preempt, intercept, and intervene with students in academic, behavioral, social, emotional, and mental health areas as well as serving as the basis for determining a student's eligibility for special services in many states and provinces.

Within the RtI/I model, data-informed decision-making is integral to implementation. Educators realize that data-informed decision-making is essential to instructional planning to address and enhance student outcomes. Data-informed decision-making is a continuous use of static and dynamic assessment data to determine *when* and *how* to intensify instruction and intervention (Wanzek & Vaughn, 2009) to address student strengths and needs. As educators collect data and adjust instruction, decisions are made about the need to intensify instruction either through frequency (additional sessions), duration (increased time), and group size.

Throughout the RtI/I model, educators use data-informed decision-making to identify students who are surpassing or achieving the instructional goals and those not responding positively to instruction. Based on students' strengths and needs, a team of educators determine specific, additional instructional goals based on the data and provide more intensive intervention (Gesel et al., 2021). Educators meet the strengths and needs of students using static and dynamic assessments sensitive to and directly linked to instruction, allowing them to make informed decisions about curriculum content, resources, and accommodations for high-progress to low-progress learners through solution-seeking data-informed decision-making within the tiers of the RtI/I model.

# Data-Informed Decision-Making within RtI/I

Data-informed decision-making, also referred to as action research, is a process of describing and testing theories through which teacher-colleagues study student learning related to classroom instruction (Yendol-Hoppey & Fichtman, 2020). This model of professional learning requires teacher-colleagues to know about data collection, research-validated instructional practices and interventions, and assessments used in classrooms. With that knowledge, teacher-colleagues systematically and intentionally reflect on their practice and make changes to their instruction based on careful analysis of current classroom performance of their students (Efron & Ravid, 2020). As teacher-colleagues continue to teach, employ new practices and resources, and reflect on results, the goal is to improve student learning (Sagor & Williams, 2016). Conducting applied action research using data-informed decision-making has been described as empowering for teachers, giving them opportunities to grow within their professional roles and responsibilities (Gesel et al., 2021; Yendol-Hoppey & Fichtman, 2020). The data-informed decision-making process of action research is so continuous and fluid that most teacher-colleagues complete data-informed decision-making cycles without realizing it. As described, the data-informed decision-making process addresses the following key steps: (1) Identify the issue at hand, (2) Develop and implement a solution, (3) Collect and analyze data related to the solution, and (4) Reflect and share the results (See Figure 9.1).

Daily, teacher-colleagues document and collect static and dynamic data through formal and informal assessment procedures, then make decisions about needed research-validated instructional methods and resources (Yendol-Hoppey & Fichtman, 2020). This knowledge empowers teachers to use the documented data collected to enact instructional changes. Data are used to support and justify decisions because documented data collection continues throughout the process from identification of the issue to implementation of instructional practices and interventions and beyond. Progress monitoring through continuous, intentional, and coherent assessments allow teacher-colleagues to not only monitor student progress to determine the impact of the instructional plan, but also make changes and adjustments as warranted by student strengths and needs.

It is important to note that documented data collection need not necessitate "extra" work on the part of the teacher. Teachers already use documented formal and informal assessments in their classroom, as well as have accessing to both district and state assessment results for their students. Implementing an RtI/I model does not mean more testing; it means carefully analyzing results from current, purposeful assessment, and then reflecting on whether the instructional methods resulted in improved students learning to master and exceed skills aligned with state standards (Efron & Ravid, 2020). Teachers analyze data from documented observations of student behavior or other informal measures in addition to data collected from more formal assessments. Classroom static and dynamic assessments provide needed information about student learning for teachers to improve their practice.

Data-informed decision-making is enhanced when done in collaboration with other professionals. It allows teacher-colleagues and other school personnel (e.g., administrator, literacy coach, media specialist, speech language pathologist, audiologist, school psychologist, etc.) to ideate by sharing ideas, comparing, contrasting, interpreting, and concluding. This is especially important if initial solutions from the data-informed decision-making process did not address the instructional concerns for all of the students. Through the data-informed decision-making process, teacher-colleagues and other educators review and interpret available documented assessment data as part of their discussions. In this way, collaborative data-informed decision-making enhances participants' depth of understanding and interpretations of static and dynamic data as a result of discussions during data meetings, lesson studies, professional learning opportunities within a professional learning community of practice, especially when the focus is to determine the impact of instruction on student learning.

# Recursive Data-Informed Decision-Making within the RtI/I Model

Response to Intervention/Instruction (RtI/I) is a coherent and intentional, data-informed model for identifying, defining, and resolving instructional issues that relies on collaborative multi-tiered systems. Central to implementation of RtI/I is the expert use of research-validated instructional practices, resources, and strategic actions within a learning environment while continuously monitoring student learning formally and informally. There are two overarching goals of RtI/I: (a) to deliver research-validated instruction and interventions to improve student learning; and (b) to collect information regarding students' response to instruction and intervention.

RtI/I procedures provide the framework to continuously use data-informed decision-making related to instruction, interventions, and program placements for specific students (Little, 2012; Little et al., 2024a). The process of data-informed decision-making is at the nexus of implementation of the RtI/I model to use multiple sources of static and dynamic assessments as the basis for specific instruction and interventions for students. The data-informed-decision making used within RtI/I occurs as members of the school-based team ideate by identifying the issue, researching, and implementing various research-validated practices, and intervening to address the instructional issue and collect data to determine the effectiveness of instruction and the intervention (see Figure 9.1).

Through continued learning to situate and address complex strengths and needs of the students in our classrooms, static and dynamic data are used to address the instructional strengths and needs of students in classrooms and schools. Teacher-colleagues, instructional coaches, and other educators review the educational issues at hand to investigate data during the team meetings to construct, deconstruct, and co-construct innovative and unique solutions. Using the data-informed decision-making process, current static and dynamic assessment data are reviewed, hypotheses are developed, and the results of specific instructional practices and interventions are investigated and shared among educators (e.g., teacher, literacy coach, teacher leaders, special education teacher, speech-language pathologist, etc.). Eventually, a gradual blurring of roles occurs, as each shares their knowledge, experiences, and expertise and learn from their collaborators. During the collective work of these RtI/I teams of teacher-colleagues and teacher leaders, important questions may include:

- What do students know, what do they need to know, and what should they be able to do?
- What will we do to assure learning?

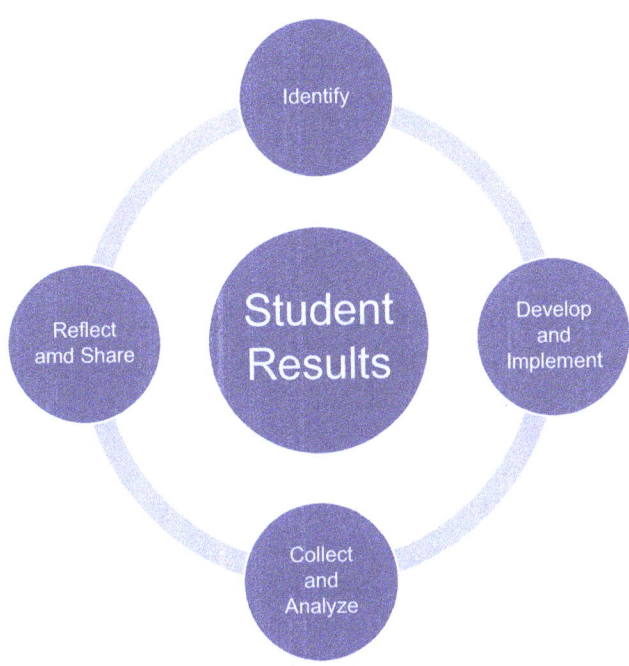

*Figure 9.1* The RtI/I Data-Informed Decision-Making Cycle

- How will we know when they have learned it?
- What additional supports may be needed?
- What are some potential challenges or unintended consequences?

This dynamic and iterative data-informed decision-making process is the foundation for professional learning and, consequently, student improvement within classrooms and schools during implementation of an RtI/I model. Whether the process is focused on grade-based assessment results from district standardized testing or on individual student results after intensive interventions, the data-informed decision-making process is implemented by teacher-colleagues and teacher leaders to develop a school-wide RtI/I system of support for all students by educators through careful examination of documented assessment data to address critical instructional questions by members of school-based teams within each of the tiers.

The RtI/I model, as well as other multi-tiered systems of support, is often depicted as a three-tier model. The cyclical data-informed decision-making process to define, analyze, implement, and evaluate is central to this model when determining instruction and intervention supports for students within the tiers of instruction. The cycle of data-informed decision-making is dynamically employed and refined teams within the RtI/I model as teams of educators develop broad-spectrum core, targeted, and/or intervention plans that address academic or behavioral issues that may be impeding student learning.

## Tier 1 Universal, Broad-Spectrum, Core Intervention/Instruction

All students are exposed to Tier 1 instruction, which is broad-spectrum core classroom instruction to receive research-validated coherent and intentional instruction to address and exceed the curricular state standards. Tier 1 instruction is designed to enhance and accelerate learning to prevent academic failure and reduce inappropriate referrals to special education and other educational services. Instruction during Tier 1 is universal, whole-class instruction, which includes flexible grouping and differentiation. This means that *all* students, with and without disabilities, are receiving well-differentiated, broad-spectrum core instruction with flexible grouping and differentiation. Teachers use multiple sources of both static and dynamic assessments to observe and address students' learning, collecting frequent data to inform their instructional decision-making. Teachers and teacher leaders are responsible and self-accountable to questioning, learning, implementing, and coaching each other to continuously improve and enhance their use of research-validated instructional practices. Collaboration is important to identify, use, and interpret multiple sources of data to ensure all students feel safe and that they are successful in the learning environment. The purpose of ongoing progress monitoring assessment is to determine the students' strengths and who may need additional, targeted interventions at Tier 2. As teachers observe the learning of the students within their classrooms, it may be helpful to note some of their concerns. Teachers often keep anecdotal observations about their students, the learning, the responses to specific lessons and activities to reflect upon for continuous planning. As teachers are involved in these reflections, it may be helpful to record specific issues as initial plans for the data-informed decision-making process.

This initial planning may include documenting initial teacher observations of possible instructional concerns for students, either a small group or an individual, within the classroom. Discussions to learn more about whole-group instruction during Tier 1 at school-wide data meetings could include the following topics:

1. Is the core research-validated instruction well-delivered? Is the literacy coach available to respond? Are lessons aligned with curricular state standards?
2. What assessments or processes were used to identify instructional strengths and needs and the students' response to instruction/intervention?
3. Is the core instruction effective? What percent of students are achieving standards/benchmarks (approximately 80% or more)? What percent of students in subgroups are achieving standards/benchmarks (approximately 80% or more)? What percent of students, in the subgroup to which the referred student belongs, achieved benchmarks?

## Tier 2 Targeted, Small-Group Intervention/Instruction

In Tier 2, supplemental, targeted instruction, supports and intervention are provided in a small-group setting with increased progress monitoring for students who have not mastered curricular goals from Tier 1 core instruction. For students who are not learning nor making adequate progress in the Tier 1 core curriculum as determined by static and dynamic assessments, teacher-colleagues then combine their core instruction with more targeted, intense instruction/interventions for a smaller group of students. It is important to understand that tiers are additive, not replacement, instruction. So, students who require more intensive intervention receive Tier 1 core instruction plus Tier 2 targeted instruction. This additional, supplemental support is called Tier 2 targeted instruction and intervention. This level of teaching consists of targeted, supplemental interventions aligned with the core curriculum. Provided that additional time is added to the school day, Tier 2 support can be provided by the classroom teacher, the special education teacher within the general education setting, or by school support faculty. These interventions are delivered in a small-group format using research-validated practices known to be effective in addressing the curriculum content for low-progress learners. Static assessments are used to inform instruction while dynamic assessments are used to adjust instruction and intervention, as well as document learning over time. Based upon student results of the static and dynamic assessments in Tier 2, students receive more or less intense instruction.

Discussions to learn more about instruction and interventions during Tier 2 at school-wide meetings could include the group reflection questions:

1. What specific supplemental instruction was implemented to improve the performance of students who are not yet mastering the curriculum content?
2. What improvements in student learning resulted from instructional changes such as more exposure, more practice, more focus, or smaller group size?
3. How effective is supplemental instruction for groups of students struggling with the curriculum content?
4. What progress monitoring assessments were used for ongoing data collection? How frequently were assessments conducted?

During Tier 2, a collaborative data-informed decision-making team, consisting of teachers, transdisciplinary literacy coaches, behavioral specialists, and/or other school-based personnel, enhance and differentiate large- and small-group instruction and interventions to support solutions during the data-informed decision-making process. Core instruction will be delivered by classroom teachers. Interventionists and/or other professionals may assist in providing interventions to small groups of identified students. Academic interventionists, transdisciplinary literacy coaches, special education teachers, and/or curriculum resource teachers may also offer collaborative, consultative, and/or coaching to enhance and support the learning by the teacher to address unique instructional strengths and needs of students not yet mastering instructional goals, as determined by static and dynamic assessments. Students who positively respond to the Tier 2 interventions may no longer need Tier 2 interventions. If more intensive interventions are determined as needed by the team of educators, Tier 3 interventions and/or services may be warranted.

# Tier 3 Intensive Individual Intervention/Instruction

Even with targeted instructional efforts in small groups, there will be a small percentage of students who will not respond sufficiently to Tier 1 instruction and Tier 2 interventions. These students will require more intensive support. In Tier 3, students are provided with one-on-one intensive instruction to meet their individual strengths and needs, and progress monitoring and intervention are augmented. Usually delivered by educators with specific training, Tier 3 intervention is intensive, in both the duration and frequency of intervention, while increasing focus on how students are processing information, not just acquiring item knowledge. *Tier 3 instruction must be provided by highly effective interventionists who have a clear understanding of literacy learning as a process and understand that scaffolding instruction can only occur when students' strengths and processing deficits are recognized.* Specific intervention plans, developed through a process called Data-Based Individualization (DBI), may be developed to address specific intervention and progress monitoring strengths, and needs of the students (NCII, n.d.). Tier 3 does replace Tier 2 instruction, but, like Tier 2, Tier 3 instruction supports and *does not* replace the general, core curriculum content – it is in addition to instruction in core curriculum content that each student receives. To determine whether instruction and interventions have been successful, teacher-colleagues and members of the school-based team continue to collect static and dynamic assessment data. It is important to collect sufficient data to determine if students are responding to high-quality instruction and interventions delivered with coherence and intentionality in order to further modify/inform instruction and interventions as determined by educators through the DBI process (NCII, n.d.).

DBI is a systematic method for using data to determine *when and how* to individualize and intensify intervention for students with severe and persistent learning and behavioral needs. DBI is grounded in experimental teaching research conducted by Deno and Mirkin at the University of Minnesota and expanded upon by others (Marston et al., 2003). The DBI process integrates research-validated intervention, assessment, and strategic practices (NCII, n.d.). It was developed and refined to address the academic and behavioral needs of students with persistent and severe needs, often within Tiers 2 and 3. With the data, meaningful decisions about the impact of the instruction and interventions are determined, as to continuation or revision of the interventions as a response to intervention/instruction.

Discussions to learn more about services and interventions during Tier 3 at school-wide meetings could include the following group reflection questions:

1 What specific supplemental interventions and/or services were implemented to improve the performance of students who are not yet mastering the content?
2 What specific, individualized, intensive instruction/intervention was implemented to improve the performance of the student (more exposure, more practice, more focus, smaller group, type of delivery, program, in addition to and aligned with core instruction, etc.)?
3 How much additional time, focus of the instruction/intervention, specific instructional practices and evidence of coherence and intentionality of instruction were implemented?
4 How effective were the intensive interventions for identified, individual students?
5 What assessments were used for on-going data collection? How frequently were assessments conducted? What is known about student processing and learning?

In reality, DBI is the technical term for what many good teachers do naturally through the data-informed decision-making process – frequently review student data and make changes to their teaching based on what works for individual students. DBI, however, makes this process coherent, intentional, systematic, explicit, and tailored to meet the strengths and needs of individual students through a multistep process that gradually intensifies instruction, interventions, and support.

To effectively deliver Tier 3 instruction, the roles of teachers, transdisciplinary literacy coaches, interventionists, behavioral specialists, and others will be expanded to enhance and synergize solutions. With the necessary credentials, curriculum resource teachers, interventionists, and special education teachers may provide the specialized, intensive interventions. We have found that it is incredibly challenging, primarily due to scheduling issues, for general education classroom teachers to deliver Tier 3 instruction. The specific knowledge and competencies of each educator are important during this process. In addition, the specified, static (summative), and dynamic (formative) assessment data collected as a result of high-quality intensive instruction using research-validated practices within an RtI/I model are important in the determination of eligibility of a possible disability (Slanda & Little, 2018), if this is warranted for an individual student.

Since Tier 3 is the most intense level of instruction/intervention, a student who does not respond to Tier 3 interventions may qualify for special education services or other school services. Therefore, throughout instruction, intervention, and assessment within the tiers, educators on school-based teams document the early intervening services provided to students during the various tiers as part of the instructional decision-making or eligibility process.

Emerging research is showing that students who receive intensive instruction are able to make significant gains when interventions are aligned with their specific strengths and needs. Individualized supports and specially designed instruction are sustained when a student is not responsive to tiered interventions and is determined eligible for special education services. In fact, data-informed decision-making is integral to the Individualized Education Plan (IEP) process and should be used in IEP design, implementation, and evaluation. Delivering special education services provides students with disabilities productive access to general education curriculum content.

High-quality instruction using research-validated practices, additional resources, collaborative expertise, interventions, differentiation, and scaffolded support must be considered and implemented in classrooms within networked systems of support during each of the tiers (Leonard et al., 2019; Little et al., 2024b). Classroom instruction may be differentiated and intensified based upon the instructional strengths and needs of the students, within the large group and as individuals within the classroom. Static (summative) and dynamic (formative) assessments are the primary sources of information, along with documented teacher observations, about the student's learning which serves as the basis for instructional decisions.

These three RtI/I tiers are integrated and implemented within other coordinated and comprehensive MTSS. Since the goal is to improve instruction and increase learning for all students, teachers and teacher leaders must be the primary participants in the data-informed decision-making process. To assist these discussions during each of the three RtI/I tiers, see the questions to consider during MTSS meetings (see Table 9.1) This comprehensive and continuous process, however, may include other educators (e.g. teachers, transdisciplinary literacy coaches, school psychologists, special education teachers, etc.) on the school-based team to help identify and participate in solution seeking to improve learning and instruction. This may require all to learn new methods and use new curricular resources to teach and differentiate instruction within a dynamic and complex MTSS in a harmonic manner.

With the common goal of improving student learning for all students, the continuous use of the data-informed decision-making process is necessary throughout the tiers within the RtI/I model to plan, implement, and reflect upon student learning as a result of classroom instruction and intervention methods, procedures, and resources. With a focus on professional learning, improving student learning requires proactive approaches in the learning and leading process. Teacher-colleagues, teacher leaders, and students must be involved in the decisions that directly affect that process. The cyclical format of data-informed decision-making is consistently used within each of the three tiers. As educators engage in data-informed decision-making as part of the RtI/I school-based model, they become empowered agents of change. Teachers are consciously planning for changes in their classroom and using data to plan and to monitor students' learning. Use of research-validated instructional methods and progress monitoring assessments continues through the tiers in an RtI/I model, with increasing intensity and interventions, until student improvement comes to fruition. This cyclical process provides a forum for harmonic, synergistic, collaborative discussions, and decision-making among members of the RtI/I team. The essence of an RtI/I model is to understand and continuously employ the data-informed decision-making process by members of school-based teams to develop unique solutions for students from multiple sources of assessment data to determine, implement, and assess specific action plans. Table 9.2 provides a sample action plan for initial planning purposes. Although the specific titles of the steps or phases of data-informed decision-making and the number of tiers and model used in RtI/I may vary, the processes and goals are similar. Teachers and teacher leaders identify instructional issues when reviewing assessment information (data) and collaboratively develop an action plan for instruction or intervention. Monitoring the results of the action plan in terms of student results provides additional information. These activities continue throughout each of the tiers within the RtI/I model to ensure increased intensity of interventions within classrooms prior to determining eligibility for other programs,

Multi-Tiered System for Response to Intervention/Instruction

*Table 9.1* Questions to Consider during RtI/I Team Meetings

| Questions to Consider | Current Status | Next Steps |
|---|---|---|
| **Tier 1** | | |
| Is core instruction research-validated and well-delivered? Is the literacy coach available to provide a response? | | |
| What assessment tools or processes were used? How were decisions re: differentiation and small groups made? | | |
| Is core instruction effective for all students? How do you know? | | |
| **Tier 2** | | |
| What specific supplemental instruction was implemented? How often? Aligned? | | |
| Was additional time, more practice, more focus, smaller group, type of delivery provided? | | |
| How effective is supplemental instruction? How do you know? | | |
| What progress monitoring assessments were used? How often? Results? | | |
| **Tier 3** | | |
| What specific intensive instruction and interventions were implemented? How often? Aligned? | | |
| Was additional time, more practice, more focus, smaller group or individual, delivery provided? | | |
| How effective is intensive intervention? How do you know? | | |
| What progress monitoring assessments were used? How often? Results? | | |
| What additional educators and/or resources were provided? | | |

Summary Discussions by Members of the MTSS Team: _____

_____

Date of Next Meeting: _____

Table 9.2 Initial Planning for DATA-INFORMED DECISION-MAKING

| DATA-INFORMED DECISION-MAKING Planning Form | | |
|---|---|---|
| School: | Classroom Teacher's Name: | Grade Level/ Subject Area: |
| MTSS Team Members: | | Date: |
| Defining an Issue | | |
| What is the expected level of performance? | | |
| What is the current level of student(s) performance? What assessment was used? | | |
| What is the current level of peer performance? | | |
| What are the areas of need? Is this a whole group, small group, or individual student problem? | | |
| What are the instructional expectations/goals for the student(s) related to the identified problem? | | |
| What is the gap between expected level of performance and the actual current level of student(s) performance? | | |

such as those concerned with special education. Even though the names and specific procedures may vary slightly, the underlying goals, concepts, necessary skills, and data-informed decision-making processes are critical to the implementation of RtI/I. Table 9.2 is a sample form to support data-informed decision-making.

# Unintended Consequences

It is important to acknowledge the initiation of Response to Intervention (RtI) as a policy. First mentioned in the *Individuals with Disabilities Education Act* (IDEA, 1997), this process of instruction, assessments, and interventions was perceived as a system to determine the eligibility of special education services, as RtI was initially described within legislation authorizing special education services. However, the Every Student Succeeds Act (2015) reemphasized the use of a multi-tier framework, describing it as a comprehensive continuum of evidence-based, systemic practices to support an immediate response to student needs through data-informed instructional decision-making (Little et al., 2024b). Specifically, the Every Student Succeeds Act (2015) recognized the use of Multi-Tier Systems of Support as necessary to "increase the ability of teachers to effectively teach children with disabilities, including children with significant cognitive disabilities, and English learners" (Section 2103(b)(3)(F), ESSA).

In addition, the Every Student Succeeds Act (2015) renewed concerns about the implementation of RtI, which have been raised by scholars (e.g., Thorius et al., 2014), highlighted in federal reports (e.g., Balu et al., 2015), and voiced by school personnel (Greenfield et al., 2010). There is a persistent issue that exists when educational reform stems from federal mandates, which often do not consider local, political, or social structures that shape implementation (Welner, 2001). Understanding how policies are applied is critical as there are multiple stages and levels at which policy is implemented, which are subject to unanticipated consequences and impacts due to local systemic and institutional effects (Slanda & Little, 2018).

When implementing federal and state policies such as RtI, district personnel, school administrators, and classroom teachers typically rely on their own interpretations of established federal and state guidelines and requirements (Spillane, 2004). Consequently, the implementation of an RtI/I model at the school level is negotiated between their understanding of policy and procedure and their access to resources. In addition, other stakeholders may be involved with implementation of various components of a policy. For example, decisions regarding curricular resources may be determined at state and/or district levels, with little input by teachers and teacher leaders within the school sites who are charged with knowledgeable implementation of policies with the use of resources provided. Given the complexity and multiple components of an RtI/I model, developing, due to time and funding, the knowledge and skills of teachers and teacher leaders may be a challenge, leading to ineffective implementation.

## Emerging Understandings

This reality of the unintended consequences and lack of fidelity of implementation of these federal and state policies provided the impetus to develop a more comprehensive model within the Multi-Tiered Systems of Support in the Every Student Succeeds Act (2015). Meeting the academic, behavioral, and social needs of all students required the knowledge, efforts, and collaboration of multiple stakeholders in schools, communities, and states. These unintended consequences also serve as the foundation for this text to expand on a MTSS model that embraces RtI/I as one of necessary systems not synonymous with MTSS but rather part of multiple systems necessary to improve instruction.

RtI was initially legislated within the Individuals with Disabilities Education Act (IDEA, 1997; 2004) to proactively address the academic and behavioral strengths and needs of students prior to identification of a disability. However, given the focus on differentiated instruction and interventions within the general education classrooms, RtI was expanded and enhanced within subsequent educational legislation and subsequent policies of Every Student Succeeds Act (ESSA, 2015) as MTSS. The broad-spectrum MTSS framework presented in this text is an integrated, harmonic comprehensive system to address behavioral, social, emotional, and academic concerns of students by teachers and other school-based educators using an asset-based, solution-seeking process.

During this process, high-quality instruction using research-validated practices, additional resources, collaborative expertise, interventions, differentiation, and scaffolded support must be considered, developed, and implemented within classrooms through cyclical systems of supports during each of the tiers within the RtI/I model. Classroom instruction may be differentiated and intensified based upon the instructional needs of the students, within the large group and as individuals within the classroom. Static and dynamic assessments are the primary sources of information about the student's learning which serves as the basis for instructional decisions at each of the tiers. Decisions regarding the amount of time, resources, and specific interventions are determined by the teacher and members of the RtI/I team based upon continued gathering and analyzing classroom performance data. Finally, given the comprehensive approaches to addressing the academic strengths and needs of students, we choose to use the term, RtI/I in this chapter and book, as one tiered system within MTSS, in order to highlight the necessary continuum of pedagogical and hebegogical classroom practices to address the academic strengths and needs of all students. Data-informed decision-making is used for many purposes, including classroom instruction, accountability, and continuous progress monitoring as part of the RtI/I system within classrooms, schools, districts, and provinces. Data-informed decision-making is a process in which teachers systematically, coherently, and intentionally reflect on their practice and make changes to their instruction based on careful analysis of current classroom performance of students. It is similar to action research. Teachers, instructional coaches, curriculum specialists, and other school-based educators must be knowledgeable and skilled in the effective implementation of the RtI/I system and data-informed decision-making process. The data-informed decision-making process impacts and influences the selection of research-validated instruction, interventions, and assessment practices for students through three tiers of instruction and interventions.

## Professional Conversation Prompts

As you and your team develop and enhance support and engagement by community members, the following illustrative questions may serve as guideposts for in-depth critical and professional discussions:

1 Describe Response to Intervention/Instruction to your colleagues.
2 Describe the current opportunities within your school to participate in data-informed decision-making on RtI/I, grade level, or data teams.
3 What processes and resources are available to you and your colleagues to conduct data-informed decision-making on MTSS teams when considering RtI/I?
4 As you explore online resources available from several national and international centers, what resources could be used by you and your colleagues' data-informed decision?
5 How will the intervention/instruction be grounded on students' strengths?

# References

Balu, R., Zhu, P., Doolittle, F., Schiller, E., Jenkins, J., Gersten, R., & Jacobson, J. (2015). *Evaluation of response to intervention practices for elementary school reading: Executive Summary*. Washington, DC: US Department of Education, Institute of Education Sciences, National Center for Education Evaluation and Regional Assistance.

Batsche, G. (2014). Multi-tiered system of supports for inclusive schools. In *Handbook of effective inclusive schools: Research and practice* (pp. 183–196). Abingdon, Oxon: Routledge.

Council for Exceptional Children. (2017). *High-leverage practices*. Council for Exceptional Children & CEEDAR Center. https://ceedar.education.ufl.edu/wp-content/uploads/2017/07/CEC-HLP-Web.pdf

Efron, R., & Ravid, R. (2020). *Action research in education: A practical guide*. New York: Guilford.

Every Student Succeeds Act, Public Law 114-95, 114th Cong., 1st sess. (2015).

Gesel, S. A., LeJeune, L. M., Chow, J. C., Sinclair, A. C., & Lemons, C. J. (2021). A meta-analysis of the impact of professional development on teachers' knowledge, skill, and self-efficacy in data-based decision-making. *Journal of Learning Disabilities, 54*(4), 269–283. https://doi.org/10.1177/0022219420970196

Greenfield, R., Rinaldi, C., Proctor, C. P., & Cardarelli, A. (2010). Teachers' perceptions of a response to intervention (RTI) reform effort in an urban elementary school: A consensual qualitative analysis. *Journal of Disability Policy Studies, 21*(1), 47–63.

Hoover, J. J., & Soltero-González, L. (2018). Educator preparation for developing culturally and linguistically responsive MTSS in rural community elementary schools. *Teacher Education and Special Education, 41*(3), 188–202.

*Individuals with Disabilities Education Act* (1997). 20 U.S.C. §§ 1400 et seq.

*Individuals with Disabilities Education Improvement Act* of 2004, 20 U.S.C. § 1400 et seq. (2004). (reauthorization of the Individuals with Disabilities Education Act 1990).

Jackson, D. (2021). *Leveraging MTSS to ensure equitable outcomes*. Washington, DC: American Institutes of Research.

Kittelman, A., McIntosh, K., & Hoselton, R. (2019). Adoption of PBIS within school districts. *Journal of School Psychology, 76*, 159–167.

Lane, K. L. (2007). Identifying and suppoRtI/Ing students at risk for emotional and behavioral disorders within multi-level models: Data driven approaches to conducting secondary interventions with an academic emphasis. *Education and Treatment of Children, 30*(4), 135–164. https://doi.org/10.1353/etc.2007.0026

Lemons, C. J., Sinclair, A. C., Gesel, S., Gruner Gandhi, A., & Danielson, L. (2017). *Supporting implementation of data-based individualization: Lessons learned from NCII's first five years*. Washington, DC: National Center on Intensive Intervention.

Leonard, K. M., Coyne, M. D., Oldham, A. C., Burns, D., & Gillis, M. B. (2019). Implementing MTSS in beginning reading: tools and systems to support schools and teachers. *Learning Disabilities Research & Practice, 34*(2), 110–117.

Little, M. (2012). Action research and response to intervention: Bridging the discourse divide. *The Educational Forum, 76,* 69–80. doi: 10.1080/00131725.2012.629286

Little, M. (2009). *Response to intervention (RtI) for teachers: Classroom instructional problem solving.* Denver, CO: Love.

Little, M., Slanda, D. D., & Spector, E. (2024a). *The educator's guide to action research: Practical connections for implementation of data-driven decision-making.* New York: Rowman & Littlefield.

Little, M., Slanda, D. D., & Spector, E. (2024b). *The educator's guide to action research: Practical connections for implementation of data-driven decision-making.* New York: Rowman & Littlefield.

Marston, D., Muyskens, P., Lau, M., & Canter, A. (2003). Problem-solving model for decision making with high-incidence disabilities: The Minneapolis experience. *Learning Disabilities Research & Practice, 18,* 187–200.

Miciak, J., & Fletcher, J. M. (2020). The critical role of instructional response for identifying dyslexia and other learning disabilities. *Journal of Learning Disabilities, 53*(5), 343–353.

National Center for Intensive Interventions. (n.d.). Retrieved from https://intensiveintervention.org/

Office of Special Education Programs. (2021). *Individuals with Disabilities Education Act (IDEA) database.* U.S. Department of Education. https://www2.ed.gov/programs/osepidea/618-data/state-level-data-files/index.html#bcc

Positive Behavioral Interventions and Supports. (2022). *What is PBIS.* https://www.pbis.org/

Pullen, P. C., van Dijk, W., Gonsalves, V. E., Lane, H. B., & Ashworth, K. E. (2018). RTI and MTSS: Response to intervention and multi-tiered systems of support: How do they differ and how are they the same, if at all?. In *Handbook of response to intervention and multi-tiered systems of support* (pp. 5–10). Oxfordshire: Routledge.

Sagor, R., & Williams, C. (2016). *The action research guidebook: A process for pursuing equity and excellence in education.* New York: Corwin.

Slanda, D. D., & Little, M. E. (2018). Exceptional education is special. In *The Wiley handbook of teaching and learning* (pp. 277–285). Hoboken, NJ

Spillane, J. P. (2004). *Standards deviation: How schools misunderstand education policy.* Cambridge, MA: Harvard University Press.

Steed, E. A., & Shapland, D. (2020). Adapting social emotional multi-tiered systems of supports for kindergarten classrooms. *Early Childhood Education Journal, 48,* 135–146.

Stoiber, K. C. (2014). A comprehensive framework for multitiered systems of support in school psychology. In *Best practices in school psychology: Data-based and collaborative decision making* (pp. 41–70).

Thorius, K. A., Maxcy, B. D., Macey, E., & Cox, A. (2014). A critical analysis of response to intervention appropriation in an urban school. *Remedial and Special Education, 35*(5), 287–299. doi: 10.1177/0741932514522100

Wanzek, J., & Vaughn, S. (2009). Students demonstrating persistent low response to reading intervention: Three case studies. *Learning Disabilities Research and Practice, 24*(3), 151–163

Welner, K. G. (2001). *Legal rights, local wrongs: When community control collides with educational equity.* New York: State University of New York Press.

Yendol-Hoppey, D., & Fichtman, N. (2020). *The reflective educator's guide to classroom research: Learning to teach and teaching to learn through practitioner inquiry.* New York: Corwin.

# Epilogue

*Words mean more than what is set down on paper. It takes the human voice to infuse them with deeper meaning.*

–Maya Angelou

If asked, what are some watchwords for this text? We would hope that readers would respond with – harmonic, comprehensive, humane, broad-spectrum, research-validated, intentional, and coherent. Our hope and scope from the start was grounded in years of experience in a sea of interactions with teacher-colleagues and teacher leaders that gave life to those words by infusing them with deeper meanings. Now the work starts. We have provided our most current thinking throughout this text for Multi-Tiered Systems of Support. Many teachers with expertise in transdisciplinary literacy, learning, and leadership in education have shared with us what it is going to take to improve instruction and grow critical thinking and mindful transdisciplinary literate citizens of the world. The book has taken us quite a while to write because of the overlapping nature of the multi-tiered systems and reaching consensus on many terms. Along the way we have constructed, deconstructed, and reconstructed, over and over, what Multi-Tiered Systems of Support needs to be for it to be implemented effectively and efficiently with little room for misinterpretation of terms and actions.

We have stated throughout the text that we believe strongly that language is a tool for critical thinking. Thank you, Lev Vygotsky. Consequently, we stand firmly that if we do not update our language, we will not upgrade our thinking. It is also an issue of positionality. The language we use can position us as collaborative and democratic or oppressive and autocratic.

# Epilogue

The collaborative nature of implementing Multi-Tiered Systems of Support demands not only updating our language but also upgrading our thinking to curate a sustainable transdisciplinary learning environment where all stakeholders learn and lead. Reflection is indicative of deep and critical thinking. Reflect on your current language use. For example, a shift from "corrective feedback" to "generative response" can make a dramatic difference in positionality among administrators and teachers, teachers and students, and schools and communities to create a more equitable and inclusive landscape for learning.

Historically, as we have mentioned earlier, corrective feedback should make us question positionality and has mechanistic and behaviorist connotations. By contrast, generative responses, as the term implies, is inclusive and nurtures independent learning behavior, putting the learner in the driver's seat. Effective and efficient implementation of Multi-Tiered Systems of Support demands developing transformational relationships, and the language employed is critical. It is about working shoulder to shoulder to improve transdisciplinary literacy instruction. It is not about pontificating from an ivory tower or office or position. Even the title of this book should prompt some meaty professional conversations. Shifting from "teaching and learning" to "learning and leading" is a big step when we are addressing transdisciplinary literacy instruction, professional learning, and distributive leadership as a tier of support toward improving and sustaining instruction. Effective teachers and teacher leaders are learners first, and they should be exemplars of learning for students and colleagues. This shift in understanding can probably be the most cathartic and transformational to enable curating a transdisciplinary learning environment via Multi-Tiered Systems of Support. If schools, school systems, teacher-colleagues, and teacher leaders are still using such ubiquitous terms as "strategies," "systematic and explicit," it may be time to investigate innovative words and terms that will challenge us and, in the process, upgrade our thinking. What if we talked about "practices" instead of strategies; and looked for solutions that were "intentional and coherent" in addition to systematic and explicit?

The examples and models we have provided along the way are illustrative; this is certainly not intended to be an exhaustive list of terms and actions or research-validated practices. Each classroom, school, district, state, and province will have to take what we have provided and adapt it to best serve the community it embraces. As we continue to learn and shift, we need to consider the mindset or perspective taken in order for worthwhile forward shifts to occur to create a mindful and sustainable learning environment. We have peppered this text with the term "pedagogy," but have also employed the terms "hebegogy" and "andragogy" to make a distinction between the art, science, and craft of working with children, adolescents, and adults, respectively. This distinction is critical for the successful implementation of Multi-Tiered Systems of Support. Consequently, successful implementation of Multi-Tiered Systems of Support rests on how we treat all stakeholders (students, teachers, teacher leaders, and community).

All texts are open for interpretation. This one is no different, and may read like Swiss cheese with many holes at times. The repetitive nature is intentional; the holes are unavoidable since our knowledge and science is ever-evolving. Although we have made claims, suggestions, and recommendations for implementing Multi-Tiered Systems of Support, our hope and scope is that this text is a living document-a seed, to prompt critical thinking about sustainable transdisciplinary education. As we end this text, or, better said, recycle our thinking, we close with seven lessons learned from Viktor Frankl, psychiatrist, Holocaust survivor, and author of *Man's Search for Meaning*. His experiences while in a concentration camp helped him theorize about the significance of finding meaning in everything we do. Here are seven pearls from Frankl that should serve as guiding principles for Multi-Tiered Systems of Support:

1. Finding purpose in life is crucial for psychological well-being and resilience.
2. Individuals have the freedom to choose their attitude and responses.
3. Meaning can be found through acts of service, creativity, and devotion to others.
4. Redirect attention away from yourself to focus on meaningful activities or relationships to find joy in service to others.
5. Meaning is not a static concept but is found in action.
6. Pursue your passions, engage in meaningful work, and cultivate relationships that contribute to a fulfilling sense of purpose.
7. Hope is a crucial element in finding meaning.

# Epilogue

Vicktor Frankl presents thoughtful perceptions into the human condition and the significance of unearthing meaning in life. Through his encounters and ruminations, he constructed a conceptual framework for how individuals can nurture strength, determination, and hope, ultimately steering us toward a more evocative reality. Transfer your passions!

Mary and Enrique

For Product Safety Concerns and Information please contact our EU representative GPSR@taylorandfrancis.com
Taylor & Francis Verlag GmbH, Kaufingerstraße 24, 80331 München, Germany

www.ingramcontent.com/pod-product-compliance
Lightning Source LLC
Chambersburg PA
CBHW061713300426
44115CB00014B/2666